BROWN IS THE
NEW WHITE

BROWN IS THE NEW WHITE

How the Demographic Revolution
Has Created a New American Majority

Steve Phillips

THE NEW PRESS

NEW YORK
LONDON

Requests for permission to reproduce selections from this book
should be mailed to: Permissions Department, The New Press,
120 Wall Street, 31st floor, New York, NY 10005.

Published in the United States by The New Press, New York, 2015
Distributed by Perseus Distribution

ISBN 978-1-62097-115-4 (hardcover)
ISBN 978-1-62097-116-1 (e-book)
CIP data available.

The New Press publishes books that promote and enrich public discussion and
understanding of the issues vital to our democracy and to a more equitable world.
These books are made possible by the enthusiasm of our readers; the support of a
committed group of donors, large and small; the collaboration of our many partners
in the independent media and the not-for-profit sector; booksellers, who often hand-sell
New Press books; librarians; and above all by our authors.

www.thenewpress.com

Book design and composition by dix!
This book was set in Scala

Printed in the United States of America

10 9 8 7 6 5 4 3 2 1

To my mother and father, who fought the fights
that opened the doors that gave me the chance to succeed;

To Reverend Jesse L. Jackson Sr., who risked his life to show
the world the power and potential of an electoral rainbow coalition
connected to the movement for social justice. I was paying attention;

To Susan, without whom none of this would have been possible,
and by "this" I mean pretty much anything meaningful
I've accomplished in the past twenty-five years;

And to all those working to change the organizations
and institutions you are a part of to make them more reflective
of the New American Majority and effective at fostering
justice and equality. This book is for you.

CONTENTS

AUTHOR'S NOTE

Names matter to people who have battled discrimination and oppression. Although I haven't seen the miniseries *Roots* in nearly forty years, there's a scene I'll never forget where the slave master forces LeVar Burton's Kunta Kinte character to accept his slave name, "Toby." Burton's character is tied to a post and whipped repeatedly while the overseer asks, "What's your name?" Each time the character says "Kunta Kinte," he receives another lash of the whip across his bare back until finally, bloodied and broken, he whispers, "Toby. My name is Toby." Flash forward two hundred years from that scene's moment in history to 1967—during the height of the civil rights and Black Power movements—when boxing legend Muhammad Ali was trying to get people to stop referring to him as Cassius Clay, his "slave name." One of Ali's opponents, Ernie Terrell, made the mistake of continuing to call him Cassius Clay. As Ali dominated the boxing match, he preceded each flurry of punches by asking Terrell, "What's my name?" and then punched his opponent in the face again. So, yes, names matter.

The choices I've made about how to describe the ethnicity and race of people and groups—terminology, style, etc.—in this book also matter. The task was complicated by the fact that how people prefer to refer to themselves continues to change (my grandmother used the word "Colored" to describe my racial group). I have tried to respect and honor the identity and history of each particular group and community discussed.

In the pages that follow, I capitalize "Black" and "White," and use the terms "Latino" (instead of "Hispanic"), "Native American," and "Asian American." I also refer frequently to "progressives" and "Democrats," the former being part of a broader movement for social change and the latter being people who generally cast their ballots for candidates of the Democratic Party. (Also, sometimes, when referring to "Democrats," I mean the leadership of the Democratic Party.) My rationale and reasoning for these choices can be found in Appendix B: What's in a Name?

INTRODUCTION

"They Said This Day Would Never Come"

They said this day would never come. They said our sights were set too high. They said this country was too divided, too disillusioned to ever come together around a common purpose. But on this January night, at this defining moment in history, you have done what the cynics said we couldn't do.[1]

—Barack Obama, January 3, 2008,
victory speech after winning Iowa caucus

At 6:00 p.m. on April 4, 1968, Jesse Jackson was in the parking lot of the Lorraine Motel in Memphis, Tennessee, waiting with civil rights leader Andy Young and others to accompany Martin Luther King Jr. to a community meeting. At 6:05 p.m., Dr. King stepped out on the balcony of the motel and called down to saxophonist Ben Branch: "Ben, make sure you play 'Precious Lord, Take My Hand' in the meeting tonight. Play it real pretty." Then Jackson and the group heard what sounded like a car backfiring and looked up to see Dr. King lying prostrate on the balcony in a pool of blood, his shoe dangling over the edge, the life draining from his body.[2] Forty years later, on November 4, 2008, standing in Chicago's Grant Park with tears streaming down his face, Jackson was again gazing upward at another young Black leader—Barack Hussein Obama, president-elect of the United States of America. In the forty years between King's death and Obama's election, America had undergone a profound transformation.

In the four decades since King's death, the percentage of people of color in the American population has tripled, ushering in a new political era, scrambling the old electoral equations, and creating the conditions for a lasting New American Majority. In 1968, America was home to approximately 25 million people of color, or 12 percent of the U.S.

population. By 2008, people of color numbered more than 104 million people, or 36 percent of the population. The civil rights movement pushed through two laws in the mid-1960s that paved the path for the demographic transformation of the American voting public. First, the Voting Rights Act of 1965—a signature accomplishment of civil rights activists such as King, Young, Jackson, and many others—eliminated obstacles to voting that had effectively disenfranchised most of the African American population since shortly after the end of the Civil War a hundred years earlier. Second, the Immigration and Nationality Act of 1965 removed race-based immigration barriers that had been in place since the founding of America. After the passage of those two laws, Blacks began to register and vote in much larger numbers, and millions of Asians and Latinos could finally legally enter the country. The color and composition of the country's electorate would never be the same.

Most of the attention paid to the country's changing demographics focuses on the trends showing that Whites will one day be a minority of America's population. Many articles and analyses look to a distant date when the United States will become a "majority minority" nation. According to the most recent census projections, that year is expected to be 2044.[3] There are two major problems with emphasizing the point when Whites will lose their majority status. First, it presumes that all White people are and will continue to be at odds with all people of color, which is untrue and unfounded. A meaningful minority of Whites have always sided with people of color throughout U.S. history. The second problem is that the focus on 2044 overlooks the equation that's been hiding in plain sight, one that shows what happens when you add together the number of *today's* people of color (the vast majority of whom are progressive) and progressive Whites. It's this calculation that reveals that *America has a progressive, multiracial majority right now* that has the power to elect presidents and reshape American politics, policies, and priorities for decades to come. Not in 2044. Not ten years down the road. Today.

Watching the tears stream down Jesse Jackson's face the night of Obama's election moved me personally because Jackson's presidential campaigns changed me. I was a delegate to Jackson's 1984 and 1988 campaigns, and I took a year off from college to serve as the California student coordinator of his 1988 campaign. Through that baptism by political campaign, I learned some lasting truths about politics and social change. Before Barack Obama went to law school, before Spike Lee made his first movie, before Shonda Rhimes could even dream of writing television shows featuring actors of color, a forty-two-year-old Black civil rights leader shook up the political system by running for president of the United States of America. To get from Martin in 1968 to Barack in 2008, we needed Jesse in 1984 and 1988.

It was during the presidential elections of the 1980s that the seeds planted in the 1960s began to sprout and become visible in national politics. Jackson was fond of saying, "When the old minorities come together, they form a new majority." The potential of this prophecy came into sharp focus in the 1988 campaign as Jackson won the presidential primaries in eleven states, led the race for the Democratic nomination near the halfway point, and finished as the Democratic runner-up with the most votes in history up to that time.

The key to Jackson's success—and Obama's electoral victories twenty years later—was the power of connecting the energy of people of color and progressive Whites seeking justice, equality, and social change to a political campaign for elected office. I'll always remember how the Jackson for President campaign organized a march with Latino farmworkers in Delano, California, that culminated in Jesse kneeling and praying with Cesar Chavez, who was on a hunger strike at the time. I witnessed Asian Americans across the country thanking Jackson for being the only presidential candidate to call for justice for Vincent Chin, who was killed in a hate crime. I walked my first picket lines with members of the Rainbow Coalition standing in solidarity with the Watsonville cannery strikers and saw those formerly disempowered workers, who were mostly Latinas, become effective political organizers. And I learned about courage and compassion watching Jackson visit and comfort gay people suffering from AIDS, at a time when their plight was unrecognized and their humanity disrespected.

As a result of these types of efforts, millions of people of color and progressive Whites were inspired to register to vote and turn out at the

xiv   INTRODUCTION

polls in 1984. Two years later, large and enthusiastic voting by people of color helped Democrats win closely contested U.S. Senate races in the heavily Black and Latino Southern and Southwestern states of Georgia, Alabama, Florida, Maryland, Nevada, and North Carolina, capturing control of the Senate from the Republicans. Because the embryonic New American Majority had begun to flex its power in this fashion, when Ronald Reagan nominated radical right-wing judge Robert Bork to the U.S. Supreme Court in 1987, the Democrats were able to defeat the pick, forcing Reagan to put forward the more moderate Anthony Kennedy. Twenty-eight years later, in 2015, Kennedy provided the swing vote that established marriage equality as the law of the land.

Although I have many criticisms of Democratic politics over the past several years, I have loved having Barack Obama as my president. From providing health care to all Americans to working to bring undocumented immigrants into the American family to saving the U.S. economy from collapse and creating millions of jobs to reestablishing U.S. respectability and relationships with countries around the globe, to the incalculable positive impact on American children in allowing them to see a Black First Family in the White House for eight years, America and the world are better places because Barack Obama became president of the United States.

Yet despite meaningful and significant progress in the public policy realm, Democrats and progressives have failed to maximize the opportunity to build and secure a lasting multiracial political majority for positive social change by investing in, strengthening, and solidifying the communities that comprised the Obama coalition. As a result, we are at risk of losing the advantage the demographic revolution has presented us, and of losing the chance to move toward becoming a more just and equitable society.

Too often, people in power in the progressive movement in general and the Democratic Party in particular have not seen the New American Majority as a political force to advance a progressive agenda and expand the terms of debate. Instead, they tend to see people of color and progressive Whites as nuisances who need to be silenced for fear of alienating White swing voters. As one national progressive leader told me in 2010, "Whenever you mention racial issues to anyone in the West Wing, White House staffers curl up into the fetal position." For example, the leaders of the Democratic Party in 2009 and 2010 defunded and dismantled the constituency desks targeting voters of color because they preferred a "color-blind" approach to voter outreach. In 2010, a top Obama advisor tried to pull the plug on a large march for jobs planned by a coalition of civil rights and labor groups for fear that it would alienate White swing voters. In 2014 an audit of Democratic Party spending confirmed that the lion's share of the money—97 percent of more than $500 million in consulting contracts—was going to White consultants. What these leaders have failed to appreciate and understand is the essential interplay between the multiracial movement for social justice and the nation's public policy process. There would have been no Voting Rights Act or Immigration and Nationality Act of 1965 without the marches, protests, bloodshed, and sacrifices that took place in the streets of Selma, Alabama, earlier that year. As Jesse Jackson observed, "The Voting Rights Act was written in blood before it was signed in ink."

The problem is not limited to the White House. Most leaders of the Democratic Party still operate under the mistaken belief that Republicans took control of Congress because White swing voters switched their allegiances to the Republican Party, resulting in the crushing losses in the midterm elections of 2010 and 2014. The real problem in those races was lack of turnout of the Democratic base, but that analysis has not been done by the Party higher-ups, and hundreds of millions of dollars are being wasted in the futile pursuit of winning back White swing voters when a permanent progressive governing coalition could be established by investing those same millions in organizing the diverse communities that make up the New American Majority.

We are at a pivotal point in history with incredible potential, but we must act boldly and decisively or else it could all slip away as conservatives make inroads with people of color while progressives are sleeping. Democrats run the risk of being lulled into complacency and false confidence by the historic election of Obama, while many Republicans are aggressively getting with the multiracial program.

•   •   •

This book seeks to provide a quantitative analysis of the numbers and math that prove the existence of a New American Majority, offer a qualitative look at the groups who make up this majority, and present a constructive critique showing what progressives and Democrats are doing wrong and need to do better.

The first two chapters unveil the New American Majority. Chapter 1, "51 Percent (and Growing Every Day): The New American Majority," identifies progressives in each racial and ethnic group and shows how their numbers add up to a majority of the country's eligible voters. Chapter 2, "Meet the New American Majority," offers a more qualitative picture of who people of color and progressive Whites are by looking through the lens of the lives of a cohort of activists and change makers, using their stories to offer a window into the historical and political dynamics of the nation's racial and ethnic groups.

The next set of chapters offers a candid critique of the progressive movement, exposing how and why it is so far behind the curve in understanding and embracing the demographic revolution and the New American Majority. Chapter 3, "Blinded by the White," explores the depth and breadth of America's longstanding preference for White people, and how that preoccupation continues to influence all aspects of politics and society. Chapter 4, "Requiem for the White Swing Voter," explains how the conventional wisdom about the importance of chasing White swing voters is both mathematically wrong and politically perilous. Chapter 5, "Fewer Smart-Ass White Boys," details how progressive politics suffers because so many of the people in charge don't reflect the composition of the New American Majority and lack the cultural competence to communicate with its members.

The next two chapters move toward solutions. Chapter 6, "Invest Wisely," draws from the world of business to identify principles of successful investing and how those principles should be applied to the hundreds of millions of dollars spent on politics and social change. Chapter 7, "What Is Justice? Policy Priorities for the New American Majority," focuses on public policy solutions for the New American Majority by rooting the inquiry in history, exploring how contemporary inequality came to be, and examining what can be done to foster greater justice and equality.

Chapter 8, "Conservatives Can Count," concludes by offering a strong warning that Democrats and other progressives need to take action urgently because many conservatives are actively responding to the demographic revolution. Examples abound of conservatives who are moving more aggressively than progressives, creating the real possibility that the progressive movement will squander this historic opportunity to solidify a lasting multiracial New American Majority.

For hundreds of years, what most mattered in America was whether you were White or not, and that question has continued to be the driving force in our politics, as consultants and candidates have competed for the support of White swing voters thought to be essential to winning elections. But the growth in the country's communities of color has created a new touchstone and starting point for assembling the majority needed for victory. It is becoming abundantly clear, through recent elections and political analysis, that the needs, hopes, dreams, conditions, and concerns of people of color should be driving politics today and into the future. The political party that gets this, and meets the needs of the New American Majority the best, will govern for decades to come.

Progressives cannot win going forward without large and enthusiastic support from people of color. White can no longer be the starting point. We must now begin with Brown, and that is why Brown is the new White.

To be clear, this is not a book about how to end racism, and it is not a book about how to build a multiracial coalition in which there are no more "isms." That's a tall task, and we've been fighting those battles for a few centuries.

What this book does do is focus on how to build political power that can go a long way toward addressing and redressing the effects of racism, discrimination, injustice, and inequality. Electing Barack Obama president didn't end racism and discrimination; far from it. In fact, if anything, it inflamed many people to see a Black "Kenyan," "socialist," and "Muslim" occupy the White House. And we don't need to look any further than any given day's news reports to see that racism and discrimination are alive and well. But electing Obama and a relatively progressive Congress resulted in millions of people getting health care coverage. It resulted in millions getting jobs. It resulted in a Black attorney general—who had been appointed by the Black president—uprooting and replacing the entire police leadership in Ferguson, Missouri, in the wake of the murder of Michael Brown in 2014. Organizing and mobilizing the New American Majority in Baltimore's 2014 election resulted in the victory of Marilyn Mosby as state's attorney, putting in power someone with the authority and accountability to arrest the police officers charged with the murder of Freddie Gray in 2015.

If these electoral victories have showed us anything, it's that we can win elections and push the progressive movement forward while we work on other, deeper, and more intractable issues such as racism, injustice, and inequality. We don't have to wait for every single person to fully understand and embrace every single racial or ethnic group to make progress toward greater racial and economic justice. In fact, we can't afford to wait. We can work and win at the ballot box while we learn and grow in the movement.

One of my early organizing experiences involved coordinating Stanford University's 1987 Martin Luther King Day celebration, which had the theme "The Unfinished Business of Martin Luther King, Jr." Law professor William Gould gave a speech during the event in which he connected King's unrealized dream to Abraham Lincoln's words at Gettysburg, where Lincoln said, "It is for us the living to be dedicated here to the unfinished work which they who fought here have thus far so nobly advanced." Lincoln and King both left unfinished work. Both gave their lives in service of the cause of democracy, equality, and racial justice. (Few know that days before assassinating Lincoln, John Wilkes Booth, in reaction to Lincoln's speech announcing the surrender of Southern general Robert E. Lee, said, "That means nigger citizenship. . . . That is the last speech he will ever make.")[4] Both Lincoln and King helped bring about changes and laws that laid the foundation for the creation of a New American Majority composed of people of color and progressive Whites.

During much of U.S. history, it must have seemed there would never come a day when the majority of American voters would embrace and elevate a person of color to the highest office in the land. But that day has come, and it is for us the living to study it and understand what and *who* made that possible and then act with courage and conviction to cement a political majority that can build and protect the kind of society for which millions of people have struggled, sacrificed, and died.

A new day has dawned in America. By strengthening the progressive, multiracial New American Majority, we can make this day one of lasting equality and justice for all.

BROWN IS THE
NEW WHITE

1

51 Percent (and Growing Every Day):
The New American Majority

The hands that once picked cotton, and grapes, and pineapple can now pick presidents, and governors, and senators.
 —Rev. Jesse L. Jackson Sr., 1984

It was not the first time a policeman shot and killed an unarmed Black person, and it certainly won't be the last. But when Alabama state trooper James Bonard Fowler put two bullets into Jimmie Lee Jackson's stomach in 1965, the events that followed would change the world.

Jackson, twenty-six years old at the time of his murder, worked in Alabama's pulpwood industry, where he helped turn trees into paper; served his community as a church deacon; and believed he had the right to vote. He had attempted to register to vote five times, and his application was rejected each time. On February 18, 1965, he joined his mother, grandfather, and four hundred local residents in a peaceful march from Zion United Methodist Church to the Marion, Alabama, jail where they planned to sing a freedom song in support of civil rights organizer James Orange. Earlier that day the police had arrested Orange, who worked as an organizer for Martin Luther King's civil rights organization, the Southern Christian Leadership Conference, and their justification for doing so was the charge that Orange had contributed to the delinquency of minors by enlisting them in voter registration drives.

When the marchers came to a police blockade half a block from the church, a local minister kneeled to pray, and a policeman struck the

minister in the head with a billy club. Fifty state troopers then waded
into the crowd, broke up the march, and chased the Jackson family and
others into nearby Mack's Café. A *New York Times* reporter covering
the events wrote, "Negroes could be heard screaming and loud whacks
rang through the square." While Jackson was attempting to protect his
mother and eighty-two-year-old grandfather from the state troopers'
blows, Fowler took out his gun and shot him. He died eight days later.[1]

Local residents were so angry about the murder that they wanted
to carry Jackson's body all the way to the state capitol—fifty miles
away—and place it on the steps of the capitol building.[2] That sentiment propelled John Lewis, Albert Turner, Amelia Boynton, and others to organize a march over the Edmund Pettus Bridge in Selma on
March 7, 1965. The event became known as Bloody Sunday after police
again unleashed their force and fury on peaceful protestors—except
this time, the carnage was caught on camera. Days later, Rev. James
Reeb, a White minister from Boston who had gone to Selma to stand
in solidarity with protestors fighting for voting rights, was beaten to
death by White segregationists. Reeb's murder shocked the nation and
catalyzed passage of the 1965 Voting Rights Act.[3]

Barack Obama became president because of the changes sparked
by the protests in Selma. As a result of two laws passed in 1965, millions of people of color—mainly African Americans—were able to vote
for the first time, and millions more people of color—mainly Latinos
and Asians—were able to enter the United States once the racial restrictions were finally removed from our immigration and naturalization
laws. The Voting Rights Act was introduced into Congress days after
Bloody Sunday when President Johnson went before a joint session of
Congress and dramatically told a national television audience, "What
happened in Selma is part of a far larger movement which reaches into
every section and state of America . . . it's not just Negroes, but really
it's all of us, who must overcome the crippling legacy of bigotry and
injustice. *And we shall overcome.*"[4] The day after giving that speech,
Johnson convened the top congressional leaders and laid out his plan
to seize the momentum by introducing three sweeping laws addressing federal aid to education, Medicare, and immigration reform.[5] Congress passed the Voting Rights Act in August of that year, and, weeks

later, Johnson introduced the Immigration and Nationality Act, which became law in October. The events of 1965, in general, and those two acts in particular marked the beginning of the modern demographic revolution.

People of color now comprise more than 37 percent of the U.S. population, greater than triple the 12 percent in 1965. The two fastest-growing groups have been Latinos and Asian Americans. In 1965 there were fewer than 9 million Latinos in the United States; by 2013 that number had soared to 54 million. During that same forty-eight-year span, the Asian American population has grown from 2 million to more than 18 million people.[6]

Once the protections of the Voting Rights Act were put in place, the percentage of African Americans participating in the political process increased almost immediately. Whereas an estimated one-quarter of eligible Black voters were registered to vote in the South prior to passage of the act, by 1968 the number had increased to 62 percent.[7] In states such as Mississippi the percentage of African Americans who were registered to vote increased from 6.7 percent in 1964 to 59 percent in 1968.[8] This long-delayed flowering of democracy resulted in the number of Black elected officials in America more than tripling from 1,469 in 1970 to 4,912 in 1980 to more than 10,500 in 2011.[9]

All of these changes created the conditions for the development of the multiracial coalition of voters that made Barack Obama the forty-fourth president of the United States. As President Obama said from the foot of the Edmund Pettus Bridge on the fiftieth anniversary of the Selma to Montgomery March, "Because of what they did [in Selma in 1965], the doors of opportunity swung open not just for black folks, but for every American. Women marched through those doors. Latinos marched through those doors. Asian Americans, gay Americans, Americans with disabilities—they all came through those doors."[10]

A LITTLE BIT OF MATH, A LOT OF POLITICAL POWER

As Obama's elections showed, the country's demographic revolution over the past fifty years has given birth to a New American Majority. Progressive people of color now comprise 23 percent of all the eligible voters in America, and progressive Whites account for 28 percent of all eligible voters. Together, these constituencies make up 51 percent of the country's citizen voting age population, and that majority is getting bigger every single day.

Cross-referencing national exit polls from 2012 with census data reveals just how many people of each racial group are progressive (see Appendix B for more on why the Obama vote in 2012, after the glow from 2008 had worn off, is a useful proxy for "progressive"). The exit polls show that 80.5 percent of people of color (93 percent of African Americans, 71 percent of Latinos, 73 percent of Asian Americans, and 58 percent of "other") as well as 39 percent of White people voted to reelect Obama in 2012.[11] The 39 percent percentage for Whites correlates with the historical average of 39.91 percent of Whites who have voted for a Democratic presidential candidate since 1972, when exit polling for presidential races began. Obama received 65 million votes, beating Mitt Romney by more than 5 million votes.[12] In a national election where people of color are 28 percent of all voters—as was the case in 2012—the New American Majority electoral equation requires securing the support of 81 percent of people of color and 39 percent of Whites.

Now, let's take a closer look at how the current components of the country's population add up to a progressive New American Majority.

As of the 2013 estimate by the Census Bureau, just over 311 million people live in the United States, and 217 million of them are citizens over the age of eighteen, and therefore eligible to vote (the data geeks use the phrase "Citizen Voting Age Population," or CVAP). Of the country's eligible voters, 62 million are people of color, and 155 million are White.[13] Using the 2012 Obama voter percentage as the definition of progressive (see Appendix B), just over 50 million eligible voters are progressive people of color (23 percent of the pool of eligible voters), and another 61 million eligible voters are progressive Whites (28 percent of the eligible voter population). The coalition of progressive Whites and progressive people of color who are eligible to vote stands nearly 111 million strong, or 51 percent of all eligible voters in the country.[14]

Composition of the New American Majority
(Percentage of All U.S. Eligible Voters)

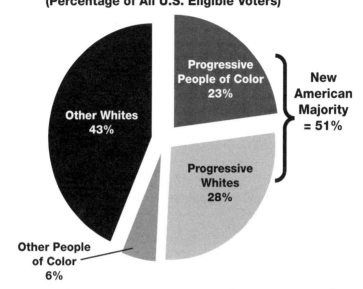

Figure 1. Source: Based on American Majority Project Research Institute (AMPRI) analyses of the Citizen Voting Age Population (CVAP) Special Tabulation from the 2009–2013 5-Year American Community Survey by the U.S. Census Redistricting Data Office, and the National Election Pool Exit Poll, 2012.

The New American Majority is growing larger every single day (every minute, actually). Each day, the size of the U.S. population increases by more than 8,000 people, and *nearly 90 percent of that growth consists of people of color.*[15] To understand this startling reality, one must look at the rate of births and deaths, and the rise in immigration.

In terms of births, as of 2011 the majority of babies born in America (50.4 percent) are now people of color.[16] A baby is born every seven seconds, resulting in 12,343 births per day.[17] At the other end of the age spectrum, the racial composition of the over-65 segment of the population is quite different. Because of centuries of racially exclusionary immigration policies (see Chapter 3), the total U.S. population was nearly 90 percent White as recently as 1950.[18] As a result, the current over-65 population is 78 percent White.[19] Using that figure to estimate the racial breakdown of the country's deaths—which occur at a rate of 6,646 per day (once every thirteen seconds)—it's clear that while a majority of births are people of color, deaths are overwhelmingly White.[20]

What this means for net population growth, then, is that the White birth number of 6,048 new babies each day (49 percent of the babies born every day) are largely canceled out by the 5,204 White deaths every day. For people of color, the 6,295 daily births (51 percent of all births) are only reduced by 1,442 deaths, leaving a net increase of 4,853 people of color every day.

And then there are the immigration numbers. Implied, feared, but unstated in America's heated immigration debate is a remarkable population statistic—more than 90 percent of all immigrants to America are people of color.[21] In terms of legal immigration alone, 2,618 people are added to the U.S. population each day, nearly all of them people of color (reflecting the reality that most of the people outside of the United States are people of color).[22] When those numbers are added to the net increase from births and deaths for people of color, the bottom line is that each and every day, 7,261 people of color are added to the U.S. population, in contrast to the White growth of 1,053 people. The chart in Figure 2 summarizes the situation.

Whether undocumented immigrants will eventually get to become voters in the foreseeable future largely depends on the political calculations of the Republican Party as it relates to providing a pathway to citizenship, but whatever the outcome of that debate, all the children born in the United States to undocumented immigrants are automatically U.S. citizens (much to the dismay and consternation of many conservatives angry about the growing numbers of human beings they derisively call "anchor babies").[23] Not all the population growth immediately translates to an increase in eligible voters (babies obviously cannot vote), but roughly 150,000 young people—nearly all U.S. citizens—turn eighteen every month, and 42 percent of them are people of color.[24] And of the legal adult immigrant population, of the nearly 1 million people who become Lawful Permanent Residents each year, more than 75 percent are over eighteen.[25] Consequently, the New American Majority percentage gets bigger every minute of every hour of every day. In fact, since the latest complete census data is from 2013,

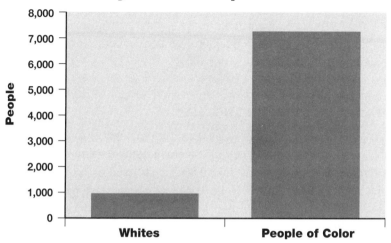

Figure 2. Source: Based on AMPRI analyses of data from U.S. Census Bureau's "U.S. and World Population Clock," U.S Centers for Disease Control and Prevention's "Number of Deaths and Percent Distribution by Specified Hispanic Origin and Race for Non-Hispanic Population: United States and Each State, 1999–2007," U.S. Department of Homeland Security's "2013 Yearbook of Immigration Statistics," and U.S. Census Bureau's Population Estimates Program (PEP) estimates of population for the United States by age, sex, race and Hispanic origin released July 1, 2014.

the numbers of the New American Majority for 2016 are likely much closer to 118 million people, 7 million more than the number from 2013.[26] To put that in perspective, since Obama was reelected in 2012, the ranks of the New American Majority have grown by more than his margin of victory in that race.

These numbers also play out in enough individual states to win the White House and control Congress for decades to come. There are 33 states where the New American Majority has an outright or soon-to-be-outright mathematical majority of eligible voters.[27] Those 33 states have 398 electoral votes, 128 more than the 270 it takes to win the White House (bear in mind Obama won 365 electoral votes in 2008, and the population has grown even more diverse since then). They elect 331 members of the House of Representatives, where it takes 218 votes to control the chamber, and 64 senators, 4 more than the 60 votes needed to overcome filibusters.[28] Republican gerrymandering has dispersed and diluted some of the immediate potential power of the New American Majority in terms of state legislative and congressional districts, but the population numbers nonetheless add up to a majority in these states.

THE EVIDENCE OF THINGS NOT SEEN

Despite the seemingly ample evidence of the dawn of a new political day brought about by the country's demographic revolution, acknowledgment of the arrival of this moment still seems mostly unseen and unspoken. It is surprising that more people have not crunched the numbers to conclude that a New American Majority exists in U.S. politics, since the evidence is there for the taking and math is supposed to be objective and fairly immune to dispute and disagreement. Fortunately, a few voices have reached similar conclusions about the imminent transformative implications of America's population metamorphosis.

Noted Brookings Institution demographer William Frey not only saw the signs but documented the trends in his 2014 book, *Diversity Explosion: How New Racial Demographics Are Remaking America*. In Frey's words, "While most people have some awareness of this growth, I have found that few truly appreciate its magnitude and potential." He added, "As a demographer who has followed U.S. population trends for decades, even I was surprised by the sheer scope of racial change that came to light with the 2010 Census. The story that the data tell is not just more of the same. I am convinced that the United States is in the midst of a pivotal period ushering in extraordinary shifts in the nation's racial demographic makeup."[29]

The Center for American Progress (CAP) has also been examining these changes, through its Progress 2050 program. A 2015 CAP report, *The Changing Face of America's Electorate: Political Implications of Shifting Demographics*, concludes, "Although demographic changes in the electorate do not fully track the seismic demographic shifts in the population, there are nonetheless obvious and significant shifts occurring within the U.S. electorate. While each state's demographics are changing at different paces and are being driven by different racial or ethnic groups, one trend is unmistakable: Non-Hispanic white voters are a shrinking share of the electorate."[30]

In the world of journalism, Ron Brownstein has been an often lonely voice in drawing attention to the political ramifications of the country's changing racial demography. Brownstein has been on this beat for several years and wrote in 2011, "Last week's release of national totals from the 2010 census showed that the minority share of the population increased over the past decade in every state, reaching levels higher than demographers anticipated almost everywhere, and in the nation as a whole. If President Obama and Democrats can convert that growth into new voters in 2012, they can get a critical boost in many of the most hotly contested states and also seriously compete for some highly diverse states such as Arizona and Georgia that until now have been reliably red."[31]

Despite these isolated outposts of analysis pointing to a developing electoral revolution, much of modern-day politics is still conducted as if the population of America is as White as it was fifty years ago.

The preceding calculations in this chapter about the size of the New American Majority represent an interesting intellectual exercise, but any recitation of facts and figures admittedly runs the risk of falling prey to the famous saying popularized by Mark Twain that there are three kinds of lies—lies, damned lies, and statistics. But these are not just abstract stats disconnected from the real world. The mathematical theorem of the New American Majority was proved in practice in Obama's election in 2008 and then tested and affirmed in his reelection in 2012.

The arrival of a new political era is perhaps best seen by contrasting the results of Obama's 2008 victory with John Kerry's defeat four years earlier. In 2004, Kerry followed the then-conventional wisdom of Democratic politics by attempting to win the White House without winning any Southern states (in an interview, he said that winning in the South was not necessary and pointed out that Al Gore would have

2004 Presidential Election Electoral Map

Figure 3. Source: Federal Election Commission, "Federal Elections 2004: Election Results for the U.S. President, the U.S. Senate, and the U.S. House of Representatives," May 2005.

won in 2000 had New Hampshire voted Democratic).[32] This 2004 election electoral map shows the results of that approach with compelling clarity. Kerry was completely shut out of the entire South and Southwest in his losing bid for the presidency.

Just four years later, Obama made significant successful incursions into the areas that Democrats had previously conceded to Republicans. Obama's mobilization of the New American Majority propelled him to victory in North Carolina and Virginia—two Southern states that Democrats had not carried in a presidential election in thirty-two years (forty-four years in the case of Virginia).[33] And support of 67 percent of Latino voters lifted Obama to first place in the Southwestern states of Colorado, Nevada, and New Mexico.[34]

Four years later, the 2012 results affirmed that 2008 was not a fluke but in fact the beginning of a trend with long-term implications. In his reelection bid, Obama carried almost all the Southern and Southwestern states he'd won in 2008 (except for North Carolina, which he lost by 92,000 votes out of 4.5 million total votes). Those victories created a gateway to a new era anchored in progressive majorities in the former

2008 Presidential Election Electoral Map

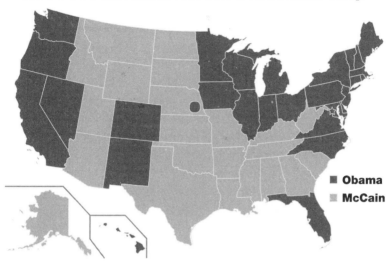

Figure 4. Source: Federal Election Commission: "Federal Elections 2008: Election Results for the U.S. President, the U.S. Senate, and the U.S. House of Representatives," July 2009.

Confederacy and what was once northern Mexico, places where people of color once picked cotton and grapes and lettuce (and, in many instances, still do).

STATE AND LOCAL LIBERATED ZONES:
10 STATES, 50 CITIES, 100 MILLION PEOPLE

Change is happening at the state and local levels as well. Although conservatives currently control Congress, the New American Majority has put Democrats (and a socialist or two) in control of the levers of government in several states and dozens of cities. Progressive voters of color and progressive White voters have won enough state and local elections and amassed enough political power to advance a progressive social justice agenda in nearly one-third of the country, offering immediate hope for tens of millions of people.

While working to take back Congress, progressives can make a real impact at the state and local levels. Plus, success locally will create momentum and pressure for change at the federal level. The marriage equality movement offers an excellent case study that the rest of the progressive movement can learn from.

Marriage equality was a "losing" issue at the national level as recently as 2004. Just over a decade ago, Republicans effectively used same-sex marriage as a wedge issue for inflaming prejudiced passions and increasing conservative voter turnout. In the 2004 election, right-wing leaders placed anti-marriage-equality initiatives on the ballot in eleven states that were key to George Bush's reelection prospects. And it worked. All eleven of those states voted to ban marriage equality, and nine of the eleven voted to reelect George Bush.[35]

But then a funny thing happened on the way to political irrelevance. The movement leaders' strategy of focusing their firepower on fighting battles in select strategic states began to show results, and the tide began to turn. From Massachusetts to New York to California, the LGBT movement weighed in at the state legislative level, backed pro-marriage-equality candidates for governor and attorney general, and won victories that created a sense of national momentum. With each of these battles, and especially with each success, public perception of the issue began to change, culminating in the 2015 Supreme Court decision that made marriage equality the law of the land. The rest of the progressive movement can follow this road map. The numbers of potential New American Majority voters in the states and cities make such a strategy particularly promising.

Seven states have New American Majority control of state government (defined, for these purposes, as having a Democratic governor and Democratic control of the state legislature). Collectively, those states—California, Connecticut, Delaware, Hawaii, Oregon, Rhode Island, and Vermont—contain nearly 50 million people.[36] In every one of these states, the voting population reflected the electorate that propelled Obama to victory, and the composition of voters in each state will only grow more diverse in coming years. The cumulative budgets of these states is $206 billion. Their gross state product (how much wealth they produce) is $2.9 trillion.[37]

Prior to the debacle of the 2014 elections, an additional three states—Illinois, Maryland, and Massachusetts—had New American

Majority control, but Democrats lost the gubernatorial elections in those traditionally heavily Blue states. If you include these three states, then the number of lives affected grows to 73.6 million people, and the cumulative budget becomes $347 billion (clearly, retaking the governors' offices in these three states needs to be a top progressive priority heading into 2018).

Across the country, New American Majority control is most manifest at the municipal level. In many of the Purple and Red states that have split governments (meaning the governor is of a different political party than the party that controls the state legislature) or total Republican control at the statewide level, there are large cities with New American Majority control. Often the population of these cities, such as New York City and Houston, is larger than the population of many (in fact, most) other states. Texas is a perfect example. Republicans have complete control of the state government there (for now), but there are five large cities in Texas completely run by Democrats, and more than 7.6 million people live in those cities (the equivalent of the thirteenth-largest state in America).[38] The top fifty cities with Democratic control in Purple or Red states represent 33 million people. The cumulative budgets of those cities exceeds $135 billion.

These state and local liberated zones offer fertile ground for promoting and passing social justice–based public policies that can improve the lives of millions (Seattle and Los Angeles, for example, led the nation in 2014 and 2015 respectively in raising the minimum wage in their cities to $15/hour). They should be seen as strategic areas for progressives to focus on in the near-term while also pursuing the more medium- and long-term challenges of taking back Congress and holding the White House.

Six months after Jimmie Lee Jackson was murdered trying to defend his family during a voting rights demonstration, his eighty-two-year-old grandfather, Cager Lee, walked into the Marion, Alabama, courthouse and registered to vote, accompanied by officials from the Department of Justice who were present to enforce the newly enacted Voting Rights Act.[39]

This is how history happens.

One hundred years after the end of the Civil War, young African American Jimmie Lee Jackson marched for democracy and the right to vote in the cradle of the Confederacy and was murdered by the police. The march for justice after Jackson's death resulted in Bloody Sunday, where courageous citizens were clubbed and teargassed with the images broadcast across the country on national television. Rev. James Reeb, a White minister, responded to King's call for help by coming from Boston to stand and march in solidarity with Black residents of Alabama seeking justice. Reeb was beaten to death by cowards calling him a nigger lover. Reeb's murder moved President Johnson to deliver a nationally televised address where he introduced the Voting Rights Act with the words, "The time of justice has now come." The speech was so successful and galvanizing that the very next day Johnson convened the congressional leadership and laid out his plans to introduce the Great Society legislation, including immigration overhaul.

Because of the Voting Rights Act and the Immigration and Nationality Act, the country's composition has changed to the point where people of color and progressive Whites are now the majority of America's population—and the majority of eligible voters. But who exactly are the inheritors and initiators of this struggle? Who is this New American Majority?

2

Meet the New American Majority

Out of the huts of history's shame
I rise
Up from a past that's rooted in pain
I rise . . .
Bringing the gifts that my ancestors gave,
I am the dream and the hope of the slave.
—Maya Angelou, "Still I Rise," 1978

WHOSE HOUSE? *OUR* HOUSE!

In April 1987 I joined thousands of other students marching through the halls of the California State Capitol chanting, "Whose House? OUR House!" We were there to demand more funding to increase access to the state's colleges and universities (and in an early lesson about the power of mass pressure, then-governor George Deukmejian reversed $600 million in cuts after our protest). At first glance, our multiracial coalition may have looked like a motley collection of loud, fired-up kids of color and progressive White students tramping through the formerly placid halls of power. A closer look at the organizers, however, would have revealed a kaleidoscopic picture representing the children and grandchildren of the very communities whose labor and land helped build America and whose growth is now transforming the national political landscape. Understanding the history, hopes, and struggles of these groups is essential to forging a lasting and progressive New American Majority.

Among the core group of organizers were five of us who had become close colleagues and friends through organizing and activism. We were all in our early twenties and concerned about the quality and accessibility of education in California. We had all become student activists working for justice and equality on California's college campuses, but we had taken vastly different journeys to arrive there. I am the great-grandson of Doke and Minnie Clark Hutchins, who were born into slavery in Alabama in the 1800s. Julie Martinez Ortega was born in San Antonio, Texas, to American-born Mexican parents and was the first in her family to attend college. Lisa Le was born in Vietnam and had taken one of the last planes out of Vietnam on the day Saigon fell in 1975. Colin Cloud Hampson, a member of the White Earth Band of Chippewa and the Winnebago tribes, had lived on an Indian reservation before going to college. Dave Brown, a White third-generation San Francisco Bay Area native, inherited the progressive outlook of his father, a public school teacher and coach, and his mother, a public health nurse.

The collective story of how we all came to march together in Sacramento that day is really the story of America: grandchildren and great-grandchildren of people who fought genocide, slavery, segregation, war, discrimination, and poverty. The legacy of those who helped build the wealth of America through backbreaking labor. Children of parents who risked their own safety and made significant sacrifices so that we could walk through the doors of America's institutions of higher education. We were the modern realization of the hopes and dreams of the slave, the abolitionist, the farmworker, the refugee, and the tribal leader.

AFRICAN AMERICANS

When my family first moved into my childhood home on Dartmoor Road in Cleveland Heights, Ohio, in 1964, my mother slept in her clothes because she was afraid our house might be firebombed. We were the first Black family to move into that previously all-White neighborhood, and some of the neighbors did not want us there. The previous owners refused to sell the house to our Black family, and a White civil rights attorney, Byron Krantz, had to purchase the home for us and deed it over to my parents. One of the neighbors, upset that the home had made it into Black hands, called a neighborhood meeting to discuss what to do about the presence of the new African American family in the 'burbs (a meeting that my father decided to crash, making for some awkward moments).

Like many African Americans before them, my parents were trailblazers. My dad became one of the first doctors in an HMO back in the 1960s. My mom became a successful real estate investor after a long career teaching in Cleveland's public schools. The income from properties my mother bought helped pay the tuition to the private high school I attended, which gave me the education to score well enough on tests to get into Stanford University. But my parents were only able to blaze those trails because others had come before to open the doors of opportunity for them. My mom's grandmother, Grandma Hutchins, was born into slavery in Alabama. My mom's father, Rev. A. R. Cochran, participated in the "Great Migration" of African Americans to the North when he moved from Mississippi to Cleveland during World War I and found work in a peanut factory before becoming a minister for fifty years. The Great Migration, what writer Isabel Wilkerson called "the first mass act of independence by a people who were in bondage in this country for far longer than they have been free," involved 6 million African Americans—nearly a quarter of the nation's Black population—leaving the South.[1]

My parents shared the experience of millions of other African Americans in that they often encountered resistance and racism as they sought the American Dream for themselves and their children. My parents were not alone in being blocked from purchasing a home in the neighborhood of their choice. As will be discussed in Chapter 7, throughout the twentieth century, banks and federal mortgage agencies consciously and deliberately "redlined" neighborhoods to prevent Black folks from moving in.

AFRICAN AMERICANS AT A GLANCE

For a long time, when Americans talked about people of color—or minorities, or non-Whites—they were mostly talking about Black folks. African Americans were the largest, most visible group of people of color in the United States from the time of the founding of America (after the decimation of Native Americans in the colonial years in the seventeenth and eighteenth centuries) up until 2001, when Latinos became the largest non-White group in the country.[2] Today, the African American population consists of more than 43 million people, 13 percent of the country's population.[3]

While it is well known that most ancestors of today's Black people were held in slavery, people generally think that happened "a long time ago" and that our history of slavery is of little relevance to contemporary politics and policy. But *legalized* racial discrimination and economic exploitation of African Americans continued all the way up until the passage of the Civil Rights Act in 1964, the year I was born. As will be discussed in chapter 7, this lengthy legacy has perpetuated conditions that contribute to the continued widening of the country's profound racial wealth gap.

Most African Americans continue to live on the land where their ancestors picked cotton and tilled soil for hundreds of years, first as slaves, then as sharecroppers. The increasing number of African Americans in Southern states is due largely to the relatively recent trend of "reverse migration," where Black people are leaving other parts of the country (mostly the North) and moving back to the South for economic and cultural reasons.[4]

Figure 5 shows the geographic distribution of African Americans.

POLITICS

African Americans are the most loyal and consistent Democratic voters in the country. Since the passage of the 1965 Voting Rights Act, the percentage of Black folks voting Democratic has never dipped below 83 percent and peaked with the 96 percent, or 15 million people, who voted for Obama in 2012.[5] An additional 9 million African Americans are eligible to vote but didn't vote in 2008.[6]

Because of their dependability, Black voters are frequently taken for granted by the Democratic Party and other progressives. Many in media and politics do not appreciate just how much of the Democratic coalition consists of African Americans. While 13 percent of the country is Black, African Americans make up 23 percent of Democratic

Where African Americans Live:
Geographic Concentration of the Black Population in the U.S.

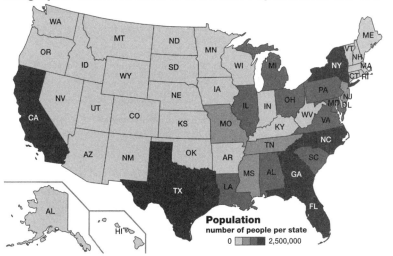

Figure 5. Source: Based on Dr. Laura Lara-Brady's tabulations of 2008–2012 American Community Survey 5-Year Estimates.

voters.[7] In several states, such as Maryland, Georgia, South Carolina, and Mississippi, the Black vote can exceed 40 percent of all votes cast in Democratic primaries.[8] That's why the media miss the mark when they mistake the Democratic "base" for the more visible and vocal progressive White activists who have shown enthusiasm for populist politicians like Senators Elizabeth Warren and Bernie Sanders. Any discussion of the Democratic base must include the acknowledgment that that base is heavily Black. As Barack Obama showed, successful candidacies require a large and enthusiastic Black vote.

In several states, the untapped Black vote can flip the political balance of power. For example, Democrats in Georgia lost the 2014 statewide elections for governor and senator by 200,000 votes, and Georgia has more than 700,000 eligible nonvoting African Americans. In North Carolina, which has 300,000 eligible nonvoting African Americans, Democrat Kay Hagan lost her U.S. Senate seat in 2014 by just 48,000 votes. That same year, Mary Landrieu lost her Senate seat in Louisiana by 117,000 votes; the Bayou State has 300,000 eligible

nonvoting Black voters.[9] The list goes on and on, and now that Obama
will no longer be on the ballot, the Democratic Party must pay particular attention to engaging and inspiring Black voters.

LATINOS

In the 1970s, White kids in San Antonio used to chase young Julie
Martinez down the street, throwing rocks at her and calling her "wet-
back." In the 1980s, she joined me and others marching through the
halls of California's state capitol. In 2014, Dr. Julie Martinez Ortega,
JD, PhD, a leading national quantitative researcher and analyst, was
named by *Campaigns and Elections* magazine as one of the top fifty key
players influencing elections in America.

Born and raised in Texas, Julie, like most Latinos, grew up in a
working-class Mexican American family. Julie's father, Julian Martinez, was born on the outskirts of San Antonio. He was among the first
Mexican Americans in his community to graduate from high school.
Eventually he was drafted and went into the armed services. Afterward, he joined the Air Force as a civil servant, where he worked as
a mechanic repairing airplanes at Kelly Air Force Base until his mid-
fifties and retired with full benefits. He was an active member of the
Machinists Union and retired as Senior Master Sergeant.

While "Remember the Alamo" is a well-known phrase in U.S. history (referencing the pivotal 1836 battle where White Texans lost Fort
Alamo to the Mexicans), for Julie's family it is closer to home. Much
closer. Julie's mom, Isabel, was born in San Antonio in a four-room
home with no indoor bathrooms, just ten minutes from Fort Alamo.
She left school after eighth grade to work various jobs with her sister
to help her family, including eight younger siblings. Isabel was twenty
and working at a frozen dinner factory when she married her husband,
Julian.

The Martinez family were regular fixtures at St. Lawrence Catholic
Church, where Julie's three nephews now attend catechism as they prepare for their First Communion. (Julie is now a lector at her parish in
Washington, D.C.) Isabel stays abreast of current events by keeping her
television tuned to CNN and MSNBC, and regularly votes in local and

national elections. She supports Democratic candidates because she proudly calls herself a Yellow Dog Democrat (an old phrase referencing loyalty to Democrats as in, "I'd vote for a yellow dog before I voted for a Republican"), and she has voted for the party that has stood for racial equality and opportunities for the working poor for as long as she can remember. Most of the Martinez family is bilingual, but when Julie was growing up they primarily spoke English rather than Spanish at home. This was Julie's parents' attempt to give their children a "leg up" in hopes that English fluency would help them excel academically and find a "way out" of their socioeconomic status.

LATINOS AT A GLANCE

Latinos are now the largest group of color in the country, with a population that exceeds 54 million people, making up 17 percent of the total U.S. population and 46 percent of all people of color in America.[10]

The countries of ancestry of the six largest subgroups of Latinos are Mexico (63 percent), Puerto Rico (9.2 percent), Cuba (3.5 percent), El Salvador and the Dominican Republic (each about 3 percent), and Guatemala (2.1 percent)—collectively comprising 84 percent of the total Latino population in the United States.[11]

Among all Latinos, 51 percent live in the Southwest[12] on land that was part of Mexico prior to the 1846 U.S. war with Mexico (a war that started because Texas—with the enthusiastic support of U.S. president James Polk—sought independence from Mexico so that it could continue the practice of slavery).[13] The military conquest of Mexico culminated in the 1848 Treaty of Guadalupe Hidalgo, which compelled Mexico to relinquish its claim to the territory that now constitutes the states of California, Texas, Arizona, Colorado, and New Mexico.[14] In the eyes of many Mexican Americans, "illegal" isn't a word to describe people who come to America without documents, but rather a term more applicable to how America took much of Mexico at gunpoint 168 years ago. As the popular saying goes among many Mexican Americans, "We didn't cross the border, the border crossed us!" This history of U.S. conquest and seizure of land resulted in the tearing apart of families and communities and is also why many Mexicans continue to come here to reunite with loved ones. Much of the recent growth in the U.S. Latino population is a result of the 1965 Immigration and Nationality Act, which provided for family reunification. In recent decades, large numbers of Latinos applied for and received visas that had formerly been denied them.

The second and third largest groups of Latinos in the United States—Puerto Ricans (4.6 million people) and Cubans (1.8 million)—are also concentrated in places tied to historical travel patterns.[15] The island of Puerto Rico has a long and complicated history with the United States, and especially relevant to contemporary politics is the fact that Puerto Ricans are all U.S. citizens and, therefore, eligible to vote. Puerto Rican migration accelerated in the 1950s as part of the first airborne migration. Many Puerto Ricans settled in New York and the surrounding states of New Jersey, Pennsylvania, Connecticut, and Massachusetts.[16] In recent years, the economic challenges on the island have prompted a new wave of migration to the mainland, with hundreds of thousands of Puerto Ricans leaving the island and many of them settling in the South, in general, and Florida, in particular.[17]

With Cuba located just ninety miles from Florida, Cuban immigrants not surprisingly immigrated to the Sunshine State, mostly after the Cuban revolution of 1959, and today 70 percent of Cuban Americans still live in Florida.[18] With the passage of time since the wave of immigration tied to the 1959 Cuban revolution, nearly half of all Cuban Americans in this country today were born in the United States.[19] And with President Obama's 2015 decision to reestablish full relations with Cuba, a new era is beginning for all Cuban Americans with family and historical ties to that island nation.

Figure 6 shows the geographic distribution of Latinos.

POLITICS

The Latino political wave is coming. As of 2012, 23 million Latinos were eligible to vote, but 12 million of them did not cast ballots in the 2012 election, more than twice the size of Obama's margin of victory.[20] The 11 million who did vote constituted 10 percent of all voters and 14 percent of Obama's total number of votes. In addition to those *currently*

Where Latinos Live:
Geographic Concentration of the Latino Population in the U.S.

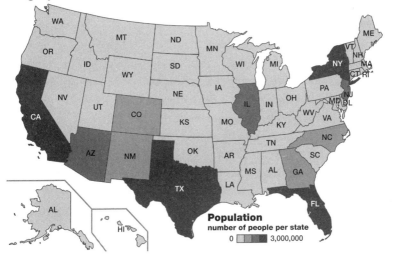

Figure 6. Source: Based on Dr. Laura Lara-Brady's tabulations of 2008–2012 American Community Survey 5-Year Estimates.

eligible to vote, 800,000 Latino children will turn eighteen every year between now and 2028, nearly all of them citizens and therefore eligible to vote.[21] To put that in perspective, if all the current Latino seventeen-year-olds were a state (just the seventeen-year-olds, mind you), that state would rank forty-fifth in the United States in population, exceeding the number of people in the states of Wyoming, Vermont, the District of Columbia, North Dakota, Alaska, and South Dakota.[22] An additional, little-noticed pool of potential new Latino voters can be found among the ranks of Lawful Permanent Residents who are eligible for naturalization, but who have not yet applied for citizenship. It is estimated that nearly 5 million Latinos fall in this category, and were they to become citizens, that would swell the ranks of Latino eligible voters to more than 28 million people, 13 percent of all eligible voters.[23]

In recent years, Latinos have tended to vote for Democrats. In 2008, 67 percent of Latino voters cast their ballots for Barack Obama, and in 2012, Obama's share of the Latino vote increased to 71 percent.[24] Despite this significant support for the Democratic presidential nominee,

Latinos do not necessarily identify as hard-core Democrats. In national surveys, 56 percent of Latinos say they are Democrats, with 26 percent identifying as Republicans, and 18 percent not aligned with either party.[25]

In the 2016 presidential race, Latinos could be particularly influential in a closely contested race in the pivotal battleground state of Florida. Obama won Florida in 2012 by just 73,000 votes (out of more than 8 million votes cast), and nearly 850,000 eligible Latinos did not vote.[26] Historically, U.S. politicians have tried to appeal to Florida's Latino voters by playing to the conservative and anticommunist sentiments of older Cuban Americans. Those dynamics are changing, however, as the composition of the Florida Latino population shifts to include younger Cuban Americans, less influenced by anti-Castro animus, and larger numbers of Puerto Ricans who have migrated to Florida in recent years. How presidential candidates respond to Puerto Rico's debt crisis will send a strong signal about respect for and appreciation of Puerto Rican people. The opportunity for Democrats to win Latino support in Florida can be seen in the trends over the past decade. Whereas George W. Bush won 56 percent of the Florida Latino vote in 2000, Obama won 57 percent in 2008 and 60 percent in 2012.[27]

While most Latinos have historically voted Democratic, the problem for progressives is that too many Latinos don't vote at all. The challenge—and political potential—is most dramatic in Texas, where Latinos constitute 37 percent of the population and 30 percent of the eligible voters.[28] Republicans win statewide elections in Texas by anywhere from 600,000 to 900,000 votes, but there are 3 million Latinos who are eligible to vote, but who did not cast ballots in the 2012 presidential election (and even more sat out the governor's race in 2014).[29] Even if *one-third* of the eligible, but nonparticipating, Latinos voted regularly, they could instantly make Texas elections much more competitive.

California is a case study of the transformative power of a growing Latino electorate. In 1992, California was considered a swing state, and before that it was reliably Red serving as the political launching pad for Richard Nixon and Ronald Reagan. Bill Clinton failed to win the support of a majority of the state's voters in 1992, and he only prevailed because the vote was split between George H. W. Bush and Ross Perot.

California Republicans controlled the governor's office and other state-wide positions until 1998. In response to a series of anti-immigrant policy measures and rising anti-Latino sentiment in the state, rates of Latino naturalization and voter registration soared in California in the mid-1990s. By 2014, Latinos had become the largest single ethnic group in the state, making up 39 percent of the state's population.[30] Today Republicans are an endangered species in California, with Democrats holding every single statewide elected office and nearly two-thirds of the state legislature. Latinos in Texas have the numbers to replicate this kind of political transformation. Such a seismic shift in the political landscape would ring the death knell for conservative politics in America.

ASIAN AMERICANS

As a ten-year-old, Phuong Le (she goes by her nickname Lisa now) liked to play with her dolls and read French comic books like *Tintin* and *Asterix*. Having grown up in Saigon, Vietnam, with her mom, dad, two younger sisters and younger brother, Lisa was a typical young girl with common childhood concerns like clothing for her dolls or the next comic book installment. Then, on April 30, 1975, her mother rushed home from her job at the U.S. Embassy and told Lisa and her siblings that they had one hour to pack because they were heading to the airport. Annoyed at the late notice and unable to take all her dolls, Lisa packed what she could and went with her family to the airport. She thought they were going on vacation. She did not know their destination, and she did not know that they would be on one of the last planes out of Vietnam on a day that would go down in history as "the Fall of Saigon," with the North Vietnamese Army seizing control of the country's capital.

By reasons of simple geography and the limits of fuel and aviation technology, the plane carrying Lisa's family, a military cargo plane, landed in Guam, and then Hawaii, the closest American state. Other Asian Americans had made that journey before them for different reasons, stopping—and many staying—in Hawaii, the only state where Asian Americans are a majority of the population. Lisa's family's next stop was Southern California and then the San Francisco Bay Area, which they still call home today. When they first arrived in the Bay Area, they stayed in San Francisco's Mission District, where Lisa's mother worked as a secretary and her father as an accounting clerk. Lisa shares her father's affinity for numbers and went on to become a certified public accountant and the treasurer of the country's first Super PAC in 2007, handling the finances and balancing the books of the multimillion-dollar effort that helped elect Obama president. English is Lisa's second language (third, arguably, as she grew up speaking French, reflecting earlier French colonization of Vietnam). Nationally, 75 percent of Asian American adults speak a language other than English at home.[31]

ASIAN AMERICANS AT A GLANCE

Asian Americans are the fastest-growing racial group in the United States, slightly ahead of Latinos. Another important fact about Asian Americans is that, like Lisa and her family, 74 percent of today's Asian American adults were not born in the United States.[32] From the Chinese Exclusion Act of 1882 through the early 1960s, Asians were subjected to eight decades of systematic exclusion and restrictive immigration policies that greatly limited their ability to enter this country and become Americans. Only with the civil rights movement's success in eliminating racial preferences in immigration policy (specifically with the passage of the 1965 Immigration and Nationality Act) did doors to Asian immigration finally open. Lisa was born in 1964, and in the span of her lifetime, the Asian population in the United States has grown by 900 percent from 2 million in 1965 to more than 18 million today. In states such as California, the number of Asian Americans has surpassed that of African Americans (14 percent of California's population, compared to 6.6 percent for Blacks).[33]

Among Asian Americans, the six largest nationalities of origin are Chinese (4 million), Filipino (3.4 million), Indian (3.2 million), Vietnamese (1.7 million), Korean (1.7 million), and Japanese (1.3 million), collectively comprising 83 percent of the total Asian American population.[34]

The histories, politics, and economics of each of these Asian

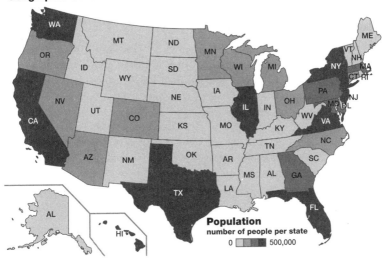

Where Asian Americans Live:
Geographic Concentration of the Asian American Population in the U.S.

Figure 7. Source: Based on Dr. Laura Lara-Brady's tabulations of 2008–2012 American Community Survey 5-Year Estimates.

American subgroups are unique and largely tied to their country of origin, but by and large those who came here traveled a similar route no matter which country they came from. Lisa's family followed a common geographic path taken by prior Asian immigrants, traversing one side of the Pacific Rim to the other and settling in the Western region of the United States. From the Gold Rush days of the 1850s to post-1965 Asian emigrations, the West Coast has served as the gateway to America for many Asian Americans. These migration patterns established today's Asian American communities and population centers. Today, 47 percent of all Asian Americans live in the West, the region geographically closest to Asia. The largest concentration of Asian Americans outside of the Western United States is in New York City, the result of historic British imperial routes as well as remigration from the West to the country's dominant economic center. Altogether, 20 percent of Asian Americans live on the East Coast, concentrated in New York, Boston, and Washington, D.C.[35]

Figure 7 shows the geographic distribution of Asian Americans.

NATIVE HAWAIIAN AND PACIFIC ISLANDER POPULATION

In her 2013 book, *A New History of Asian America*, Professor Shelley Sang-Hee Lee noted, "A number of recent developments have kept questions regarding the boundaries and meanings of Asian America at the forefront of discussion regarding identity." High on that list of developments is "a movement among Filipino American activists to reclassify or at least disaggregate their group from the larger 'Asian' category on the U.S. Census and debate over whether or not Pacific Islanders ought to be included in the larger Asian American grouping."[36]

Pacific Islander Americans are often associated with Asian Americans because their nations of origin are in proximity to Asia, and many Asian American activists still use terms such as API (Asian Pacific Islander), AAPI (Asian American Pacific Islander), or APA (Asian Pacific American). Until relatively recently, the census included a category that combined the two groups. In 1997, responding to pressure from Native Hawaiian and Pacific Islander activists, the Census Bureau created the new category, Native Hawaiian and Other Pacific Islanders, more clearly distinguishing those populations from the Asian American population.[37] This category was offered for the first time in the Census 2000 questionnaire.[38]

According to the 2010 Census, 1.2 million people in the United States identify as Native Hawaiian and Other Pacific Islander, either alone or in combination with one or more other races. The top six Pacific Islander American subgroups are Native Hawaiians (527,077), Samoan Americans (184,440), Guamanian/Chamorro Americans (147,798), Tongan Americans (57,183), Fijian Americans (32,304), and Marshallese Americans (22,434).[39] An estimated 58 percent of all Pacific Islander Americans live in two states: Hawaii and California.[40]

POLITICS

Of the 18 million Asian Americans, 9 million are eligible to vote; 5 million are registered to vote, and 3.7 million cast ballots in the 2012 presidential election.[41]

In terms of partisan political self-identification, Asian Americans are somewhat more evenly split than Latinos and African Americans, but they have tended to vote increasingly Democratic over the past decade. A large national survey of Asian Americans in 2012 found that 49 percent of Asian Americans identify as Democrats, and 39 percent identify with or lean toward the Republican Party. Indian Americans are the most heavily Democratic Asian subgroup (65 percent), while Vietnamese Americans are the most Republican (Vietnamese reported 25 percent Democrat, 35 percent Other, and 37 percent Republican).[42] In 2008, 62 percent of Asian Americans voted for Obama. Those numbers climbed in 2012 when 73 percent voted to reelect him.[43] This is a significant shift from 1992, when George H. W. Bush received 55 percent of the Asian American vote compared to 31 percent for Bill Clinton.[44]

The Asian American population has grown large enough in several states and cities that their votes can sway elections. In Washington State, Chinese American Gary Locke was elected governor in 1996, becoming the first and only Chinese American to serve as governor of an American state. California now has three Asian American statewide elected officials: Treasurer John Chiang, Controller Betty Yee, and Attorney General Kamala Harris. (Harris, who is half Indian American, became the first female, first African American, and first Asian American state attorney general in the United States in 2010.) In New York City, John Liu served as city comptroller and then waged a competitive campaign for mayor in 2013. San Francisco and Garden Grove, California, are among the cities that have Asian American mayors (Ed Lee and Bao Nguyen, respectively). As of 2015, there were eleven Asian Americans in the House of Representatives and one in the Senate.

NATIVE AMERICANS

Colin Cloud Hampson was an active leader in the Stanford American Indian Organization when I met him in 1988. I was active with the Black Student Union and our respective organizations worked together with other student-of-color groups and individual progressive White allies to advocate and agitate for more faculty of color. In 1989, we had to resort to taking over the university president's office in order to bring attention to the need for change. Through Colin and other friends, I learned about Native American history, culture, and struggles. Colin was active with Stanford Powwow, the West Coast's largest gathering of Native Americans, which brought together more than twenty thousand people each year, changing the complexion of Palo Alto, in the heart of Silicon Valley, for a few days.

Colin's maternal grandmother was from the Winnebago tribe and the White Earth Band of Chippewa (his father is White), two of the 595 federally recognized tribes in the continental United States (meaning they have a government-to-government relationship with the United States). Colin's mother enrolled in the Winnebago tribe in Nebraska, and later moved to Oregon, where Colin lived on the Umatilla Indian Reservation. The history of Colin's tribe, in general, and his great-grandfather, in particular, were closely connected to the legacy of two U.S. presidents.

The history of the Winnebago tribe stretches back hundreds of years and includes a major battle in 1811 that killed many Indians and ended up advancing the political career of a future U.S. president. The Winnebago Nation was part of a confederacy of Native Americans resisting White American westward expansion into Native territory, and a major battle took place near the Tippecanoe River (in present-day Indiana). Led by William Henry Harrison, the U.S. Army destroyed the town in which the Winnebago lived, "burning the town, destroying the granary, and looting, even digging up graves and mutilating the corpses." This murder and destruction established Harrison's reputation and earned him the nickname "Tippecanoe," a nickname popularized in his 1840 presidential campaign with the phrase, "Tippecanoe and Tyler too" (referring to Harrison and his running mate John Tyler).[45]

One hundred and ten years after the destruction at Tippecanoe, Colin's great-grandfather Henry Roe Cloud became an advisor to presidential administrations working on overhauling U.S. policy regarding Native Americans. Cloud was the first full-blood Native American admitted to Yale College and was instrumental in the 1920s in shifting U.S. education policy regarding Natives away from the assimilation model to one that supported the preservation of the Native students' cultures. He also advised President Roosevelt and helped draft the Indian Reorganization Act of 1934, which has been described as the "Indian New Deal" and marked a significant reversal of the then-U.S. policy toward Native Americans in that the act moved away from promoting assimilation of Native Americans into mainstream White culture and emphasized preservation of historic traditions and cultures.[46] In 1947, Cloud was appointed superintendent of the Umatilla Indian Reservation in Oregon, the same reservation where Colin would live nearly forty years later.

Life on the Umatilla Reservation, like many reservations, was difficult in that the community was very poor, with significant economic and social challenges that resulted in widespread loss, hardship, and tragedy. The overwhelmingly White high school nearby that Colin attended was frequently hostile and inhospitable to students from the reservation. But at the same time, Colin's family lineage included relatively significant success in mainstream White society. In addition to his great-grandfather's accomplishments, his grandfather became a professor at Stanford, where Colin's mother wound up matriculating (exposing Colin at an early age to the possibility of higher education).

Today, Colin holds a law degree from Stanford and is a partner in a prominent law firm focused on representing Native American interests across the country, and in recent years he has returned to Umatilla Reservation to provide legal services for the residents there.

NATIVE AMERICANS AT A GLANCE

Native Americans were once the sole occupants of what is now the East Coast of America. The fact that most of them now live in the middle of the continent says a lot about U.S. history. As White America moved westward in the nineteenth century it forced Native Americans farther and farther west until they were ultimately concentrated in the Western half of the continental United States.

At the western edge of the continent, many indigenous peoples also lived, loved, and worked. The historian Roxanne Dunbar-Ortiz captured this reality by writing, "In the Pacific Northwest, from

present-day Alaska to San Francisco, and along the vast inland waterways to the mountain barriers, great seafaring and fishing peoples
flourished, linked by culture, common ceremonies, and extensive
trade."[47] Contrary to the conventional wisdom that the U.S. government's practice of disrupting—if not destroying—indigenous land
and culture is a colonial era artifact, that course of conduct continued
as recently as 1959 when Alaska was made the forty-ninth state. With
passage of the Alaskan Statehood Act, "103 million acres were allotted
for federal land without regard for the indigenous tribal properties or
hunting, fishing, and gathering areas."[48]

It is important to remember that the group we call "Native Americans" is not one homogeneous racial group. This population actually consists of many different "peoples" or "sovereign nations," all of
whom faced and battled the violent assault of the U.S. government.
As recognized nations, Native peoples have signed treaties with the
United States, outlining rights and relationships to land, water, and
other intergovernmental matters (however, many treaties have been
broken when their terms were particularly inconvenient for the federal government). A legacy of wars waged and promises broken has
shaped the experience of the constellation of peoples we call Native
Americans.

As of the latest available census data, 5.2 million people, or 1.7 percent of the total U.S. population, are at least part Native American.
There are eight tribes with populations greater than 100,000 people,
the largest being Cherokee (819,105), followed by Navajo (332,129),
Choctaw (195,764), Mexican American Indian (175,494), Chippewa
(170,742), Sioux (170,110), Apache (111,810), and Blackfeet (105,304).
The Alaska Native population is 138,850.[49]

An estimated 40 percent of Native Americans now live in the geographic band that runs from South Dakota in the North, down through
Oklahoma, to Arizona and New Mexico in the Southwest. The four
states with the largest concentration of Native Americans are, respectively, Arizona, Oklahoma, New Mexico, and California (notably, North
Carolina is fifth, making it the main East Coast state to still have an
appreciable Native American population).

Figure 8 shows the geographic distribution of Native Americans.

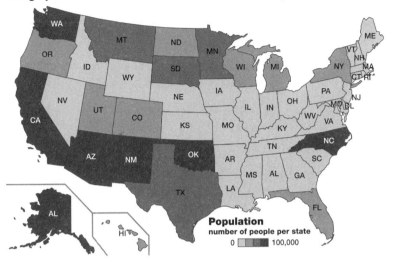

Where Native Americans Live:
Geographic Concentration of the Native American Population in the U.S.

Population
number of people per state
0   100,000

Figure 8. Source: Based on Dr. Laura Lara-Brady's tabulations of 2008–2012 American Community Survey 5-Year Estimates.

POLITICS

Notwithstanding the distinct nationhood of the various Native peoples, Native Americans have always occupied a complicated space in terms of their relationship to the United States, and this applies to the realm of voting as well. In an effort to accelerate assimilation, the U.S. government imposed citizenship on the indigenous peoples with the Indian Citizenship Act of 1924.[50] Ironically, the attempt to dilute the Native American identity has, in some ways, provided the tools, through the vote, for Native Americans to inject their voice into the political arena. Of the 5.2 million people who identify as Native American today, an estimated 3 million are eligible to vote.[51]

Because of their concentration in select regions and the steady population growth of the past several decades, Native Americans constitute a meaningful—and potentially decisive—swing vote in specific strategic states. In Alaska, they are 19.5 percent of the total state population (the largest percentage of Native people in any state), and in South Dakota and Arizona, for example, Native Americans comprise

8.5 percent and 4.6 percent of those states' populations, respectively. In North Dakota (the state itself is named after the Lakota and Dakota Sioux tribes), there are 50,000 eligible Native American voters, more than enough to influence the outcome of elections in a state where the 2012 U.S. Senate race was decided by just 2,936 votes.[52] Native American voters have sufficiently large numbers to also influence statewide electoral outcomes in Arizona, New Mexico, Montana, and Washington State.

ARAB AMERICANS

When I went to college in 1982, I had no idea my life, and my friends' lives, would be so influenced by Abdulfattah Jandali's son. From the tools we used to organize the 1987 March on Sacramento to how we listen to music and watch movies today, the lives of my circle of activists—and many others—bear the unmistakable stamp of the son of the immigrant teaching assistant from Syria. Jandali came to America from Syria in 1954 at the age of nineteen to attend graduate school at the University of Wisconsin, Madison, where he studied political science. He fell in love with Joanne Schieble, a White Wisconsin woman, also attending graduate school. When Schieble learned she was pregnant with Jandali's child, her father threatened to disown her if she married her Arab lover. Not wanting to incur the wrath of her father or the disapproval of her small town in Wisconsin, Schieble traveled to San Francisco to have the baby, and they gave the boy up for adoption. The son of Abdulfattah Jandali and Joanne Schieble was adopted by a nice White couple in Silicon Valley, Paul and Clara Jobs, and their adopted son—Steve Jobs—went on to found Apple Computer.[53]

Like Steve Jobs's biological father, the largest numbers of Arab Americans hail from Syria and its neighboring nation Lebanon.

WORDS MATTER: MUSLIMS, ARABS, ISLAM, ISLAMISTS— WHAT'S THE DIFFERENCE?

Arab Americans occupy a large place in American political discourse because they are frequently featured as scapegoats and used by politicians and others to fan the fears and anxieties of non-Arabs. Because of 9/11, the word "terrorist" has often become associated—if not used interchangeably—with "Muslim," "Islam," and "Arab" in the American mind-set. The conflating of religion and terrorism (something that doesn't happen, for some reason, when Christians commit terrorist acts) reached the point where, in 2015, leading Republican candidates for president were saying unapologetically that a Muslim should not be allowed to become president of the United States. For this reason, it is vitally important that we choose our words properly and know what we're talking about when referring to groups of people who may either come from a certain region of the world, practice a certain religion, or speak a certain language.

One area of great confusion involves the vocabulary associated with the intersection of the religion of Islam and the people from Arab countries. Although a consensus definition of "Arab" is actually somewhat elusive, the American-Arab Anti-Discrimination Committee says *Arab* is a "cultural and linguistic term" that "refers to those who speak Arabic as their first language. Arabs are united by culture and by history." Most of the countries where Arabs live and Arabic is spoken are in the Middle East and North Africa, a region consisting of twenty-five countries.[54]

In terms of religion, those who belong to the faith of Islam are called Muslims. The fact that different words refer to the religion and those who practice it can be confusing to Americans used to a situation where those who practice the religion of Christianity are called Christians, those who practice the religion of Judaism are called Jews, and those who practice Buddhism are called Buddhists, etc. Further complicating the picture is the usage of the term "Islamists," which is frequently used to refer to "someone who seeks to blend Islam and politics."[55]

Additional misperceptions frequently result from conflating religious identity with national identity. For a point of comparison, the largest religion in the United States is Christianity, and many, if not most, Americans identify as Christian. Christianity is a global religion, however, so obviously Christians are not all Americans. Such clarity is frequently missing in discussions of the Middle East. The

countries in the Middle East have the same three large religions as in
the United States—Christianity, Judaism, and Islam—except that in
those nations, Islam is the dominant religion. But that doesn't mean
that all Muslims are Arabs (in fact, just 15 percent of the world's Muslims are Arabs; the largest numbers of Muslims live in Indonesia, Pakistan, India, and Bangladesh).[56] The converse is also true. Not all Arabs
are Muslim (although a high percentage of Arabs are in fact Muslim).[57]

In the United States, 75 percent of Arab Americans are Christian,
and 25 percent are Muslim (the percentage of Muslims is higher—
60 percent—among those who immigrated since 1965).[58] Of Americans who practice the religion of Islam, 40 percent of first-generation
Muslims in the United States are Arab Americans (13 percent of U.S.
Muslims are African Americans born in the United States, many of
whom, like Malcolm X, Muhammad Ali, Congressman Keith Ellison,
and others, converted to Islam from Christianity).[59]

ARAB AMERICANS AT A GLANCE

As has been the case with Asian Americans and Latinos, the Arab
American population has grown significantly since the passage of the
1965 Immigration and Nationality Act. According to the latest census data, there are 1.7 million Arab Americans in the United States,
up more than 51 percent since 2000.[60] (The Arab American Institute
Foundation estimates there are nearly 3.7 million Arab Americans
living in the country. That number is likely more accurate since the
foundation takes into account the statistical shortcomings of the U.S.
census form.)[61]

Of those Arab Americans identified by the census, the largest subgroups are, in order of size, Lebanese Americans (502,000), Egyptian
Americans (190,000), Syrian Americans (148,000), Iraqi Americans
(106,000), Palestinian Americans (93,000), Moroccan Americans
(82,000), and Jordanian Americans (62,000).[62]

The geographic patterns of Arab Americans are more disparate
than those of other groups of color in the United States. The states with
the largest numbers of Arab Americans are, respectively, California,
Michigan, New York, Florida, and New Jersey. The largest concentrated

Where Arab Americans Live:
Geographic Concentration of the Arab American Population in the U.S.

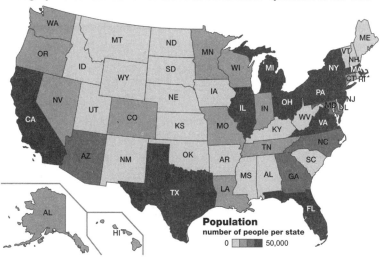

Figure 9. Source: Based on Dr. Laura Lara-Brady's tabulations of 2008–2012 American Community Survey 5-Year Estimates.

Arab American population is in Detroit, Michigan. With the more recent waves of Arab immigration, many newer arrivals have settled in California, in particular Southern California.

Figure 9 shows the geographic distribution of Arab Americans.

IRANIAN AMERICANS

There is another sizably significant group of people who have Middle Eastern heritage who are not Arabs, but also not White, and that is Iranian Americans. One article describes why Iranians and other people of Iranian descent are not Arabs by saying, "Alone among the Middle Eastern peoples conquered by the Arabs, the Iranians did not lose their language or their identity. Ethnic Persians make up 60 percent of modern Iran, and modern Persian is the official language." [63] And yet by virtue of skin color, speaking a language other than English, and coming from the Middle East, Iranians are generally not embraced as White folks in America. In terms of population size, the constricted categories of the Census Bureau make it difficult to arrive at an accurate figure, but most estimates settled around 1 million people (the Census Bureau figure is 448,722),[64] and half the country's Iranian Americans live in California, with the largest area of concentration being Los Angeles.

POLITICS

Exit poll data about Arab American voters is unfortunately not available due to the small sample size used by most pollsters, so we don't know as much as we should about this electorate. Much of what we do know is because of the work of two Lebanese American brothers, James and John Zogby. James helped found the Arab American Institute, and John runs Zogby Analytics, a leading national polling firm. John conducts regular polling of the Arab American electorate, and his 2014 poll found the following:

- 44 percent of Arab Americans identify as Democrats, 23 percent as Republicans, and 15 percent as Independent;
- In the 2012 election, 59 percent of Arab Americans who were surveyed said they voted for Obama, 23 percent for Romney, and 11 percent said they didn't vote;
- 65 percent of Arab American women voted for Obama, as did 53 percent of the men;
- 76 percent of Arab American Muslims supported Obama, compared to 48 percent of the Protestants and 51 percent of the Catholics.[65]

In areas of their greatest geographic concentration, Arab Americans can make a meaningful difference in election outcomes. Many analysts credit a large Arab American vote in Michigan with helping propel Jesse Jackson to victory over Michael Dukakis in the 1988 presidential primary. And as shown in Chapter 4, the Arab American vote was pivotal in the election of the mayor of Garden Grove, California, in 2014.

PROGRESSIVE WHITES

At first glance, Dave Brown was an unlikely radical. A successful White male Stanford graduate who'd served as president of Stanford's student government and then gone on to win election to the West Contra Costa school board in California in the district where he'd attended high school, Dave fit the profile of a typical ambitious young White guy on the fast track to an influential and prestigious career. So, in 2006, at just thirty-six years old and in the early stages of a promising political career, he didn't have to risk his prestige to stand up for low-income students of color whose futures were being held hostage by California's high-stakes testing, but that's what he did. At the time, California's "Exit Exam" required all high school seniors to pass a standardized test to graduate. If students didn't pass, the state would withhold their diplomas—a practice leading educators criticized as racially discriminatory and educationally ineffective since many low-income and immigrant students had not received proper training and instruction to pass the exam. Dave challenged the state's practice by introducing a resolution to reject the state's punitive move and award diplomas, a move the local paper described as "a call to rebel against the controversial graduation requirement."[66] Dave proposed allowing students to complete a research project or present a portfolio of their work in place of taking the exit exam as a graduation requirement.

Dave's colleagues lacked the courage to join him in challenging the state standards, resulting in the measure's defeat by a 4–1 vote—another example of how progressive Whites are frequently in the minority in the struggle for social change.

The seeds of Dave's political activism were sowed in his early experiences witnessing his parents working in the public sector with low-income families and children in the racially diverse San Francisco Bay Area. Dave's parents were the first in their families to attend college. Dave's father, Fred, is half Scottish and half Italian and was a public school teacher and coach. Dave's mom, Carol, is Jewish with Ukrainian ancestry and worked for years as a public health nurse. His parents gravitated to the public sector in part because their parents modeled racial tolerance during the early years of the civil rights movement in the 1950s. Dave's grandfather worked as an ironworker, and the casual racism of his colleagues and neighbors made an impression on Dave's father, who noted the different and more open attitude of his own father. Such open-mindedness stayed with Fred as the population of the Bay Area diversified in the 1960s, and eventually Fred became a public school teacher in one of the Bay Area's more racially diverse schools. Dave's mother went into nursing, where she worked with families attempting to navigate an often confusing social service sector. Through his parents' work, Dave received early exposure to society's inequality that left him disquieted and with the sense that something was wrong. When he got to Stanford, he found friends, colleagues, and teachers who helped him develop an analysis of structural racism, the power of the movements for racial justice, and the important role that progressive White allies could play in supporting the struggle for social change. It wasn't long before Dave was joining students of color in taking over the university president's office to demand more faculty of color, and from there it was a natural step to rebel against California's standardized tests, which were disproportionately harming hundreds of students of color in his school district.

PROGRESSIVE WHITES AT A GLANCE

Looking back at the bloody and racist saga of U.S. history and politics, it would be easy to condemn all White people for a fairly relentless assault on the lives, property, and prospects of people of color for the past four hundred–plus years. Largely lost to history, however—and critically important to the future—is the role of progressive Whites, those who took stands against American White supremacy in favor of an inclusive multiracial democracy. At practically every step of U.S. history, progressive Whites have stood up, spoken out, and fought back on the side of social justice and equality for people of color.

Like the late comedian Rodney Dangerfield, progressive Whites just don't get any respect. Scholars, academics, journalists, politicians, pollsters, and operatives have historically neglected this vitally important demographic. As a result, the body of knowledge about who progressive Whites are, where they are, and how they behave is grossly inadequate. All contemporary analyses—including this book—are therefore diminished by that deficit. It is my hope to catalyze a conversation and redirect attention and resources so that, in future years, we deepen our collective understanding about this essential element of the New American Majority equation. Until then, here is what we do know.

The media, popular culture, and conservative critics like to promote caricatures of progressive White people. One of the most entertaining exaggerations was the 2004 television ad criticizing Howard Dean's presidential campaign supporters by presenting purported Iowa residents saying to the camera, "Howard Dean should take his tax-hiking, government-expanding, latte-drinking, sushi-eating, Volvo-driving, New York Times–reading, body-piercing, Hollywood-loving, left-wing freak show back to Vermont." [67] While it's true some progressive Whites drive Volvos, read the *New York Times*, and drink lattes, that picture is decidedly inaccurate.

Not all stereotypes are completely baseless, and there is some truth to the perception about the preponderance of liberals on both coasts, as California and New York boast the largest numbers of progressive Whites.[68] Less appreciated is the fact that meaningful numbers of progressive Whites live in the South. Texas, for example, has more than 2 million progressive Whites, and in North Carolina their number tops 1.6 million.[69] Many have observed that some of the staunchest White progressives are those who come from the South because they have had many chances to observe overt racism close up and have had to make a more conscious stand against racism and discrimination.

Figure 10 shows the geographic distribution of progressive Whites.

POLITICS

The percentage of Whites who voted for the Democratic nominee for president has fluctuated from a low of 32 percent in 1972 to a high of 58 percent in 1964, the last year a Democratic presidential candidate (Lyndon B. Johnson) won the majority of the White vote.[70] In the most recent election, Obama received the support of 39 percent of White voters. The historical average since 1972 is 39.91 percent.[71]

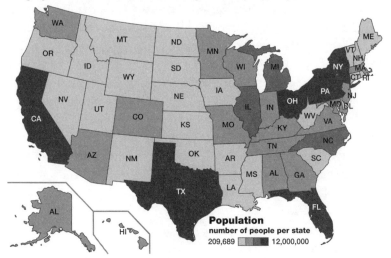

Figure 10. Source: American Majority Project Research Institute (AMPRI) tabulations from the 2012 Current Population Survey, November supplements, and National Election Pool Exit Poll, 2008.

The 2008 and 2012 national exit polls provide the following information about progressive White voters:

- 73 percent make over $50,000 per year;
- They are evenly split between those who graduated from college and those who did not (51 percent are college grads);
- 56 percent are women (as compared to 50.8 percent of the total U.S. population);
- They are relatively evenly dispersed throughout the country (that is, they don't all live in Vermont, or Berkeley). The South and East are each home to slightly less than one-quarter of the country's progressive Whites, and the West and Midwest each contain slightly more than one-quarter of that population.
- Slightly more of them identify as being "Born Again" (19.6 percent) than identify as having "No Religion" (18 percent);
- The majority (56 percent) are over 45 years old;

- A higher percentage of young Whites (18 to 29 years old) vote progressive compared to older Whites (40 and over), 44 percent compared to 39 percent.[72]

In 2014, the Pew Research Center conducted a large-scale survey that engaged 10,000 people (five times the sample size of most national surveys) in exploring what they call the "typology" of Americans. They divided the population into eight "types" or groups based on attitudes and values, and then asked all participants a set of questions to determine which type they fell into.[73] The results are illuminating and instructive, especially when matched with census data to determine relative sizes of the population represented by each group.

Progressive Whites largely fell into three of the eight types: Solid Liberals, Faith and Family Left, and Next Generation Left. The number of Whites who identify with those three groups is 37 percent of all Whites, and that comes close to the 39 percent percentage of Whites who voted for Obama.[74] Pew describes these groups as follows:

SOLID LIBERALS (42 PERCENT OF PROGRESSIVE WHITES)

Highly educated and affluent, Solid Liberals strongly support the social safety net and take very liberal positions on virtually all issues. Most say they always vote Democratic and they are unflagging supporters of Barack Obama. Solid Liberals are very optimistic about the nation's future and are the most likely to say that America's success is linked to its ability to change, rather than its reliance on longstanding principles. On foreign policy, Solid Liberals overwhelmingly believe that good diplomacy—rather than military strength—is the best way to ensure peace.

NEXT GENERATION LEFT (33 PERCENT OF PROGRESSIVE WHITES)

Young, well educated, and financially comfortable, the Next Generation Left have very liberal attitudes on many issues, including homosexuality and abortion, the environment, and foreign policy. They are supportive of an activist government but wary of expanding the social safety net. They also have relatively positive views of Wall Street's impact on the economy. While most affiliate with the Democratic Party or lean Democratic, few consider themselves strong Democrats.

FAITH AND FAMILY LEFT (25 PERCENT OF PROGRESSIVE WHITES)

The Faith and Family Left combine strong support for an activist government with conservative attitudes on many social issues. The Faith and Family Left favor increased government aid for the poor even if it adds to the deficit and believe that government should do more to solve national problems. They oppose same-sex marriage and legalizing marijuana. Religion and family are at the center of their lives.

When my friends and I marched through the California State Capitol in 1987, we didn't fully understand the journeys we'd all taken to get to the same place. While we were marching for educational equity and access, we did know intuitively that our parents, grandparents, and ancestors had walked even harder roads, literally and proverbially. Our ancestors had traveled the Trail of Tears, the paths of the Underground Railroad and Great Migration, the waterways of the Pacific Rim, the Atlantic and Pacific Oceans, and the roads of what was once Mexico. We were more united in a common cause than we'd realized. We knew that something powerful happened when you brought these disparate communities of color together with their progressive White allies at one time in one place. In many ways, that is what is happening all across the country politically now. The separate roads walked by the communities of color and progressive Whites have ended up in common destinations of communal power. The regions where we were once repressed separately can now be the cornerstones of a new political structure if we come together, work together, and vote together.

3

Blinded by the White

The record is there for all to read. It resounds all over the world. It might as well be written in the sky. One wishes that Americans, white Americans, would read, for their own sakes, this record and stop defending themselves against it. Only then will they be enabled to change their lives. The fact that they have not yet been able to do this—to face their history to change their lives—hideously menaces this country. Indeed, it menaces the entire world.[1]
—James Baldwin, "The White Man's Guilt," 1965

As an American raised in this society with negative implicit biases against black people, you are not a bad person. You are simply a normal American.[2]
—David Williams, Harvard sociologist, 2015

It's impossible to fully understand modern American politics without coming to terms with the fact that this country has been obsessed with White people for 409 years. Since 1607, the year the first English immigrants landed in what is now Jamestown, Virginia, the fears, concerns, and prejudices of Whites have shaped American public policy, politics, and culture in deep and lasting ways that continue to influence our society today. Conventional wisdom holds that conservatives are the ones who have the problem with racial issues, but progressives are also complicit. Even at this time, when a racial demographic revolution has transformed the composition of the electorate and elected and re-elected a Black president, much of the progressive movement and many progressive campaigns are still dominated by White leadership, fixated on White voters, and focused on policies preferred by White people.

This reality did not develop in a vacuum. There is a context for the continued and disproportionate dominance of Whites, mainly White men, in most of the country's leading political organizations and institutions. There is an explanation for the persistent and baseless focus on White swing voters. There is a reason the overwhelming majority of people of color support social change and progressive public policies.

Looking at the ugly and unvarnished history of the United States reveals three truths that are critically important for understanding contemporary politics. First is that the political character of the New American Majority is inherently progressive, as it rests on the foundation of the communities who have historically battled discrimination and exploitation in the pursuit of justice and equality. This reality means that the political agenda of those communities is much further to the left than that of the more moderate swing voters who are the perennial focus of the country's political parties, and a choice has to be made about which voters to prioritize. The second truth is that many of the leaders and funders of the current progressive movement have been infected by the deep-seated preference for Whites to the extent that they are blinded to the potential and power of the rapidly growing communities of color. The modern successor to old-school, explicit, widespread White supremacy is equally widespread but more implicit, often unconscious, bias that continues to influence and inhibit the potential of the progressive movement. The third relevant reality is that the obsessive focus on "what will White people think?" and the fear of alienating White voters has led progressive leaders frequently to surrender their highest hopes, ideals, and dreams, resulting in a pattern of repeated capitulation to and compromise with conservative Whites that continues apace today.

A lot of people don't want to hear about the White supremacist roots of the United States. Many deflect discussion and divert attention by saying, "That happened a long time ago," "I didn't kill Native Americans," "My family didn't hold slaves," or "People should stop complaining about ancient history." We have seen multiple manifestations of this willful amnesia in the past couple of years. In the fall of 2015, five million public school students in Texas began using new textbooks that treat slavery as a "side issue" of the Civil War. One Texas State Board of Education member explained the thinking behind adopting the new curriculum materials by saying, "There would be those who would say the reason for the Civil War was over slavery. No. It was over states' rights."[3]

The problem is not confined to Texas. High school students across the country who take Advanced Placement History now receive a neutered version of history after the College Board caved to conservative criticism in 2015 about the course's content. According to the *Washington Post*, "The chief complaint was that the 2014 AP history course taught the story of the United States as 'identity politics'—a series of conflicts over power and control between various groups, as opposed to explaining historical events through commonalities and shared ideals of the American people."[4] The *Post* article lacked specific examples of exactly which shared ideals existed between Native Americans and the people who massacred them and what the commonalties were between Black people held in slavery and the owners who whipped them.

Even after the June 17, 2015, Charleston, South Carolina, massacre—committed by a Confederate flag–loving White supremacist who reportedly said, "You're raping our women and taking over our country," as he pumped bullets into the Black bodies of nine church members gathered for Bible study at Mother Emanuel Church—many people still refused to acknowledge the power and persistence of White supremacist symbols in this country. Days after the Charleston massacre—and 150 years after the end of the Civil War—elected political leaders from the South Carolina state legislature to the U.S. House of Representatives defended the fictional notion that the Confederacy and the Civil War were about preserving Southern "heritage" rather than protecting the right of Whites to buy and sell darker-hued human beings like "an ordinary article of merchandise and traffic whenever a profit could be made by it," as the Supreme Court unapologetically held in its infamous 1857 *Dred Scott* decision.[5]

Despite the sense of shame brought on by the murder of the parishioners, the South Carolina legislature was still reluctant to remove the Confederate flag from the grounds of the state capitol and instead endured sixty-eight amendments designed to block passage of the bill calling for removal of the flag, during a marathon thirteen-hour legislative session.[6] The South Carolina House of Representatives only acted after Republican state representative Jenny Horne, a descendant of Jefferson Davis, president of the Confederate states during the Civil War, made a tearful and impassioned plea that finally set the debate in its proper context, saying, "The people of Charleston deserve swift and immediate removal of that flag from these grounds. I cannot believe that we do not have the heart in this body to do something meaningful. . . . I am sorry; I have heard enough about heritage. I am a descendant of Jefferson Davis, O.K., but that does not matter."[7]

However uncomfortable it may be, finally facing the facts of how the United States has privileged Whites and exploited and oppressed people of color for hundreds of years is essential to developing effective contemporary public policies and crafting winning political campaigns in an increasingly multiracial nation. The record is there for all to read. Examining it holds the key to unlocking the answers to why things are the way they are and what it will take to make progressive change possible.

THE REJECTED STONE SHALL BE THE CORNERSTONE OF THE NEW ORDER

In this era of big data, computers can perform sophisticated analyses that slice and dice the population in a lot of different ways. Using age as a filter, one sees the aging of the baby boom generation and the rise of the millennials. A geographic lens shows population increases in the South and Southwest. Focusing on employment, one can identify a decline in blue-collar workers. These examples yield interesting and useful information, but it is the changes in the racial demographic composition of the country that hold revolutionary implications for American politics.

There is a reason why people of color are progressive. It has nothing to do with the amount of melanin in one's skin and everything to do with the history of America's treatment of people of color. The New American Majority is inherently progressive because it is a direct outgrowth of centuries of exclusion and exploitation. The foundation of the coalition that elected Obama is a constellation of groups who were formerly oppressed, still battle discrimination, and maintain a hunger for equality and justice. In a country that ended legalized racial discrimination only in 1964—three years after Obama was born—nearly half the president's voters (45 percent) in 2012 were people of color. The rejected stone has become the cornerstone of the new order.

THE HISTORICAL RECORD

In order to appreciate the progressive potential of this new majority, it helps to understand the depth, breadth, and duration of America's preference for White people. Many minimize, skim over, or rationalize the legacy of American White supremacy by suggesting that it was limited to a small number of bad actors. In reality, the view that Whites were superior to people of color was the majority mind-set in America for most of U.S. history, and it was ratified by laws that enjoyed widespread public approval.

Consider just a few examples of U.S. laws that have enjoyed majority support in America:

- Prior to the formal formation of the United States, many colonies passed laws to establish the relative relationships and positions of the country's racial groups. South Carolina's 1712 Slave Code read, "Negroes and other slaves brought unto the people of this Province for that purpose, are of barbarous, wild, savage natures, and such as renders them wholly unqualified to be governed by the laws, customs, and practices of this Province."[8] The "wild and barbarous" nature of Black people required the establishment of laws to "restrain the disorders, rapines and inhumanity, to which they are naturally prone and inclined."[9]

- Article I, Section 2 of the U.S. Constitution states that Black people were only to be counted for tax purposes as three-fifths of a human being. The language of the Privileges and Immunities clause (Article IV, Section 2) includes the "Fugitive Slave Clause," which made it illegal for anyone to interfere with slave owners who were tracking down human beings who managed to escape captivity.[10] (Incidentally, this tendency of Black folks wanting to be free was eventually diagnosed as a mental disorder and given the name drapetomania, "the disease causing negroes to run away." Google it.)[11]

- As a young nation looked west and saw that the rest of the continent was replete with rich and fertile land, America's leaders sought to secure this region for White people despite the fact that Native Americans already occupied the territory. In 1823, the U.S. Supreme Court cited the "superior genius" of Whites in its ruling that Native Americans—"fierce savages," in the language of the Court—could not legally hold title to land.[12] Buoyed by this legal authority, President Andrew Jackson then convinced Congress to pass the 1830 Indian Removal Act, which granted him authority to clear a path—by any means necessary—for White westward expansion.[13]

- The idea that White people had a Manifest Destiny to conquer the continent was translated into laws that were backed by guns and force. The land formerly belonging to Mexico was taken through violence that killed 26,000 Mexicans, forcing Mexico to cede much of its territory to the United States in the Treaty of Guadalupe Hidalgo in 1848.[14]

- The discovery of gold in California in 1849 and the prospect that Whites could get rich from that mineral wealth motivated the California legislature to, among its very first acts, pass a law authorizing more than $1 million ($29 million in today's dollars) to reimburse the White "Indian hunters" for expenses they may have incurred in killing Native Americans to clear the way for gold prospectors.[15]

- Even after slavery was finally eliminated with the passage of the Thirteenth, Fourteenth, and Fifteenth Amendments to the Constitution—at the price of a bloody Civil War and the first assassination of an American president—racial discrimination remained perfectly legal and widely practiced for another hundred years. The Supreme Court declared in 1896 in *Plessy v. Ferguson*, "We cannot say that a law which authorizes or even requires the separation of the two races in public conveyances is unreasonable." The Court added, "If one race be inferior to the other socially, the Constitution of the United States cannot put them upon the same plane."[16] Sixty years later, the seminal *Brown v. Board of Education* decision (1954) outlawed racial segregation in schools but left untouched legalized racial discrimination in public accommodations and transportation.[17] It wasn't until adoption of the 1964 Civil Rights Act that racial discrimination was officially outlawed throughout the country.

"FREE WHITE PEOPLE": THE DEFINITION OF AMERICAN

America's fixation with White people at its most clear, explicit, unapologetic, and uninterrupted can be found in the history of the country's immigration policy. The common modern expressions of "They should speak English," "They should go back where they came from," and "They are illegals" have deep roots in American history. For most of the country's first century, only White people could become U.S. citizens. For most of the second century, only White people could enter America and stay.

- As one of its initial acts, the first U.S. Congress passed the Immigration and Naturalization Act in 1790, stating that citizenship was reserved for "free White persons."[18]
- The "free White persons" framework then guided immigration policy for 164 years (until 1954), and the Supreme Court regularly reaffirmed the validity of the "Whites only" sign on the doorway to the United States. In 1857, the court ruled "citizenship was perfectly understood to be confined to the White race."[19] In 1920 the court reexamined the 1790 law, upheld its validity, and ruled in *Ozawa v. United States* and *United States v. Bhagat Singh Thind* that Asians could not become U.S. citizens, because they were not White.[20]
- In 1882, Congress passed, and President Chester Arthur signed, the unambiguously titled Chinese Exclusion Act, which barred most Chinese from immigrating to the United States.[21]
- In the 1920s, the national origin quota system was created to guide immigration policy. That system allocated a limited number of slots—or visas—to each country, determining how many

people from any country could come to the United States.[22] In devising this system, the plan's architect, Dr. Joseph A. Hill, a Census Bureau statistician, tellingly said in 1926, "The stream that feeds the reservoir should have the same composition as the contents of the reservoir itself."[23] By "reservoir," Hill was referring to the racial composition of the United States, which was nearly 90 percent White at the time. Accordingly, countries of color received very few slots, and most people from Asian countries were banned outright from entering the United States until 1965 (which explains why 74 percent of Asian American adults today were born outside the United States).

- It wasn't until passage of the Immigration and Nationality Act of 1965 that the official policy of excluding non-Whites from entering the country and becoming citizens was consigned to the dustbin of history.[24]

And now, the recipients of these hundreds of years of racially oppressive policies, practices, and attacks have the numbers—along with their progressive White allies—to elect presidents. Little wonder that *The Daily Show*'s then-host Jon Stewart jokingly asked Barack Obama in 2008, "If you are fortunate to become President of the United States . . . will you enslave the White race?"[25]

Many of today's 119 million people of color in America look at politics, politicians, and their political choices through the filter of this racially charged history and racially unequal present, so it really should come as no surprise that the vast majority of people of color support progressive social, economic, and political change.

OLD HABITS ARE HARD TO BREAK: BLINDED TO THE POTENTIAL OF THE NEW AMERICAN MAJORITY

These centuries of celebrating Whiteness have taken their toll on the American psyche. The White superiority mind-set is now so deeply embedded in the cultural fabric of the nation that it infects—and devalues—nearly every facet of modern life.

Old-fashioned racial violence is not nearly as anachronistic as most people would like to believe. Although the kinds of terrorism practiced by hate groups such as the Ku Klux Klan have gone out of style, they haven't gone out of existence. The Charleston shooting was not an aberration. Justice Department statistics show that more than 250,000 hate crimes still occur every year.[26]

The spate of high-profile police murders of unarmed Black people in recent years and the attendant Black Lives Matter mass protests across the country have highlighted the criminal justice system's abuses, failures, and disproportionate incarceration of Blacks and Latinos. African Americans were 13 percent of the country's population in 2013, but 36 percent of the people locked up in prison. Latinos comprised 17 percent of the country in 2013 and 22 percent of the prison population.[27]

Less visible, but no less meaningful, are the ways in which the tradition of catering to and showing preference toward White people influences leaders and institutions in politics; business; art, culture, and entertainment; academia; and the media, among other sectors of society. From decisions about who is most qualified to run political campaigns to judgments about whom to fund, hire, and promote in the business world, to assessments about which artists and entertainers deserve backing in Hollywood, to determinations of whose scholarship is worthy of study and tenure in academia, to assessments about what stories to pursue and which reporters to elevate in journalism, the unspoken American mantra still seems to echo the phrase made popular by the old Big Bill Broonzy song: "If you're White, you're right."[28]

Unlike the more blatant forms of racism that defined most of the civil rights battles in the 1950s and 1960s—legalized segregation marked by "Whites only" signs and enforced through terrorism, cross burnings, and murder—implicit bias is much more subtle and insidious. It is also much more widespread.

According to Alexis McGill, executive director of the Perception Institute, implicit bias refers to "embedded stereotypes that heavily influence our decision-making without our conscious knowledge."[29] Commenting on research showing that bias is so extensive that even children in studies have displayed racialized responses, UC Berkeley's john a. powell noted that, "It would be absurd to claim that young

children are racist. Negative racial associations are socially and culturally embedded: these are not only, or even primarily, individual
thoughts . . . these biases are socially communicated and supported."[30]
Harvard's David Williams, a leading social scientist who has studied
implicit bias and written more than 350 scholarly papers, put it this
way: "We have to come to grips with the reality that this racism is so
deeply embedded in our culture that it shapes how we see the world, it
shapes our beliefs, our behavior, our actions toward members of other
groups."[31]

One of the most powerful studies illustrating how implicit bias
works in hiring is a 2003 report titled, *Are Emily and Greg More Employable than Lakisha and Jamal?* In this investigation by professors from
the Massachusetts Institute of Technology and the University of Chicago, researchers sent out résumés that were identical in content but
had different names. Those with more "Black-sounding" names such
as Lakisha and Jamal received 50 percent fewer callbacks for interviews
than those with more "White-sounding" names such as Emily and
Greg.[32]

When one thinks about hiring, funding, and promotion decisions
in the context of implicit bias, in general, and the Lakisha and Jamal
study, in particular, it's not hard to understand why there are still such
widespread racial disparities in our country. White people constitute
62 percent of the people in America, but 96 percent of Fortune 500
companies in America have White CEOs.[33] In the venture capital
world—where investment decisions are made about whom to fund—
87 percent of venture capital funding goes to Whites.[34] On America's
college campuses, 84 percent of full-time faculty are White.[35] In media
and journalism, Whites make up 87 percent of newspaper reporters
and 85 percent of newspaper editors.[36] In the world of arts and entertainment, 95 percent of the lead roles on broadcast television shows go
to Whites and 96 percent of those shows' creators (including writers,
producers, and directors) are White.[37] In government, nearly 90 percent of all elected officials are White,[38] and, as we'll see in Chapter 5,
in politics nearly all of the hundreds of millions of dollars spent on
Democratic politics are controlled by Whites.

Because of the resistance to reviewing the historical record, it is fashionable to try to separate contemporary inequality from America's history of racial discrimination and oppression. For those who argue that racism no longer exists, I like to ask, "When, *exactly*, did it end?" Race-based discrimination was completely legal and widely practiced until the mid-1960s, when the 1964 Civil Rights Act, 1965 Voting Rights Act, and 1968 Fair Housing Act were adopted. Racism clearly didn't end before then, so maybe one could argue it ended sometime between 1968 and today. But the Lakisha and Jamal study shows that documented racial bias has persisted into the twenty-first century. That leaves a very small window for proponents of the end-of-racism theory to locate a point when hundreds of years of comprehensive racial discrimination withered away.

Most pertinent to those seeking to succeed in modern-day politics is the fact that an increasingly large sector of the American electorate still believes that racial discrimination is real and relevant today. According to a 2015 poll, 69 percent of African Americans and 66 percent of Latinos believe racial discrimination is a problem.[39] The poll also found that 45 percent of Whites think racial discrimination remains an obstacle (even higher than the 39 percent of Whites who have historically voted for Democrats for president). A separate poll in 2013 showed that 61 percent of Asian Americans identify racial discrimination as a problem as well.[40]

When it comes to building an electoral majority in a multiracial country one can spend one's time trying to refute the reality of racial inequality by searching for alternative explanations for current disparities, or one can get busy championing those hurt by inequality and discrimination and help fix the problem.

THE TYRANNY OF THE WHITE SWING VOTER

Over the course of our history and to the present day, our elected leaders have repeatedly made decisions that have harmed millions of people, and they made those decisions because they have been blinded by the perceived power of White swing voters.

To understand this pattern better, it is useful, and more or less accurate, to think of America's White population as divided into roughly equal thirds. We're not talking about mathematically precise 33.33-percent segments, mind you, but broadly speaking, three large chunks of White folks. One-third can be classified as progressive, one-third as solidly conservative, and one-third in the middle. Over the course of U.S. history the specific issues that have mattered to Whites in the middle have differed according to the dominant concerns of the day. But one issue that has remained a constant top concern for all three White groups is this country's relationship to and treatment of its residents of color. About one-third of Whites have generally tried to side with and stand for justice for people of color. One-third has consistently opposed racial equality and inclusion. And one-third has swung back and forth.

Since neither progressives nor conservatives have had a consistent majority of the population, politics has historically been a battle for the support of the Whites in the middle. In pursuit of the support of White swing voters, even those White political leaders who had a more progressive mind-set frequently ended up surrendering their highest hopes and dreams as they capitulated time and again to those with baser political instincts and goals. This reality dates back to the founding of the Republic and continues today.

In drafting the Declaration of Independence, Thomas Jefferson recognized that slavery was a moral abomination that made a mockery of the claims of the colonies for "independence." As British abolitionist Thomas Day wrote, "If there be an object truly ridiculous in nature, it is an American patriot, signing resolutions of independency with the one hand, and with the other brandishing a whip over his affrighted slaves."[41] Jefferson sought to address the contradiction by including language in his early drafts condemning King George III for being "determined to keep open a market where men should be bought & sold." The Southern delegates, however, refused to sign any version of the document that acknowledged the basic human rights of Black people. Jefferson signaled the coming centuries of compromise on racial justice issues by striking the passages that the slave owners found objectionable.[42]

While Abraham Lincoln is rightly credited with helping lead the nation to abolish slavery, he also tempered his tongue and moderated his actions for fear of alienating White swing voters. In the famous Lincoln-Douglas debates that preceded his election, Lincoln went to great pains to reassure moderate and conservative Whites that he had no intention of disturbing their privileged place in the world. In the 1858 debate, Lincoln opened his remarks by stating that an elderly gentleman had asked him at his hotel that morning if he really intended to bring about "perfect equality between the negroes and white people." The Great Emancipator responded by putting to rest the fears of White people, saying, "I am not, nor ever have been, in favor of bringing about in any way the social and political equality of the white and black races." He went on to add that so long as there was going to be inequality, "I as much as any other man am in favor of having the superior position assigned to the white race."[43] After the Civil War, the prioritization of the concerns of Whites led to one of the great tragedies of U.S. history when the North abandoned Reconstruction-era efforts to compensate and empower the people formerly held in slavery, out of deference to and fear of inconveniencing the people who had made financial fortunes through holding humans in bondage.[44]

The New Deal reforms enacted in the 1930s to lift the nation out of the Great Depression are correctly considered to be some of the most progressive policies of modern history, but their scope was curtailed and limited at the insistence of Southern Whites who didn't want progressive protections to extend to people of color. Ira Katznelson's book *Fear Itself* illustrates how Roosevelt made significant concessions to Southern conservatives who sought to block or limit many of the New Deal's most progressive policy measures. Farm laborers and domestic servants—occupations filled largely by African Americans—for example, were excluded from the Social Security Act.[45] As discussed more fully in chapter 7, the benefits of the massive GI Bill that propelled the creation of the modern middle class were largely limited to Whites.

Lyndon Johnson, America's top general in the War on Poverty and champion of the Great Society when he was president, was limited and constrained by the conservatism of Southern Whites for most of his career. Although he's known in part for supporting the kinds of sweeping civil rights legislation covered in Chapter 1, LBJ led much of the early opposition to civil rights legislation in the 1940s and 1950s before he became president in 1963. In 1957, when the Senate took up the first civil rights bill in eighty-two years, Johnson, Senate majority leader at the time, removed provisions for the enforcement of voting rights and school desegregation and "whittled the bill down to minimal form on what he thought was the political center of gravity."[46]

As much as Bill Clinton was hailed as "America's first Black president," he also had his moments of concession and compromise out of fear of alienating White swing voters. This played out especially on matters of criminal justice. During his 1992 election, Clinton left the campaign trail to return to Arkansas to oversee the execution of partially brain-damaged African American Ricky Ray Rector, sending a message that he was a "law and order" Southerner in what the *New York Times* described as a move "that could help pre-empt Republican attacks on the crime issue."[47] And, in 1994, he signed off on draconian federal sentencing guidelines that led to a dramatic increase in mass incarceration. In 2015, Clinton admitted that that decision had been a mistake, saying, "I signed a bill that made the problem worse and I want to admit it."[48]

As we'll explore in the next chapter, even our first real Black president has made compromises and trade-offs to avoid alienating Whites he thought he needed to maintain political viability. Prior to the 2014 midterm elections, moderate Democrats prevailed on President Obama to mute his progressive policy agenda and delay taking action on immigration reform, among other policy proposals. Ironically, after the elections, which resulted in Republicans thrashing Democrats, taking the Senate and winning House and statehouse races across the board, when Obama had nothing left to lose, he rolled out one progressive proposal after another on issues such as immigration, access to higher education, a higher minimum wage, and climate change and his approval ratings actually rose, proving the popularity of a New American Majority agenda.

America faces a contradiction that contains the seeds of a solution for building a more just and equal society. On the one hand, the racial record of exploiting people of color and elevating Whites is extensive and ultimately irrefutable. This record undermines the cherished concept that "all men are created equal" in a nation that values "liberty and justice for all." On the other hand, because of the population changes of the past fifty years, the very groups that were formerly oppressed now have the numbers to secure the political power necessary to set the country on the course toward true justice and equality. To realize this potential will require facing the fact of the country's past and present preference for White people, and making major changes in priorities so that time, attention, and massive amounts of resources are directed toward the country's communities of color.

In the aftermath of the Charleston shootings in 2015, for the first time in a long time, the country grappled with its legacy of White supremacy, the meaning of the Confederate flag, and the persistence of other symbols of slavery. During those deeply depressing days, President Obama lifted the nation's spirits in his moving eulogy for Reverend Clementa Pinckney and the other victims of the shooting. The president's remarks were centered on the theme of grace, and he concluded his speech by leading the congregation in singing the old spiritual "Amazing Grace," which includes the words, "I once was blind, but now I see."[49] Hopefully, the very fact that a Black man named Barack Hussein Obama could be elected and reelected as president can help those who have been blinded by centuries of celebrating Whiteness to now see that a new, multiracial, social justice majority is finally within our grasp.

4

Requiem for the White Swing Voter

The only middle-aged white men who voted for me were myself and my brothers. We have to speak to majorities. And we're probably never going to have a majority made up of middle-aged white men.[1]
— Connecticut governor Dannel Malloy, 2015

On election day in 1992, Sharen Hewitt pulled up alongside my car and yelled out, "Steve, get out to the Bayview for your final Get Out the Vote push." I was running for a seat on the Board of Education (trying to become the only Black person on the board), the race was close, and Sharen was a leader in San Francisco's Bayview/Hunter's Point neighborhood, the area of the city with a large Black population. I smiled, nodded, waved at Sharen, and proceeded to head out instead to St. Francis Woods, the Whitest and wealthiest part of San Francisco. At that time, the largest number of people who actually cast ballots in school board races lived in St. Francis Woods and other largely White neighborhoods, and that is how a school district where 90 percent of children were students of color had a governing body dominated by a grouping called "the White ladies." My campaign's strategy of targeting the mainly White pool of likely voters was successful, and I won the election, so I understand quite well the instinct, impulse, and inclination to prioritize the pursuit of White swing voters. But the electorate of 2016 is very different than that of 1992, and we can finally stop the relentless—and increasingly ineffective—courtship of that shrinking sector of the population.

The idea that White votes matter most has dominated American politics for the past four hundred years, forty years, and even the past four years. The name given to the White swing voters has changed over the years, but the basic concept has remained constant. As Bill Clinton's campaign manager James Carville put it, "The highest-premium voter in '92 was a voter who would vote for one party some and for another party some." [2]

In the early 1980s, the phrase du jour was "Reagan Democrats," those registered Democrats who broke with their party and backed Ronald Reagan over Jimmy Carter in 1980 and then Walter Mondale in 1984. Democratic pollster Stan Greenberg described them as "non-college-educated white voters" and said that he had made a "career of spotlighting their middle-class anger and frustrations about race and Democratic politicians." [3] In the 1990s, the description became "soccer moms." *New York Times* writer Neil MacFarquhar wrote in 1996 that "pollsters and demographers find the term useful as a catchall for suburban women, most married and working at least part-time outside the home, with children under 18." [4] MacFarquhar noted that they were candidates for the "Swing Voters' Hall of Fame" because "there has been a big change in the voting inclinations of white women." In the early 2000s, the terminology of choice was "exurban voters" who, according to the *Los Angeles Times*, were "fleeing built-out areas near cities for the newest ring of developments beyond the suburbs . . . searching for more house for less money, better schools, less traffic and all-around easier living. Exurban areas are booming and, according to demographers and GOP strategists, rapidly drawing a concentration of culturally conservative but unregistered, unaffiliated voters." [5] Now, in a spate of recent articles and analyses in the wake of the Democrats' defeats in 2014, the focus is on "working-class Whites," with whom the Democrats supposedly still have a problem.

Whatever you call them—Reagan Democrats, White working-class voters, or White swing voters—the idea is the same, and the idea that they are needed to win elections in modern, multiracial America is fundamentally fact-free and flat-out wrong. Democrats do not need to chase White swing voters in order to win, and, in fact, their determination to do so is responsible for their devastating losses in the midterm elections of 2010 and 2014.

WHAT REALLY HAPPENED IN THE 2010 AND 2014
MIDTERM ELECTIONS

For a brief period in 2008, some leading political opinion leaders entertained the idea that "demography is destiny," and that the Obama coalition may have reconfigured the electoral calculus in the country. Immediately after Obama's election, Stan Greenberg wrote an op-ed in the *New York Times* titled, "Goodbye, Reagan Democrats," in which he said, "I'm finished with the Reagan Democrats," because the much more diverse voters were now ascendant and represented "the New America."[6] He bid them "good riddance." But such sentiments were short-lived.

The resurrection of the Reagan Democrat obsession stems from an incorrect and flawed summation of what happened in the 2010 and 2014 midterm elections, when Democrats lost control of the House (2010) and Senate (2014). The general consensus in the media and among political leaders of both parties about why Republicans won so many congressional seats is that White swing voters switched their preferences from progressive to conservative, thereby flipping control of Congress.

Rather than seeing the Obama election as the dawn of a promising new era for a progressive multiracial majority, David Wasserman, an analyst for the highly respected *Cook Political Report*, concluded that the explanation for the losses in the midterms can be traced to Obama's victory in 2008, which, in Wasserman's view, actually sowed the seeds of the party's eventual destruction. In "The Great Democratic Crack- Up of 2016," a 2015 *New York Times* article previewing the 2016 presidential election, Wasserman said:

> When Obama swept the 2008 primary and general elections, Democrats' image suddenly came to be defined by a city-dwelling law-school professor whose life experiences had been far different from those of most working-class whites. . . . It was the culminating moment of a half-century of realignment. Democrats had already ceded Southern whites, but in the last few years they have lost droves of Midwestern, small-town and

working-class whites who feel like they have little in common with the party anymore.[7]

Prominent columnists such as David Brooks of the *New York Times'* wrote in early 2015 that the country's demographic shifts did not add up to an electoral advantage for Democrats because "Democrats continue to lose support among the white working class."[8] The *National Journal*, which describes itself as "the most influential publication in Washington," published an article after the 2014 election, concluding, "Support for Democrats among white, working-class voters was especially sparse this year: A measly 34 percent of them backed Democratic House candidates, exit polls found, while they fled in almost equal measure from Senate candidates."[9]

The media echo chamber has reinforced this narrative to the point that it is now unquestioned gospel truth. Nearly 75 percent of the first two pages of results from googling "Democrats white working class voters" in mid-2015 were articles from mainstream or progressive outlets after the 2014 election bemoaning the alleged crisis of Democrats losing White working-class voters to Republicans. (The other results were from conservative sites celebrating the Dems' supposed White working-class problem.) Here are just a few of the alarmist headlines: "Can We Talk? Here's Why the White Working Class Hates Democrats" (*Mother Jones*, 11/13/14); "Why Democrats Can't Win Over White Working-Class Voters" (*Slate*, 11/14/14); "Can Clinton Win Back the White Working Class?" (*National Journal*, 11/30/14); "Have Democrats Failed the White Working Class?" (*New York Times*, 12/9/14); "Democrats' Problem: White, Working-Class Voters" (NPR, 1/2/15); and "How Democrats Lost White Voters" (*Chicago Tribune*, 2/20/15).

Even Stan Greenberg changed his tune seven years after announcing his breakup with the Reagan Democrats. In a 2015 article, Greenberg wrote, "Democrats cannot win big or consistently enough, deep enough down the ticket or broadly enough in the states, unless they run much stronger with white working-class and downscale voters."[10]

As I'll show in a minute, all of this is absolutely incorrect, but it also raises the threshold question: What's wrong with the White people we have? Can't we show them some love? Can't we appreciate the progressive Whites of all socioeconomic backgrounds, including working-class White *progressives*, who consistently vote Democratic year after year? When people like Greenberg argue that Democrats have to do much better with White working-class swing voters, my question is, how much better, and where is the evidence to support that contention? The numbers show that *additional* working-class White voters are not a necessary component of a progressive majority given the current racial composition of the electorate.

No Democratic candidate for president has won the White vote since LBJ's landslide in 1964.[11] Obama received just 39 percent of the White vote in 2012 and still beat Romney by 5 million votes. Obama would have beaten Romney in the popular vote with just 36.5 percent of the White vote.[12] At their lowest ebb in the past forty years—the landslide of 1984, where Reagan wiped out Walter Mondale with 525 electoral votes to Mondale's 13—the Democratic nominee still earned 34 percent of the White vote. The average of White support for Democratic nominees for president since 1972 is 39.91 percent, and that's more than enough to win elections in a country that is getting Browner by the hour. The bottom line is that a multiracial progressive coalition can achieve an electoral majority *with the current level of White working-class support.*

Proponents of the view that Democrats lost in the midterms because White working-class voters switched their allegiance display a troubling ignorance of proper statistical analysis. Democrats did not lose the House in 2010 and the Senate in 2014 because working-class Whites fled the Party. *They lost because voters of color and their progressive White allies stayed home.* Failure to understand this point, and the difference between voters staying away from the polls versus going to the ballot box and voting for the other team, could be fatal to the future prospects of progressive politics in America.

Before we look at the numbers in detail, let's explore for a minute how statistics can be misinterpreted and misunderstood. Imagine a family with four children: two girls and two boys. We'll call them the Garcia family. The two Garcia girls like to read books while the two Garcia boys prefer to play video games. One summer the oldest Garcia girl goes away to summer camp. Suddenly there is great alarm in the neighborhood about the drop in support for book reading in the Garcia household. The neighborhood newsletter runs an article that trumpets the headline "Why the Garcia Family Can't Win Over Book Readers!" David Brooks jumps in and writes a column bemoaning a situation where "the Garcias continue to lose support among book readers," and he notes that the percentage of book readers among the children in the Garcia home has dropped from 50 percent to 33 percent. The talk of the town that summer is that the Garcia family must be doing something wrong since the percentage of video game players in their house has jumped from 50 percent to 67 percent.

What happened in the Garcia family illustrates the point of what is happening in national politics. With the Garcia family, there was not a shift in support from book reading to video game playing. One of the girls was gone for the summer, altering the mathematical percentages so that video game aficionados outnumbered book readers in the home. Similarly, White working-class voters did not *shift* their support from Democrats to Republicans in 2010 and 2014. The number of Republican White working-class voters—like the boys in the illustrative Garcia family—seemed to comprise a bigger *percentage* of that election's voters because progressive people of color and progressive Whites stayed away from the voting booths—they didn't participate.

Historically, off-year elections see *some* drop-off (on average 24 percent for Democrats and 28 percent for Republicans in the decade before 2010),[13] but in 2010, the Democratic drop-off was almost twice as bad as usual, and the Republican turnout was almost twice as good as usual. As Algernon Austin explains in his book *America Is Not Post-Racial: Xenophobia, Islamophobia, Racism, and the 44th President*, many conservative Whites experienced a visceral negative reaction to the election of America's first Black president.[14] And in 2010, at the height of Tea Party animus for Obama, more conservatives than usual turned out to the polls in the midterm elections of the Obama administration.

In 2008, 65 million people voted for Democratic candidates for the House of Representatives while Republican House candidates received 52 million votes.[15] Two years later, Republicans experienced a

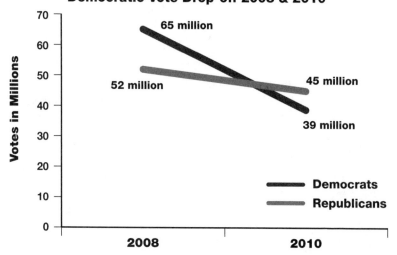

How the House Was Lost:
Democratic Vote Drop-off 2008 & 2010

Figure 11. Source: Office of the Clerk, U.S. House of Representatives, 2009 and 2011.

modest drop-off with 7 million fewer Republican voters turning out (45 million people) to vote in the 2010 midterms, but *26 million* fewer Democrats (39 million people) showed up at the polls.[16] In that year, Republicans picked up 63 seats in the House of Representatives and captured control of the chamber.[17]

The chart in Figure 11 tells the story of the loss of the House of Representatives.

This pattern repeated in 2014 when Democrats lost nine contested Senate seats, resulting in Republicans gaining control of that body. The 2014 Senate contests saw Democratic turnout plummet 42 percent—or 14 million votes—from 2008 (the year the senators up for election in 2014 last faced voters).[18] Meanwhile, Republicans—still mad at the president who had saved America from an economic depression, killed the world's number-one terrorist, lowered unemployment to its lowest level in six years, presided over the stock market smashing all previous records, and provided health insurance to millions of hardworking Americans—came out to vote against his Party in numbers closer to

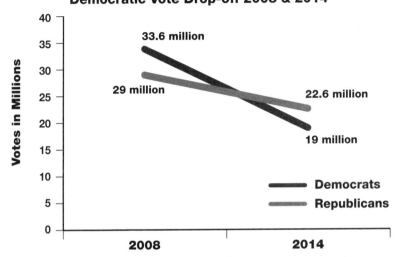

How the Senate Was Lost:
Democratic Vote Drop-off 2008 & 2014

Figure 12. Source: Office of the Clerk, U.S. House of Representatives, 2009 and 2015.

those in 2008. (The Republican drop-off was just 22 percent, or 6 million votes.)[19]

Figure 12 shows the drop-off in the Senate races in 2014.

What is critical to understand about these numbers—and what Brooks, Greenberg, and other analysts miss—is that while the number of Whites voting for Democrats did in fact decline, Republicans also received fewer White votes in the midterms than they did during the 2008 and 2012 presidential elections.[20] If White working-class voters were *switching* from voting Democratic to voting Republican, the number of total White votes for Republicans would go *up*. Instead it went *down*, just not nearly as dramatically as the Democratic number went down. The problem Democrats face is not that the White working class "fled" to the Republican Party. The problem is that Democratic voters—progressive Whites and people of color alike—sat out the midterms. Studying how and why that happened should preoccupy progressive strategists and analysts from now until the problem is corrected.

DANCE WITH THE ONE THAT BRUNG YA

The reason Democrats lost in the midterms so badly is precisely that they were obsessed with chasing the shrinking sector of the electorate comprised of working-class White swing voters. The saying "Dance with the one that brung ya" is a popular phrase for expressing the importance of reciprocating loyalty, but it's a message that too many progressives and Democrats fail to grasp. By focusing so much of their time, attention, and resources on White swing voters, Democrats neglected and ignored the very voters who elected them in the first place in 2008 and 2012—the multiracial New American Majority. After being overlooked and underappreciated, large numbers of these voters were uninspired and disaffected by the campaigns of Democrats in the midterms and stayed home in 2010 and 2014, resulting in crushing defeats for Democrats and the loss of both houses of Congress.

TWO ROADS DIVERGED IN A MULTIRACIAL COUNTRY

After winning a historic election in 2008 on the strength of the New American Majority with the highest voter turnout in forty years, Obama's advisors and strategists faced a significant decision about what path they could choose going forward in terms of governance and public policy. They could advance a progressive movement and gear their policies and proposals toward the needs, concerns, issues, and priorities of this new majority, or they could do what Democrats have historically done: curtail their ambitions and cater their agenda to the fears and prejudices of White swing voters.

Since Obama's election was unprecedented in many ways, for the White House inner circle to go down the path of prioritizing the New American Majority in governing would definitely have been choosing the road less traveled. But unlike Robert Frost's traveler, Obama's brain trust took the more well-worn path of catering to White swing voters. Having chosen their path, in 2009 Democrats proceeded to ignore the New American Majority in their policy priorities and political plans.

GEARING POLICY TOWARD THE WRONG PEOPLE

One of Obama's pollsters told me early in 2009 that White swing voters were the only group that the White House asked his firm to poll on a regular basis. Failing to recognize that they already have a multiracial majority and that the smarter, more cost-effective approach would be to nurture that existing majority, progressives and Democrats have tended to make decisions around policy and politics through the prism of "How will White swing voters react?" This fear affected nearly all White House decisions after 2009, resulting in strategic and tactical choices that, at best, failed to inspire, and, at worst, alienated the New American Majority. Dan Pfeiffer, a top senior advisor to Obama for seven years, described this hand-wringing mind-set in an interview in *New York* magazine in 2015:

> Whenever we contemplate[d] bold progressive action . . .
> whether that's the president's endorsement of marriage equal-
> ity, or coming out strong on power-plant rules to reduce cur-
> rent pollution, on immigration, on net neutrality, you get a lot
> of hemming and hawing in advance about what this is going to
> mean: Is this going to alienate people? Is this going to hurt the
> president's approval ratings? What will this mean in red states?[21]

On the policy front, the Democrats' focus on the wrong voters was evident shortly after the 2008 election. Time and time again, excessive caution and concern about how White swing voters would respond led Democrats to compromise, delay, and water down policy proposals that would have galvanized the New American Majority. Two key examples of this can be seen in how the Obama administration and other Demo-crats handled the messaging and execution of health care reform and immigration reform.

HEALTH CARE REFORM

How the White House went about pursuing health care reform pre-sents a painful paradox of politics in this new racially diverse era. On the one hand, the substance of the Affordable Care Act (ACA) is exactly what the New American Majority needed and wanted. Latino, African American, and Native American communities had significantly higher rates of uninsured people than the population as a whole.[22] The boldness and moral leadership exemplified by Obama and other Democrats in championing universal health care spoke to New American Majority members of all races (and who can forget the Democratic members of Congress breaking into a spontaneous "Yes We Can" chant on the House floor after passing the historic legislation?). On the other hand, the way in which health care reform was described, discussed, and defended by the Obama administration and Democrats was all about reacting to the fears of White swing voters.

When President Obama took office in January 2009, the Democratic Party had more political power—and more members in Congress—than at any time in the past sixteen years.[23] The New American Majority had flexed its muscle up and down the ticket, and a new political moment was at hand with Democrats having nearly sixty votes, a filibuster-proof margin in the U.S. Senate.

There is a reason people talk about the importance of the "first hundred days" of an administration. That's the period of peak leverage, influence, and momentum. But rather than seize that moment and push through the kind of health care overhaul that liberal lions like the late senator Ted Kennedy had been pursuing for fifty years, they turned the process over to Senator Max Baucus, a conservative Democrat from Montana, whose Committee on Finance dragged its feet for months in a vain attempt to achieve a bipartisan compromise, squandering the energy from Obama's election. By the time the legislation finally passed after a full year of delay, it received zero Republican votes in either house of Congress, demonstrating how futile and wasteful the efforts to win bipartisan support had been.

The legislative missteps in pursuing the ACA were compounded by the weak messaging and communications surrounding the legislation. From the beginning, the message was all about appeasing White swing voters. Phrases such as "bend the cost curve" were regularly used to describe the reforms.[24] And the main talking point was a defensive one: "This won't affect *your* coverage."[25] In his memoir, *Believer: My Forty*

Years in Politics, David Axelrod—one of Obama's top strategists—quotes from an August 2009 memo he wrote the president saying, "Many Americans . . . suspect that this is about spending and taxing more to take care of someone else."[26] What is clear, but not explicit, in Axelrod's memo is that the "Americans" he was talking about were White swing voters, not those Black and Brown folks whose families needed health insurance.

Allaying such fears was obviously necessary, but that shouldn't have been the top talking point of the Democrats' message. A communications plan should have included messages geared toward the New American Majority, making the moral argument about how caring for the sick is the responsibility of a humane society, a just civilization, and a true democracy (a message with such biblical overtones would have had the added benefit of putting religious conservatives on the defensive for their un-Christian position that society should shirk its responsibility of providing health care for all). The plan also should have taken advantage of the bully pulpit of the presidency by placing the president in a strategic state every month (hell, every week), and inviting media to cover Obama hugging happy people who now had health coverage thanks to the ACA. Since Democrats failed to defend the ACA in the face of unrelenting—and false—attacks, it's no surprise that public confidence and support for the reforms waned in the years after its passage.[27]

Even after the law passed, Democrats, fearful that White swing voters might think the country was giving government handouts to undeserving people of color, backed away from embracing their historic achievement, refused to loudly herald this important policy accomplishment, and instead went into a defensive crouch. Failure to shout about their win from the rooftops was self-defeating on two fronts. First, the defensive nature of the responses seemed to validate the attacks from the right wing that there was something wrong with extending health care to millions. Second, it failed to rally New American Majority voters by making it clear that something they cared about was under attack.

Six years after introducing the Affordable Care Act, President Obama modeled the kind of language that speaks to the New American

Majority when he defended the ACA in mid-2015 while the country was awaiting the Supreme Court's decision in *King v. Burwell*, the latest legal assault on Obamacare. In a speech to the Catholic Health Association, Obama said:

> For decades . . . [l]eaders from Teddy Roosevelt to Teddy Kennedy wanted to reform [the health care system]. For as long as there were Americans who couldn't afford decent health care, as long as there were people who had to choose between paying for medicine or paying rent, as long as there were parents who had to figure out whether they could sell or borrow to pay for a child's treatment just a few months more, and beg for God's mercy to make it work in time—as long as those things were happening, America was not living up to our highest ideals.[28]

Using that kind of language in 2009 and 2010 would have inspired the New American Majority and shown them they had a reason to turn out and vote in the midterm elections. Instead, the Democratic Party spent the 2010 election season worrying about those people who, Axelrod admitted, thought "health reform was just another giveaway to poor black people at their expense."[29] Democrats won the policy but lost the argument, and that loss has had disastrous political effects that continue to reverberate to this day.

IMMIGRATION REFORM

The other, unintended, outcome of the health care fight is that it delayed action on comprehensive immigration reform. This was another example of the painful paradox of trying to deliver for the New American Majority by catering to the concerns of White swing voters.

The missteps on immigration reform began early in the Obama administration. In 2009 some White House strategists thought it would be a good idea to inflict untold suffering on millions of people (more than 80 percent of them Latino)[30] by breaking up families and ramping up deportations of people who didn't have the requisite papers. The thinking was that by showing how "tough" Democrats could be on immigration issues they could then win Republican support for com-prehensive immigration reform.[31] A 2010 *Colorlines* article captured the mind-set: "Congressional Democrats and key Beltway advocates came together around a troubling political strategy: They would en-dorse a hawkish buildup of deportation and border security in hopes of creating space for broader reforms."[32]

It was only after millions of families had experienced the trauma of disruption through massive deportations and after activists had pro-tested, picketed, fasted, and marched in opposition to the deportations that the White House finally changed course—not coincidentally, as the 2012 election neared. In June 2012, the president announced that he was taking unilateral action—the kind of action immigration activ-ists had been demanding for years—to provide relief to "the Dream-ers," people under age eighteen without documentation. This step and signal was well received by Latinos, who turned out and gave 71 percent of their votes to Obama, up from the 67 percent who backed him in 2008.[33]

After Obama was reelected and conservatives recognized the size of his Latino support base, even Republican leaders began changing their tune on immigration. House Speaker John Boehner said in a 2012 interview, "I think a comprehensive approach is long overdue, and I'm confident that the president, myself, others, can find the com-mon ground to take care of this issue once and for all."[34] In a nod to the growing political power of the New American Majority, the Senate actually passed a robust Comprehensive Immigration Reform bill. In the House, however, where most Republicans had few New American Majority voters in their districts, the legislation ran into a brick wall. At this point, the Democratic habit of being blinded by their focus on White swing voters resurfaced as several Democratic senators began looking toward the 2014 elections, when control of the Senate was at stake.

In 2013 and early 2014, Latino activists and families continued to deplore the pace of deportations (with some going so far as to call the president the "Deporter in Chief")[35] and urged Obama to use the full-est extent of his executive authority to bypass Congress and provide protection and relief to millions of undocumented Latinos and other immigrants living and raising families in the United States. But the Democratic senators up for reelection were more afraid of a backlash from White swing voters than of losing Latino votes. They prevailed on the president to delay action on immigration until after the election, and Latino voters, seeing little reason to trek to the polls, stayed home in droves.

GEARING POLITICAL CAMPAIGNS TOWARD THE WRONG PEOPLE

Democrats' misguided focus on the wrong voters has carried over from the policy realm to political plans, campaigns, strategies, and tactics. The results have been palpable and predictable. Their infatuation with Reagan Democrats and failure to appreciate the power of the New American Majority has caused campaign operatives and decision makers to misdirect time, attention, and money in ways that contributed to the dramatic drop-off in New American Majority voters that resulted in the 2010 and 2014 midterm defeats. In several—if not most—of the Senate races the Democrats lost in 2014, the candidates and campaigns focused their efforts on catering to the fears and anger of White swing voters who were unhappy with Obama and, by extension, the members of his party.

Colorado is a state where Latino voters were indispensable in helping Democrats win statewide in 2010 and 2012, comprising a full 20 percent of Obama's total votes in 2012. Senator Mark Udall, however, pinned his hopes instead on the possibility that moderate White women voters—the soccer moms—would swing in his direction after learning about the Republican challenger's anti-choice track record. Accordingly, Udall's campaign spent its time and money chasing the soccer mom mirage rather than organizing and energizing the Latino electorate (Latinos make up 14 percent of Colorado's voters).[36] Deepak Bhargava, executive director of the Center for Community Change Action (CCCA), one of the country's leading immigration reform advocacy organizations, observed that the voters in Latino communities in Colorado were fed up with delays around reform. Bhargava said door-to-door canvassers had never encountered as much hostility, anger, and resentment toward Democrats as they did while canvassing for the

2014 election. A 2014 CCCA memo about the Colorado canvassing efforts observed, "Each interaction at the door is longer and much more complex than in previous election cycles. One of the most important lessons to draw from this experience is that robust voter participation in low-income communities requires not only year-round civic engagement, but also a sense that the issues and priorities of these communities are being addressed directly and authentically by the nation's leaders."

To compound the problem, Udall's campaign failed to prioritize outreach to Latinos until it was too late. An MSNBC article right before the election documented how Colorado leaders feared Udall's outreach was "too little, too late" and had completely ignored the differences between the candidates on immigration. When Election Day rolled around in 2014, nearly 300,000 fewer Colorado registered Democrats voted than had turned out in 2008 (*42 times the Republican drop-off of just 7,000 votes*) and Democrats lost the Colorado U.S. Senate seat by 40,000 votes. In that election, 211,000 Latinos who were eligible to vote sat out the race, more than enough to give Udall the victory had Latinos been mobilized and prioritized.[37]

In Kentucky, Democratic U.S. Senate candidate Alison Lundergan Grimes's campaign went to astonishing lengths in courting the wrong constituents. Despite having attended the 2012 Democratic National Convention as an Obama delegate, she absurdly refused to answer questions during her 2014 Senate race about whether she had ever voted for Obama. On immigration reform, she not only distanced herself from the push for Comprehensive Immigration Reform sought by many people of color, but her campaign actually released an ad attacking her opponent, Mitch McConnell, for being too supportive of immigration reform—the same Mitch McConnell who, as head of the Republicans in the Senate, had sought to block President Obama at every turn. Lundergan Grimes lost badly and received fewer votes than Obama had received in Kentucky two years earlier.[38]

In other races that led to Democrats losing control of the Senate— North Carolina, Georgia, Arkansas, Louisiana, and Alaska—the fundamental dynamics of those races also involved candidates distancing themselves from the Black president and suffering consequences in terms of significant drop-off in Democratic turnout among voters who had come out in large numbers to elect and reelect that president. The loss of so many 2014 Senate seats was particularly problematic and maddening because all of the incumbents who lost had won their elections six years earlier when Obama swept into office on the strength of an enthusiastic New American Majority.

Syndicated columnist Ruben Navarrette Jr. surveyed the wreckage of the 2014 elections and wrote a biting commentary in an article titled, "Latinos Aren't a Cheap Date for Democrats Anymore." In his piece, Navarrette wrote, "In some races, Democrats didn't just ignore Hispanics but went out of their way to antagonize them as a way of appealing to conservative white voters." He cited as evidence the North Carolina Senate race, where Democratic senator Kay Hagan "ran television commercials touting her opposition to 'amnesty' for 'illegal aliens.' Here's a tip: Those kinds of nativist buzzwords will not endear you to many Hispanics."[39]

Cutting through all the numbers and analysis, what happened in 2014 was fairly simple. After being ignored for most of the six years since the 2008 election, one that saw significant Democratic gains in the U.S. Senate, the New American Majority in 2014 ignored the last-minute pleas to turn out at the polls, and the Democrats lost control of the Senate.

On many levels, it's important to ensure that the correct conclusions are being drawn about the Democratic Party's drop-off problem. The worst possible thing Democrats could conclude is that the country's voters had moved to the right. That conclusion could lead to a downward death spiral where progressive values and policies are watered down or jettisoned altogether out of fear of offending White swing voters, and the resulting milquetoast agenda fails to inspire the participation of the New American Majority.

James Baldwin described the dynamics of gaining and losing the loyalty of people of color when he wrote about why so many African Americans were suddenly coming out to see Lorraine Hansberry's 1959 play, *A Raisin in the Sun*, the first Broadway show written by a Black woman:

I had never in my life seen so many Black people in the the-ater. And the reason was that never before, in the entire his-tory of the American theater, had so much of the truth of Black people's lives been seen on the stage. Black people had ignored the theater because the theater had always ignored them.[40]

Similar to what Hansberry proved back in the day, when you speak to the truth of the lives of the New American Majority, they respond—in large numbers, as they did in electing and reelecting President Obama. And when you ignore them in a futile fascination with White swing voters, they will ignore you, whether it's at the box office or bal-lot box. To win in today's multiracial, multicultural America, we need more Lorraine Hansberrys writing the script and articulating the vi-sion of progressive politics.

5

Fewer Smart-Ass White Boys

They are a bunch of smart-ass white boys, who think they know it all.
—Atlanta mayor Andrew Young, August 1984[1]

Andy Young had run out of patience. Having spent his life working in the trenches of social change and politics—supervising Martin Luther King's voter registration drives, organizing civil rights protests across the South, and winning his own races for Congress and then mayor of Atlanta—he was trying to help Walter Mondale's team develop a strategy for the 1984 presidential race against Ronald Reagan. When he was elected to Congress in 1972, Young had successfully applied grassroots organizing practices that included transporting 6,000 Black voters to the polls on election day, and he repeatedly urged Mondale's team to invest resources in registering and mobilizing voters of color, but his words were falling on deaf ears.[2] Finally, he had had enough and his frustration boiled over at the National Association of Black Journalists convention (NABJ), where he made his now-famous "smart-ass white boys" comment. Thirty years later, Young stood by his words. "Unfortunately, I was right," he said at the NABJ conference in 2014. "Mondale let the experts there take over the campaign and put the money into television and did not get out the vote."[3]

More than thirty years later, progressive politics are still dominated by "White boys." White men comprise 31 percent of the American population and just 23 percent of Democratic voters[4] but they control nearly 90 percent of what happens in Democratic politics and progressive advocacy. Whether the current crop of largely male Caucasian consultants is equally "smart-ass" as in the eighties depends on who you ask, but what is clear is that what I call Smart-Ass White Boy Syndrome continues to this day. By the way, you don't have to be White or a man to be afflicted with the syndrome. Its symptoms are a persistent disregard for the country's communities of color as a political force and an inability to do the basic math necessary to appreciate the size and power of the electorate of color. Also, not all White guys suffer from this; some actually "get it."[5] The fact remains, however, that the world of progressive politics is dominated by White men at a time when the future of the progressive movement depends on solidifying the support of the growing number of people of color in America.

WHITE GUYS RUN EVERYTHING

Despite the fact that we have a Black president, the Democratic Party is still largely dominated and controlled by White men. Not exclusively, but overwhelmingly. In particular, the key people who decide how and where the Party's hundreds of millions of dollars are spent are White guys.

In 2014, I commissioned an audit of Democratic Party spending to see where the Party's money was going.[6] Named *The Fannie Lou Hamer Report* to honor the work of Hamer, a Southern civil rights leader, and other members of the 1964 Mississippi Freedom Democratic Party (Hamer and her colleagues stormed the floor of the Democratic National Convention in Atlantic City to protest the all-White, pro-segregation Mississippi delegation that the Democratic Party planned to seat),[7] the report looked at national Democratic Party spending in the 2010 and 2012 elections. Conducted by researchers at the American Majority Project Research Institute, the findings were not pretty.

Over those two cycles (2010 and 2012), Democrats awarded $514 million in contracts to political consultants. Of that half-billion-plus dollars, nearly all of it (97 percent) went to White consultants and businesses (and 83 percent to White men).[8] The report was updated to include 2014 spending, and the results were not much better. Of the $193 million spent by the Democratic Party in the 2014 cycle on consulting firms, 97.9 percent of contracts went to White consultants.[9]

This means the vast majority of all Democratic Party spending—and, by extension, the strategizing, planning, and execution—was and still is carried out by White men in a party where 46 percent of its voters are people of color.

The same handful of White consultants also control most of the political work for national labor unions, political action committees, and independent expenditure groups that make up the remaining parts of the progressive politics universe. Those organizations spent more than $200 million in 2014, and most of those dollars were also handled and spent by White consultants.[10] In fact just one consulting shop, GMMB, receives hundreds of millions of dollars each cycle for television ads. Based on looking at photos and bios on its website in late 2015, it appeared GMMB's nineteen-member leadership team was made up overwhelmingly—if not exclusively—of Whites.[11]

For all the attention paid to high-profile progressive billionaires like hedge fund investors George Soros and Tom Steyer, it is labor unions and their members who are actually among the most dominant financial forces in progressive politics. Collectively, the union movement spends more than $600 million a year on politics.[12] Who's in charge in labor isn't much different than who's leading the rest of the progressive movement. Of the fifty-six unions in the AFL–CIO, the largest federation of unions in the United States, more than 80 percent were run by White men as of mid-2015.[13]

Paul Frymer, associate professor of politics at Princeton, notes in his 2008 book, *Black and Blue: African Americans, the Labor Movement, and the Decline of the Democratic Party*, that the main challenge facing the labor movement today is that it seeks to represent and mobilize an increasingly diverse workforce, while the top leadership of the movement remains White. Frymer notes that union struggles have "found energy from immigrant workers in the Justice for Janitors, Wal-Mart, and anti-sweatshop campaigns. Victories against the United [States] Postal Service, transit industries, hospitals, and casinos have also shown the face of a diverse workforce—not just more African American faces but large influxes of Latinos, women, and immigrants from Eastern Europe." And yet, Frymer observes, "The highest echelons of the movement remain largely white and male."[14]

The problem extends into the world of nonprofit advocacy as well. One of the highest-spending sectors in the progressive nonprofit space is the environmental movement. According to a study by the Foundation Center, environmental causes received $1.4 billion in funding in one year (2009).[15] The twenty largest environmental organizations collectively spend close to half a billion dollars every year (that's their total budget; not all of it is spent on politics), and White men largely determine what happens with those dollars. Green 2.0, an initiative launched in 2014 to examine diversity in the environmental movement, commissioned a study of the gender and racial diversity of 191 environmental nonprofits, 74 government environmental agencies, and 28 leading environmental grant-making foundations. The study revealed the following:

- None of the largest conservation and preservation organizations (those with budgets over $1 million per year) had a president of color. (There was some improvement in 2015 when the Natural Resources Defense Council named Rhea Suh, an Asian American woman, as its president, and the Sierra Club elected Aaron Mair as its first Black board president.);
- 76.2 percent of the organizations' presidents were men (again, all of them White); and
- People of color comprised fewer than 12 percent of the leadership positions in all environmental organizations surveyed.[16]

Against this backdrop, in 2014 five of the largest environmental groups embarked on what they described as "by far the biggest investment that the environmental community has ever made in politics."[17] All told, these organizations—the Environmental Defense Fund, the Natural Resources Defense Council, the League of Conservation Voters, NextGen Climate, and the Sierra Club—spent more than $85 million on elections that year. That spending was driven in 2014 by their leadership, which consisted of four White men and one White woman (who worked in partnership with a White male executive director).

Nondiverse leadership in the nonprofit arena also extends to the philanthropic sector, the realm of those who fund environmental groups and other progressive nonprofits. D5, a coalition working to increase diversity in the philanthropic world, surveyed 864 foundations in 2013 and found that 92 percent are run by Whites. The figures for foundation boards and senior staff mirror the findings for foundation presidents, with boards being 87 percent White and senior staff being 84 percent White.[18]

DIVERSITY IN HIRING: WHY DOES IT MATTER?

In 1992, President-elect Bill Clinton was criticized for insufficient diversity in his cabinet picks. Annoyed by the criticism, Clinton lashed out at those who were holding him accountable for failing to appoint more people of color and called them "bean counters."[19] Clinton's angry words reflect the sentiments of many well-meaning Whites who may often wonder, "When it comes to hiring, why does a person's race or cultural background matter?" That's a fair and important question.

Paying attention to race and culture in hiring, specifically in politics, matters because "the color line," identified by W. E. B. DuBois in his seminal 1903 book, *The Souls of Black Folk*, has been the fault line of U.S. politics since English settlers first landed at Jamestown in 1607. It matters because we continue to operate today in a political landscape littered with racial land mines. It matters because the growth in the communities of color has made a permanent progressive majority possible in America. It matters because this New American Majority depends on people of color voting at high rates and casting at least 81 percent of their votes for Democrats and progressive causes. It matters because in order to get that kind of voter turnout and loyalty, you need to develop trust, and to develop trust you need profound insight into the hopes and dreams and conditions and concerns of the people you're trying to reach; generally, those who have the lived experience and shared culture with the people we want to vote and support our causes have deeper knowledge and understanding of the communities we need to engage. It matters because when we don't master the politics of race, we lose.

What Andy Young was warning about when he made his "smart-ass White boys" comment was a dangerous combination of arrogance and ignorance on the part of political consultants and operatives. Not knowing what one needs to know is dangerous in any endeavor, and the particularly insidious aspect of arrogance is that it blinds one to one's own ignorance. So, for example, some White consultants become so intoxicated with fawning media clippings about their work that they start to believe they don't need to learn anything about solidifying the support of people of color. As a result, they neglect studying how to mobilize the New American Majority and fail to take the steps necessary to win elections and further the progressive movement. A non-arrogant—and more successful—approach was summed up by Intel CEO Andy Grove, author of the book *Only the Paranoid Survive*: "Success contains the seeds of its own destruction. Success breeds complacency. Complacency breeds failure. Only the paranoid survive."[20] Rather than being paranoid about the need to learn more about the electorate, the smart-ass White boys Andy Young complained about thirty-plus years ago ignored his advice, and many continue to do so today, by not prioritizing voters of color.

MYTH BUSTING

The arrogance of today's political consultants is based on a powerful and popular myth surrounding Obama's historic election. According to the myth, Obama was elected because his team of brilliant strategists—nearly all White guys—mastered cutting-edge technological tools in ways that ran circles around the Hillary Clinton and John McCain campaigns. Many otherwise intelligent people have talked about "the Obama magic" in reference to the so-called mojo mastered by the tech wizards who ran his campaigns.

Buying into this mythology fuels arrogance, and arrogance keeps one ignorant about how Obama was *actually* elected. As discussed in the previous chapter, failing to appreciate who the real drivers of change were in 2008, the White House and Democratic political machine directed their attention to the wrong sectors of the electorate in 2009 and neglected the New American Majority voters who had put them in power in the first place. As a result, progressives all paid the painful price in midterm elections in 2010 and 2014 when Republicans trounced Democrats from coast to coast.

To avoid repeating these mistakes, it's essential to do some myth busting. The Obama election myth has two components: the myth of an unprecedented technological revolution and the myth of brilliant strategists.

MYTH 1: THE OBAMA CAMPAIGN PIONEERED UNPRECEDENTED TECHNOLOGICAL BREAKTHROUGHS IN POLITICS

The 2008 election took place in the context of breathless media hype and adulation of all things digital. David Carr of the *New York Times* typified this when he wrote in 2008, "[B]y bolting together social networking applications under the banner of a movement, [the Obama campaign] created an unforeseen force to raise money, organize locally, fight smear campaigns and get out the vote that helped them topple the Clinton machine and then John McCain and the Republicans." [21]

While technology was indeed put to good use in 2008, it wasn't the first time technology had been used. Previous political campaigns, often discussed in similarly breathless tones, also used digital tools and tactics:

- In the 1992 presidential election, Jerry Brown took a great technological leap forward by waging a "small dollar revolution" that relied on donations (capped at $100) using a 1-800 number that donors could call to make contributions. A reporter in April 1992 described the operation as follows:

  "With 72 telephones, dozens of computer screens, and a pizza bill last month that totaled $2,000, the 800 number began last September as a bold experiment, a cross between schmaltzy late-night salesmanship and brilliant political one-upmanship. . . . So far, the 800 number has raised more than $4 million in pledges of $100 or less, with roughly $1.5 million of that $4 million already in hand." [22]

  (Amusingly, Brown's 1992 number, 1-800-426-1112, was, like your grandparents' durable landline, *still* active as recently as mid-2015 and being answered by Brown staffers.) [23]

- In 2003 and 2004, Howard Dean took American politics by storm and captured the imagination of the political world and its reporters with his aggressive, then-cutting-edge tactics of meet-ups, blogs, and money bombs.[24] *Wired* magazine wrote: "The biggest news of the political season has been the tale of this small-state governor who, with the help of Meetup.com and hundreds of bloggers, has elbowed his way into serious contention for his party's presidential nomination. . . . Dean has used the Net to raise more money than any other Democratic candidate. He's also used it to organize thousands of volunteers who go door-to-door, write personal letters to likely voters, host meetings, and distribute flyers."[25]

- Somewhat lost to history is the precision of George W. Bush's reelection campaign in effectively using technology in 2004. By matching consumer data to voter files, and obtaining membership lists from churches and gun rights groups, Bush's campaign advanced the field of what is now called "modeling." Articles at the time declared, "The Bush campaign's use of targeted data and its exploitation of cable was likely to be the beginning of a trend, particularly as advertisers pursue new ways of reaching consumers using technology like text-messaging and cellphones."[26]

- Looking back a bit in history, civil rights activists—people like Andy Young—mastered the use of a then-new technology called television to dramatize oppression in the South and build national support for the cause of civil rights. It was only after the police violence of Bloody Sunday in Selma in March 1965 was broadcast on national television that President Johnson, Congress, and the nation were moved to finally pass the Voting Rights Act.[27]

- If one really wants to go back, the abolitionists of the 1800s were shrewd in their adoption and deployment of that era's technology—the printing press.[28] They printed thousands of flyers calling for an end to slavery and mailed them by steamboat to South Carolina, nearly precipitating a constitutional crisis when the postmaster refused to deliver the pamphlets. In a backhanded compliment to the effectiveness of the abolitionists' use of technology, Virginia congressman John Jones lamented that "two great revolutionizers of the world . . . steam power and the press" were creating "large numbers of newspapers, pamphlets, tracts, and pictures, calculated, in an eminent degree, to rouse and inflame the passions of slaves against their masters, to urge them on to deeds of death." [29]

Not only is the use of technology not new in elections and other political movements (and, hence, a cause for humility), but effective use of technology was only one part of the picture in Obama's 2008 victory. And not even the dominant part.

MYTH 2: BRILLIANT WHITE CAMPAIGN STRATEGISTS GOT OBAMA ELECTED

The part of the 2008 election myth that credits White campaign strategists for Obama's win is particularly dangerous because it obscures the decisive role of voters of color in electing the first Black president of the United States of America.

CBS's *60 Minutes* perfectly captured the outsize attention given to the all-White consulting crew in a segment that aired right after Obama's election. The story diminished not only the role of voters of color, but the role of Obama himself:

With the candidate's help, they orchestrated what some consider one of the most improbable and effective campaigns in American political history. They took a little-known senator with a foreign sounding name and almost no national experience and got him elected as the 44th president of the United States. They did it by recruiting and vesting millions of volunteers in the outcome, by raising more money than any campaign in history, and by largely ignoring that their candidate happened to be a black man.[30]

What *60 Minutes* and many others failed to understand is that Barack Obama became the Democratic nominee for president precisely because Black people across the country turned out in droves eager to take the next step on a journey that began when their African ancestors were placed in chains and stuffed in the cargo holds of ships for a transatlantic crossing that only some would survive. Writer Trey Ellis accurately, and humorously, predicted the phenomenon when he wrote in 2007: "Every black person in America is going to vote for Obama. If you're black, you already know this and if you're not, I'm sure you've suspected it."[31] At the time of Ellis's essay, summer 2007, polls were showing Obama trailing Clinton by 23 points.[32] Ellis went on to explain the mind-set behind his prediction by saying, "If there is even a chance that there will be a black president in my lifetime, I'll be damned if I won't be one of the millions out there that helped row that boat. For black folks, an Obama presidency would be as miraculously uplifting as sending a man to the moon."[33]

A careful analysis of the 2008 presidential primary calendar and delegate battle shows the central role Black voters played in giving Obama his insurmountable delegate lead (in a bit of historical poetic justice, he took that lead in February, Black History Month). As a quick review: Obama shocked the world in early January 2008 by winning the Iowa caucuses. Two weeks later, Hillary Clinton made a surprising recovery and won the New Hampshire primary. The two then traded wins the rest of January in South Carolina (Obama) and Nevada (Clinton, in the popular vote), leading up to the megacontest on February 5—Super Tuesday—when twenty-two states held primaries across the country.[34] Super Tuesday was supposed to decide the Democratic nominee, but the two campaigns battled to a standoff. If anything, Clinton was seen by many as having the upper hand.

When the dust had settled on Super Tuesday, the candidates were separated by just two dozen delegates (Obama held that small lead), with 1,524 more delegates to be fought over in the coming months.[35] It was then that Black folks, largely in the old Confederate states, fulfilled Trey Ellis's prediction. What African American voters did over the ensuing three weeks gave Barack Obama the lead that secured the Democratic nomination for president.[36]

On February 6, 2008, Obama led Clinton by 24 delegates. By February 28, 2008, his lead had quintupled, growing to 127 delegates, the size of his final margin of victory (technically, he ended the primary season ahead by 124 delegates). Obama won eight states in a row in a two-week stretch that month. Five of those states—52 percent of the delegates Obama won during that period—came from former slave-holding states and territories: Louisiana, Washington, D.C., the U.S. Virgin Islands, Maryland, and Virginia.[37]

The powerful role of Black voters in the primaries was further boosted months later in the 2008 general election by the overwhelming support of millions of Latino and Asian American voters.[38] Collectively, the expanded ranks of voters of color—in solidarity with the meaningful minority of Whites who almost always vote Democratic—carried the Obama campaign all the way to and through the gates at 1600 Pennsylvania Avenue.

William Frey, the Brookings demographer, analyzed the 2008 election in the context of the country's changing demographics and emphatically declared that voters of color provided Obama's margin of victory. "Obama reached into Republican territory to take five new South and West states—mostly due to minority votes," Frey wrote. Even outside the South and Southwest, Frey attributes Obama's success to voters of color, noting that in traditional Democratic states on the coasts and in the industrial Midwest, "Minorities were largely responsible for his wins."[39]

The voters of color who provided the margin of difference in 2008 and 2012 didn't cast their votes for a historic candidacy because the White hands of tech-savvy whiz kids typed fancy code on computer keyboards. They were carrying on the legacy of hundreds of years of struggle. They were making real what Martin Luther King dreamed of and worked for before he was struck down on the balcony of the Lorraine Motel in 1968. They were overcoming centuries of discrimination and propelling one of their own to the highest office in the land, causing their chosen candidate of color to observe, "They said this day would never come."

WHAT IS CULTURAL COMPETENCE?

In 2016 and beyond, progressives will not be able to rely on the historic opportunity to elect the first president of color as a way to motivate

voters of color. Going forward, great cultural competence and expertise will be required to inspire and mobilize the New American Majority. Turning today's multiracial movement for justice and equality
into a *lasting* political force will not be easy. As Obama's Harvard Law
professor Chris Edley once remarked, "Dealing with race is not rocket
science; it's *harder* than rocket science."[40] In order for the Democratic
Party and the progressive movement to succeed in a racially charged,
multiracial society, great cultural competence is imperative.

The business world offers instructive lessons about how to develop
and apply cultural competence. Starbucks has been working for fifteen years to develop a toehold in the Chinese market, opening five
hundred new stores and working on fifteen hundred more. By 2016,
China is expected to be Starbucks's largest market outside the United
States.[41] To make these inroads, the coffee company is not just exporting the products and services that work in the United States. In order to
achieve success and market penetration in China (a nation of tea drinkers, mind you), Starbucks has turned to local leaders and embraced
the local culture by forging partnerships with local companies, holding
meetings with the parents of employees in a nod to the importance of
family culture, and even developing products that incorporate green
tea.[42] CEO Howard Schultz explained his understanding of the essence of a culturally competent approach when it comes to business:

> What we want to do as a company is put our feet in the shoes
> of our customers. What does that mean, especially in China? It
> means that not everything from Starbucks in China should be
> invented in Starbucks in Seattle. . . . We want to be highly re
> spectful of the cultural differences in every market, especially
> China, and appeal to the Chinese customer. So as an example,
> the food for the Chinese stores is predominantly designed for
> the Chinese palate.
>
> In the past, we were fighting a war here between the people
> in Seattle who want a blueberry muffin and the people in China
> who say, "You know what, I think black sesame is probably an
> ingredient that they would rather have than blueberry." And
> I would say that goes back to the hubris of the past, when we

thought, we're going to change behavior. Well, no, we're not going to change behavior. In fact, we're going to appeal with great
respect to local tastes . . . for the first time, [we're] trusting that
the people in the marketplace know better than the people in
Seattle.[43]

Schultz's reference to hubris suggests that Starbucks had to first
get past the business world's equivalent of Smart-Ass White Boy Syndrome in order to succeed in a new, non-White market. And just as
one wouldn't go into China without cultural consultants and guides,
American politicians shouldn't go into Asian American, Latino, Native
American, Arab American, or African American communities without culturally competent advisors. Who better to craft compelling political messages than people who have lived and personally experienced
the cultural realities of those whose votes are being sought?

In the world of arts and entertainment, African American screen-
writer, director, and producer Shonda Rhimes's phenomenal success
with the TV shows *Grey's Anatomy, Scandal*, and *How to Get Away with
Murder* illustrates how presenting characters who authentically look,
sound, and talk like the shows' target audiences can resonate in a deep
and lasting way and result in traction and loyalty. *Scandal* star Kerry
Washington—the first female African American lead in a network television show since Teresa Graves in *Get Christie Love!* in 1974—talked
about Rhimes's influence, saying, "Shonda has changed the culture of
television in that more and more people can turn on the television and
see themselves." Rhimes's shows were among the most watched on
television in 2015.

Learning lessons from Rhimes's success, 2015 was a breakout year
in television as Hollywood discovered the impact of providing fresh
and compelling culturally diverse programming with actors of color
cast in lead roles. Fox Network's *Empire*, a Black hip-hop King Lear
story, was the most successful new show on television that year. Additional successful new people-of-color-led shows included *Fresh Off
the Boat*, the first sitcom featuring an Asian American family in twenty
years, the Mexican telenovela-inspired *Jane the Virgin*, and the African
American sitcom *black-ish*, all of which secured strong ratings.

In politics, one of the best and most well-known examples of cultural competence occurred during the 2008 presidential primaries when White Americans had their sensibilities shocked by being exposed to an angry Black preacher. Rev. Jeremiah Wright was the pastor at the Chicago church the Obamas attended, and like many Black preachers, he was known to engage in colorful rhetorical flourishes. During one lengthy sermon condemning America's history in relation to people of color, Wright said, dramatically and with great inflection, the following:

> The United States of America government, when it came to treating her citizens of Indian descent fairly, she failed. She put them on reservations. When it came to treating her citizens of Japanese descent fairly, she failed. She put them in internment prison camps. When it came to treating her citizens of African descent fairly, America failed. She put them in chains . . . [the government] builds bigger prisons, passes a three-strike law and then wants us to sing "God Bless America." No, no, no, not God Bless America. God *damn* America—that's in the Bible—for killing innocent people.[44]

The video of that segment of the speech—especially the "God damn America" part—was then broadcast repeatedly on television and spawned more than three thousand news stories in one month.[45] Of course it's no accident that this sermon—which had been delivered *five years earlier*—came to light during the height of Wright's most famous parishioner's campaign to become the first Black president of the United States.

Many Black folks thought little of Wright's flourishes and critiques of America. (In fact, my aunt Janis was so excited that she texted me, "Go tell it on the mountain and write that Wright is right!" I texted back, "Do you want Obama to be president?") The mainstream media and White swing voters, however, were horrified. ABC News typified the tone of media coverage with a headline that blared, "Obama's Pastor: God Damn America, U.S. to Blame for 9/11." The first sentence of the article perfectly illustrated the alarmist coverage: "Barack Obama's pastor says blacks should not sing 'God Bless America' but 'God damn America.' "[46]

Obama's White consulting crew didn't know what to do. Obama, however, did. He understood that he had to give a speech directly addressing the country's racial fears and anxieties. Afterward, advisor Anita Dunn reflected that the decision to deliver the speech was Obama's and had there been a discussion among the staff, "most of the people in the campaign would've advised against it."[47]

Obama insisted on giving what became known as the "race speech," where he straddled the color line by affirming the Black American experience while educating Whites and allaying their fears. Unlike most of his other speeches, Obama didn't turn to his White speechwriter, Jon Favreau, but took the lead in drafting that crucial address himself.[48] In the speech, "A More Perfect Union," Obama placed Wright's comments within historical and sociological contexts. He said, "The fact that so many people are surprised to hear that anger in some of Reverend Wright's sermons simply reminds us of the old truism that the most segregated hour in American life occurs on Sunday morning . . . the anger is real; it is powerful; and to simply wish it away, to condemn it without understanding its roots, only serves to widen the chasm of misunderstanding that exists between the races."[49]

After affirming the experience of African Americans, Obama went on in his speech to let White Americans know that he understood their frustrations. "When [whites] are told to bus their children to a school across town; when they hear that an African American is getting an advantage in landing a good job or a spot in a good college because of an injustice that they themselves never committed; when they're told that their fears about crime in urban neighborhoods are somehow prejudiced, resentment builds over time."[50]

Finally, he challenged Whites and Blacks alike to bridge the racial divide. "We have a choice in this country. We can accept a politics that breeds division, and conflict, and cynicism. . . . Or, at this moment, in this election, we can come together and say, 'Not this time.' This time we want to talk about the crumbling schools that are stealing the future of black children and white children and Asian children and Hispanic children and Native American children."

It was, by all accounts, a masterstroke and a case study in cultural competence. MSNBC host Chris Matthews said it was "one of the great speeches in American history,"[51] and a *New York Times* editorial said, "It is hard to imagine how he could have handled it better."[52] Black voters identified with Obama's words, White voters's concerns were alleviated, and the Obama juggernaut marched on.

A month after the Rev. Wright controversy, Obama again had a chance to show off his mastery of cultural competence. During an April 2008 debate, Obama was pummeled with attacks by both the moderator, George Stephanopoulos, and his opponent, Hillary Clinton. The next day, during a speech before his supporters, he referenced the attacks, displayed his knowledge of hip-hop culture, and, without saying a word, brought the crowd of young people and students to its feet, clapping their hands and pumping their fists.

What Obama did was reference hip-hop mogul Jay-Z's popular 2003 song, "Dirt Off Your Shoulder." The song was on *The Black Album*, which sold more than 3 million copies and was well known by the younger, multiracial hip-hop community. The song's message: Leave negative people and experiences behind by brushing them off like dirt on your shoulder. The refrain goes:

> *If you feelin' like a pimp nigga, go and brush your shoulders off,*
> *Ladies is pimps too, go and brush your shoulders off,*
> *Niggaz is crazy baby, don't forget that boy told you,*
> *Get, that, dirt off your shoulder.*

In the song's video we see young Black men and women brushing off their shoulders, the men after they had been stopped and searched by police and women after dealing with catcalls.

In his speech, Obama talked about the attacks he'd weathered in the previous night's debate and said, "I understand [the attacks] because that's the textbook Washington game. . . . And when you're running for the presidency, then you've gotta expect it, and you know you've just gotta kinda let it. . . ." Then, just like in the Jay-Z video, he silently brushed off his shoulder. *Boom!* The crowd went wild. Obama smiled, and the message was clear: Ain't nobody got time for that.[53] *That* was cultural competence in action.

Cultural competence also makes a huge difference in assembling the nuts and bolts tools necessary to win an election. In 2014, Rida Hamida, an Arab American organizer in California, was working to turn out the Arab American and Muslim vote in Orange County (total population 3.1 million). The campaign's tech needs and voter lists were controlled by a White consultant. Hamida asked the consultant for a list of Arab American voters that her team of volunteers could call as part of their get-out-the-vote program. The consultant gave her a list with fewer than 5,000 names. Surprised at the low number, Hamida asked if she could have access to the voter file so that she could assemble the call list herself. When she was done, she'd identified 62,912 Arab American and Muslim voters.[54]

Technically, what the White consultant did is understandable since he probably looked to see how many people in that area had checked the box "Arab American." But census forms are woefully deficient in terms of their design vis-à-vis many people of color.[55] Fortunately, Hamida has deep knowledge about Arab Americans and how they identify themselves. She knew to search by individual Arab and Muslim majority countries—Syria, Iraq, Iran, Saudi Arabia, etc.—and found *ten times* more people than the White consultant in charge of the voter file had. Hamida's team contacted and turned out many of those voters. One of their preferred candidates, Bao Nguyen, won the race for mayor of Garden Grove, California, defeating the White incumbent by fifteen votes (yes, one-five). Hamida's story illustrates the invaluable difference a campaign consultant with cultural competence can make in an election.

Notably, both Rhimes's shows and Obama's race speech exemplified how the same vehicle can be highly effective in speaking to Whites as well as people of color, illuminating another aspect of cultural competence: the most truly cross-cultural people in America are people of color. Due to the dominance of White culture, many people of color have to master *at least two* cultures in order to succeed—mainstream, middle-class White culture and their own racial group's culture.

Clearly there are always exceptions to the rule, and it would be silly to suggest that every person of color has cultural competence. But when 97 percent of political contracts go to White consultants, as our audit of Democratic Party spending found, the message from the political world seems to be that people of color are in fact *worse* at reaching their own communities than White consultants are. In truth, it's both common sense and verifiable that generally people who have lived a particular cultural experience have more insight into how to communicate with those who share that experience.

Smart-Ass White Boy Syndrome is a serious threat to the prospects of the progressive movement overall and the Democratic Party in particular. Too many people in political leadership are ignorant of the power and potential of the New American Majority and believe that ours is still mainly a White country where White swing voters are the most important demographic to pursue. As long as progressive leaders and decision makers keep following this belief, one compounded by arrogance and the refusal to recognize and address one's ignorance, progressives will increasingly fail and flail in future elections and battles.

Cultural competence in campaigns and the rest of the progressive movement is needed now more than ever in order to connect with the New American Majority. It's been thirty years since Andy Young cast down the gauntlet. We can't afford to wait another thirty.

6

Invest Wisely

Are we really going to spend $100 million without a plan?
—Democratic Party billionaire donor in a 2004 e-mail
to a consultant hired to unseat George W. Bush

When progressive major donors mobilized to try to defeat George Bush in 2004, they raised $200 million for the task, a then-unprecedented sum of outside spending. As often happens in the early stages of campaigns, there was a fair amount of confusion about—and competition over—exactly how the work would be organized among various groups, operatives, and consultants. Despite the lack of clarity, however, fund-raisers were asking the country's wealthiest Democratic donors to make seven- to eight-figure donations. It was in that context that a top donor, the CEO of a Fortune 500 company, who was very unimpressed with the fund-raising materials he had received, sent an e-mail to the leading consultant of the outside effort, asking, "Are we really going to spend $100 million without a plan?" It's the kind of question that more people in progressive politics need to ask the Democratic Party and other progressive organizations and efforts, and they need to ask it more often.

At best, Democratic and other progressive campaigns are failing to maximize their potential by applying best practices and lessons learned from successful large-scale organizations. At worst, they are wasting tens, if not hundreds, of millions of dollars each election on losing strategies. Building a permanent progressive majority in America requires investing resources wisely.

WE HAVE A LOT OF MONEY TO INVEST

In the wake of the Supreme Court's 2010 *Citizens United* decision, which opened the floodgates to billionaires spending millions of dollars to influence elections, many progressives are rightly concerned about the role of big money in politics. While those concerns are understandable and justified, at the same time, the progressive movement actually has a lot of money, but much of that money is not being spent well.

The Democratic Party and progressive independent groups spent nearly $2 billion in the 2012 election cycle.[1] During the nonpresidential election of 2014, the spending topped $700 million.[2] In the 2016 election, the progressive Big Money machine will roll on unabated, and the billion-dollar mark will almost definitely be broken again. For comparison purposes, when Bill Clinton won the White House in 1992, Democrats spent $74 million (the equivalent of $124 million today).[3] That was the amount raised in a *month* by Obama in 2012 (in his best month, October 2012, Obama raised $181 million).[4] And Hillary Clinton will likely put both her husband and President Obama to shame in the fund-raising department in the 2016 election. Her first fund-raising report in 2015 showed that she'd brought in $45 million, the most money ever raised by a presidential candidate in the first three months of a campaign.[5]

Progressives haven't even reached their fund-raising potential yet. As the Obama campaigns demonstrated, the latest technology tools can offset the conservative billionaires by connecting millions of people who can make small and medium-sized contributions. In 2012, conservative billionaires and centi-millionaires bankrolled outside groups that spent $400 million trying to defeat Obama's reelection bid.[6] The Obama campaign fought off the attacks with the help of 4 million people who gave the president's campaign more than $1 billion, with an average contribution of $65 per donation.[7] Bernie Sanders's 2016 presidential campaign also adopted this model by raising $40 million in 2015 from more than 600,000 donors giving an average contribution of $30.

As a nation we have just scratched the surface of the democratizing fund-raising power of cellular and computer technology. Roughly 90 percent of all American adults have a cell phone,[8] so there is virtually no technological barrier to small-dollar fund-raising. However, the vast majority of American adults have never donated by computer, personal device, or cell phone. As of 2012, just 20 percent of U.S. adults had ever made a charitable contribution online, and just 9 percent had ever used the contribute-by-text function.[9] While the 4 million Obama donors made up the largest number of political contributors to a single campaign in U.S. history, they still just represented 1.6 percent of all American adults. There is nowhere to go but up.

While one can always use more money, *having* enough money isn't the biggest problem for progressives and Democrats. Investing it wisely in the context of demographic shifts in the electorate is where the challenge lies. Progressives are *spending* a lot of money, but *investing* very little.

PRINCIPLES OF SOUND INVESTMENT

Progressives and Democrats are not handling their assets as wise investors. Successful investors apply at least three key principles in putting their money to work. First, they look for a growing market. "The most important requirement," according to Russell Siegelman, a partner at Kleiner, Perkins, one of the first venture capital firms to invest in Google, "is a large-market opportunity in a fast-growing sector."[10] Second, they ask tough questions. If the financial meltdown of 2008 taught Americans anything it's to understand how one's money is being invested (for example, collateralized debt obligations are a good thing to avoid). And third, as exemplified by legendary investor Warren Buffett, they invest for the long term. All of these principles are equally applicable to political investing.

INVEST IN GROWING MARKETS

Apple now sells more iPhones in China than it does in the United States; sales there have been growing four times faster than U.S. sales.[11] That's one of the main reasons Apple has become the most valuable company

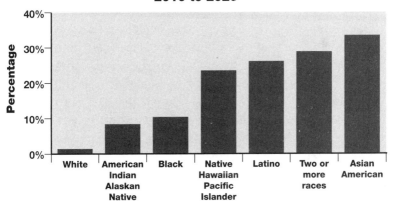

Figure 13. Source: U.S. Census Bureau, "Methodology and Assumptions for the 2012 National Projections," December 12, 2012.

in the world. Smart and effective leaders know that success entails prioritizing and investing in markets that are growing over those that are shrinking.

It defies logic and common sense to target a market that has been shrinking for forty years and will only get smaller over the coming decades, but that's what progressives are doing by chasing the declining demographic of White swing voters. The data could not be clearer about which population groups, states, and regions are growing fastest in America. The two fastest-growing groups, Asian Americans and Latinos, each grew by 43 percent from 2000 to 2010. African Americans grew by 12.3 percent. White Americans, by contrast, grew by just 5.7 percent.[12] Future projections indicate that these trends will only accelerate in coming years. The latest estimates for the current decade are illustrated in Figure 13.

Since most Latinos and African Americans live in the Southwest and South, respectively, it's not surprising that the states in those regions are growing the most each year.[13] Of the eight states that were allocated additional electoral votes after the 2010 Census due to population shifts, six are in the South or Southwest: Arizona, Florida, Texas, Georgia, Nevada, and South Carolina.[14]

Too many in the progressive infrastructure do not appreciate the size and strategic significance of the country's communities of color. Had John Kerry received 96 percent of the Black vote in Ohio in 2004—instead of the 84 percent he actually received—he would have defeated George Bush and been elected president.[15] Similarly, had Kerry won just 128,000 additional votes in the heavily Latino states of Nevada, Colorado, and New Mexico, he would have won those states and, by extension, the White House. Despite that data, one advisor to a prominent Democratic donor responded to a 2008 request for funds to target Black voters in Ohio and Latinos in the Southwest by saying, "We're not focusing on the fringe voters."

The fight to hold the Senate in 2014 saw a similar disconnect. Michelle Nunn's U.S. Senate campaign in 2014 presented an attractive opportunity to take a seat from the Republicans and preserve Democratic control of that body. Georgia elections are usually decided by 200,000–300,000 votes (Obama lost the state by 205,000 votes in 2008 and 305,000 votes in 2012). Georgia has nearly 1 million people of color who are eligible to vote but currently not participating in elections.[16] Simple math shows that those voters of color could shift the balance of power and determine electoral outcomes if they were registered and mobilized. In 2014, the representatives of several progressive billionaires held a conference call to discuss how to help Democrats win in Georgia. At the time, Georgia house minority leader Stacey Abrams had organized a very promising program that needed $6 million to register and turn out 200,000 voters. Despite the extraordinarily deep pockets of the people whose representatives were on the call and their evident interest in Georgia, most of them were not interested in investing in a voter of color registration and mobilization program. Their preferred form of engagement was to fund television ads targeting the largely White pool of "likely" voters.

Clearly, the wisdom of investing in growing markets is not yet conventional wisdom in progressive major-donor circles. Better decisions must be made about where to invest progressive resources. It's equally, if not more, important *how* those dollars are spent, and that involves following the second rule for successful investing: ask tough questions.

ASK TOUGH QUESTIONS

One of the fundamental causes of the financial crisis of 2008 was that too many people shoveled money into investment products they did not understand. In his book *The Big Short*, Michael Lewis described how "[t]he subprime-mortgage market had a special talent for obscuring what needed to be clarified."[17] "A bond backed entirely by subprime mortgages," Lewis went on to explain, "wasn't called a subprime-mortgage bond. It was called an 'A.B.S.,' or 'asset-backed security.' If you asked Deutsche Bank exactly what assets secured an asset-backed security, you'd be handed lists of more acronyms—R.M.B.S., HELs, HELOCs, Alt-A." In the political world, there's a similarly confusing cacophony of terms that have the effect of disempowering investors by obscuring how money is being spent. Political consultants talk about "GRPs," "models," "random digit dialing," "cross-tabulation," and "sample sizes."[18]

Asking tough questions is the best way to find out what an investment is actually supposed to do. Frequently those who are reluctant to give honest answers to hard questions will do their best to make a potential investor feel stupid for even asking the questions—all the more reason to keep asking. There really are no stupid questions. Asking questions leads to understanding, and hard questions create transparency and accountability, even if they make people uncomfortable. Especially if they make people uncomfortable. In the words of the late Black Arts Movement poet Amiri Baraka, "If you ask 'why?' enough, you just might get wise." In the spirit of moving toward wisdom, here are some key questions every political investor should ask:

1. WHAT IS OUR PLAN?

The goal of every political campaign is to win 50 percent +1 of the voters. This is often referred to as the "win number." To get to the win number, you have to stitch together clusters of support from various constituency groups. One constructs a campaign plan based on assumptions and projections about how many people from each group can be won over to support the cause or candidate. In Minnesota, Congressman Keith Ellison has proven that an intelligent plan tied to New American Majority demographics can not only win elections, but also defy the odds and increase voter turnout, even when internal stack is down across the state and country. In 2014, statewide voter turnout in Minnesota was down 3 percent, but Ellison's team increased turnout in his district by 5 percent, and they did it by having a plan and working that plan.

After doing a detailed and data-rich analysis of the electorate, Ellison's team identified their most likely supporters and crafted tailored efforts to reach each population. Recognizing that many of their core supporters lived in apartments and changed residences fairly frequently, they focused on 90,000 people living in 525 apartment buildings that had more than 51 units. Dozens of volunteers were then deployed to those buildings, where they knocked on 50,000 doors, registering people to vote, identifying supporters, and securing commitments to cast ballots. Seeing the racial diversity in the district—including Minnesota's relatively large population of African immigrants—the campaign developed a specific canvassing operation targeting Somali immigrants as well as Latinos. To reach African Americans, they devised a "Souls to the Polls" program that focused on 124 area churches and sent staff to encourage early and absentee voting in those churches. Through this kind of sophisticated, data-driven, culturally competent plan, the Ellison campaign defied the national trends of decreased turnout in a midterm election and also contributed to the statewide success of the Democratic candidate for secretary of state.[19] If all Democratic incumbents had emulated Ellison's detailed and meticulous plans for ensuring voter turnout, the Party would not be in nearly as deep a hole as it is now.

Campaign activities fall into two broad categories—mobilization and persuasion. Mobilization involves getting your supporters out to vote and usually consists of canvassers calling and personally contacting voters. Persuasion entails convincing undecided voters to support your side and is generally carried out through television ads and other forms of mass communication. An intelligent plan will incorporate both mobilization and persuasion with a data-driven understanding of how many votes each set of activities should yield.

Most campaigns don't direct their resources to turning out large numbers of people of color, and instead choose to try to persuade the moderate-to-conservative Whites they consider "likely" voters. Generally, those assumptions are not explicit, and that's why it's critical to ask questions. How many voters of color is the campaign seeking to secure? How many progressive Whites? Is that enough to win, and if not, how many White swing voters are required? What is the plan to close the gap, and, most important, how many votes does the campaign expect to win through advertising?

Many progressive campaigns proceed on the assumption that they will win by running ads, mostly on TV, that will persuade White swing voters to come to their side, but there is little empirical evidence for these kinds of assumptions. By contrast, the demonstrably reliable support of voters of color is regularly neglected in campaign priorities, plans, and resource allocation.

North Carolina democrat Kay Hagan's loss of her U.S. Senate seat in 2014 is a painful example of what happens when progressive forces don't have a plan. When Hagan was elected in 2008, 46 percent of her votes came from people of color.[20] In her reelection bid in 2014, more than $40 million was spent by the Democratic side, $20 million of that by outside groups working to help Hagan win.[21] Of that outside money, $18.8 million of those funds were spent on negative television ads opposing Hagan's opponent, Thom Tillis. One can't argue with a straight face that directing $19 million to attack ads was the result of an intelligent plan based on sound data and empirical evidence.

Nobody has ever tried to pretend that attack ads are the best way to retain your supporters and motivate them to turn out at the polls for you. Those ads were focused on trying to persuade a smaller pool of White swing voters that Tillis was a bad guy. That same $19 million could have paid for 400 full-time staff members to go door-to-door in communities of color for an entire year, talking to and mobilizing the voters who had turned out for Hagan when she won in 2008. If each of those 400 staff members, working full-time for a year making calls and knocking on doors, managed to get just *three* additional Democratic voters every *week* (and taking two weeks off for vacation), Hagan could have secured an additional 59,000 votes and won the election.[22]

2. DOES THE BUDGET MATCH THE PLAN?

Having a plan is just the first step. A plan is only real and relevant if there is a budget to back it up. A budget is a statement of priorities, and smart campaigns prioritize their allocation of resources to give them the best possible chance of securing sufficient support from various sectors of the population needed to assemble a winning coalition. Campaign stakeholders need to be vigilant about finding out whether field programs to mobilize voters are properly funded, how much money is allocated to television ads, and whether the campaign is reaching New American Majority market segments using the most targeted and cost-effective means.

An excellent postelection article in *Vox* in 2014 summarized what really works in mobilizing voters. According to the article by David Broockman and Joshua Kalla: "By far the most effective way to turn out voters is with high-quality, face-to-face conversations that urge them to vote. How do we know? Nearly two decades of rigorous randomized experiments have proven it."[23] From experiments by Yale's Donald Green and Alan Gerber summarized in their book *Getting Out the Vote!*, to the excellent scholarship and research of the University of California, Berkeley's Lisa Garcia Bedolla, Emory's Andra Gillespie, the University of Maryland's Janelle Wong, Menlo College's Melissa Michelson, UC Riverside's Karthick Ramakrishnan, UC San Diego's Marisa Abrajano, and others, there is widespread agreement among researchers and scholars about what works in getting people—especially voters of color—to the polls. Hiring canvassers and community-based organizers to do the unsexy but highly effective work of going door-to-door, identifying supporters, and following up with them to turn out at the polls is the proven approach to increasing voter turnout. But proven does not necessarily mean popular.

Despite the ample evidence pointing toward mobilization as the most effective route to marshal votes, the overwhelming amount of money is still spent on persuasion, usually in the form of broadcast television ads. Despite what research and data show about the lack of cost efficiency of such ads, the dollars continue to flow to TV. In 2012 and 2014, 80 percent of outside spending on Senate races went to television ads.[24]

Excessive expenditures on broadcast television ads are wasteful on several levels. One major problem with overemphasizing TV ads in campaigns is that their proliferation is certainly correlated with, if not caused by, inherent financial conflicts of interest on the part of consultants. Many consultants still take a flat 15 percent fee (from the campaign)—based on the cost of the ad buy—for each television ad that airs.[25] If the campaign places a $1 million ad buy, the campaign must pay $1 million for the ad buy to the outlet/channel running the ad and an additional $150,000 to the consultant for making the ad. What's absurd about that is that it costs a consultant the same amount to *produce* the ad whether it's run as part of a $1,000 ad buy (for example, local cable channel) or a $1 million ad buy (for example, national network). Fifteen percent of $1 million is a lot of money. Spending so much money on broadcast television ads may be good for the college funds of the children of the consultants, but it's not the smartest way to invest limited campaign resources. In addition to the money, there's a laziness factor. For consultants it's easier to sit in one's office brainstorming and editing a commercial than it is to hire, train, and coordinate dozens or hundreds of human beings to go door-to-door interacting with potential voters and then capturing, tracking, and analyzing all the data coming back from the canvassing.

An additional problem with overemphasizing television ads is that they frequently miss the target market—literally. Broadcast television commercials are at best blunt instruments in that they are aired in broad media markets that do not align neatly with the political districts where candidates are running. As a result, in many cases the television ads reach large numbers of people who can't even vote for the candidate in question. One study found that of $111 million spent in 2014, *$80 million of that was wasted* communicating with voters outside the target district.[26]

If the campaign plan does allocate resources to reaching out to voters of color, then investors and stakeholders in the campaign must make sure that those dollars are also being spent wisely and informed by hard data rather than old stereotypes.

When a prominent White consultant working on a California ballot measure campaign I was involved in a few years ago was asked about his strategy to reach voters of color, he replied: "They watch the same commercials everyone else does." Well, no, they don't. And even when they do, many of them pay more attention to ethnic media. (This consultant went on to a role of national prominence with the Obama campaign.) As former NAACP president Ben Jealous observed from his time working with the National Newspaper Publishers Association, the nation's largest association of Black papers, "If you just advertise in mainstream publications, Black folks might see the ad, but they won't know you're talking to *them*."

When most campaigns target Latinos the default mode is to run some Spanish-language ads and call it a day. But that's the result of lazy thinking, unchallenged by hard questions. In fact, Spanish-language ads may actually be ineffective with some portions of the Latino electorate. Digging deeper into the demographic data uncovers the truth: while 82 percent of all Latinos speak Spanish,[27] the vast majority of Latinos *who are eligible to vote* speak English very well. According to the Pew Center's analysis of 2012 census data, at least 73 percent of Latino eligible voters speak English exclusively at home or speak English very well (one-third of Latino eligible voters speak English exclusively).[28] While there is a place for Spanish-language advertising in campaigns, it's important to keep in mind that the overwhelming majority of Latino eligible voters speak English (which is not to say they shouldn't receive targeted communications; English language ads also need to be culturally compelling and relevant).

Communicating with Asian Americans also requires detailed dissection of pertinent data. As discussed previously, the Asian American population has skyrocketed since passage of the 1965 Immigration and Nationality Act. As discussed earlier, 74 percent of all Asian American adults are foreign-born, and not surprisingly, three-quarters of Asian American adults speak a language other than English at home. Among Asian American voters, however, approximately 63 percent speak English very well.[29] And, to state the obvious, Asian Americans speak many different languages and dialects: Mandarin is different from Cantonese, which is different from Tagalog, which is different from Gujarati, which is different from Vietnamese, and so on. Reflecting the growth of this diverse group, the number of Asian American media outlets has grown more than tenfold, from 102 in 1999 to 1,239 in 2010.[30] All campaigns should be asked how they are communicating with Asian Americans, whether they are using the right Asian languages to reach those who prefer to receive communications in those languages, and if they are targeting the right Asian American media outlets.

3. HOW ARE WE DOING AND HOW DID WE DO?

There's a great story in the book *Googled* by Ken Auletta, about how Mel Karmazin, then CEO of "old media" television giant Viacom, responded to a 2003 presentation by Google's cofounders on how the search engine was able to precisely measure the impact of advertising dollars. Karmazin, whose business model depended on revenue from broadcast television ads, responded by saying, "You're fucking with the magic!"[31] What Karmazin was referring to was the adage that everyone knows half the money spent on advertising is wasted, but nobody knows which half. Many political consultants depend on this ambiguity to justify their value to campaigns and pay their bills. The idea is that "brilliant" consultants will develop devastating ads that will capture the imagination of the voters, transform the dynamics of the election, and propel the candidate to victory and the fast track to the White House. "Trust me, I've run hundreds of campaigns" is a line proffered countless times by consultants offering lots of testosterone, bravado, and swagger, but few data or metrics. With the abundance of data and analytics now available, political campaigns can and must be much more evidence based in assessing what works and what doesn't in a campaign.

A useful model for tracking the progress of investments can be found in the business world. In the realm of investing, reputable financial advisors have regular meetings with their clients to review how various investments performed that quarter, what worked, what didn't, and whether any adjustments are necessary. The advisors provide spreadsheets showing the percentage performance of each component of the portfolio as well as the gain or loss of the total investment assets. If a mutual fund or investment isn't performing well, the advisor and client discuss whether to stay the course or switch things up. That kind of regular review and analysis is easily achieved but rarely performed in the world of political and social change.

Just as stock prices and profit-and-loss statements provide the data to assess how a financial portfolio is doing, election and voting data offer insights into the effectiveness of a political program. Public voting records reveal exactly who turned out to vote—information that can be analyzed by local precinct and neighborhood and compared with the outreach and communication activities that were designed to influence those potential voters. To take advantage of this analytical capacity, however, campaign stakeholders have to insist on accountability and reporting based on detailed and relevant metrics.

The problem is that many donors want to see large numbers of potential voters contacted, and they tend to accept metrics that are suboptimal, if not irrelevant, as evidence of success. A common inadequate metric frequently reported by campaigns consists of campaign "contacts" as a way of demonstrating the scale and scope of the campaign's efforts. But a contact is very different from a vote. If you send someone an e-mail, that's a contact. You can send 10 million e-mails (well, there are spam laws, but there are also ways around them), make hundreds of thousands of automated calls, and mail tens of thousands of direct mail letters. Those are all contacts. But at the end of the day, they're not votes.

Fortunately, there are now ways to measure who actually turned out to vote—and who didn't. The Texas Organizing Project, a leading organizing and advocacy group, for example, follows the practice of reporting meaningful metrics. Their preelection update to supporters in 2014 stated, "To date, we've turned out 52,415 of our target voters."[32] Their metric was "turned out actual voters to the polls," and that's what campaign stakeholders should be looking for, not calls, door knocks, or mailings (as many political trainers say, "Don't believe any number that ends in zero; it was probably made up"). These meaningful metrics can have impact, but only if people ask for them, regularly review the effectiveness of the campaign's investments, and insist that future campaign plans operate based on evidence of what has been proven to work. That is the thinking behind the saying, "You are what you measure."

Progressives have the tools, but not necessarily the temperament or inclination, to insist on detailed, data-rich accountability and reports. For example, where are the detailed analyses of what happened in the 2010 and 2014 midterm elections when Democrats lost their majorities? The Democratic National Committee is supposed to be doing a "postmortem" of the 2014 midterms but its preliminary findings lacked any data at all.[33] Many Party leaders don't even seem to be aware of the size of the drop-off in Democratic votes that led to the loss of control of Congress. Asking "What happened and why?" would have yielded greater insights based on real data.

DO *SOME* INVESTING FOR THE LONG TERM

Success in investing requires a lengthy time horizon, and smart and savvy investors allocate at least *some* people and *some* resources to long-term planning. As Warren Buffett has said about his investing philosophy, "If you aren't willing to own a stock for ten years, don't even think about owning it for ten minutes." Too often the preferred time horizon for progressives in politics is closer to ten minutes.

Political campaigns are, by nature, short-term endeavors, so it's logical that the lion's share of money spent in each election cycle goes toward short-term needs. But *some* of the $1 billion raised each cycle can and should be spent with an eye toward the long term. Despite the desperation each campaign inevitably produces, it is still possible to spend money in ways that increase the prospects of short-term victory while also improving the terrain for the future.

Broadly speaking, long-term investments should fall into three categories: people, organizations, and places.

PEOPLE

The progressive movement needs to change the complexion of the leadership of its organizations, campaigns, and institutions. In order to succeed in the long term, the movement must be connected to and largely led by those who understand the lived experience as well as the hopes and dreams of people of color and progressive Whites. Since White guys still control the vast majority of progressive politics, transforming the composition and leadership of the progressive movement to truly reflect the New American Majority will require a long-term investment of patient capital.

It is possible to forever ban the phrase, "We couldn't find any people of color to hire." Instead of just complaining about the inability to find talent of color, progressive organizations, funders, and leaders need to start putting their money where their mouth is in terms of addressing both the supply and demand sides of diversity in hiring. In terms of supply, heads of organizations should set aside 1 percent of their budgets to invest in a LinkedIn-like online platform for diverse talent. I was pleased to join with Quentin James, Alida Garcia, Greg Cendana, and a network of other talented young organizers of color in 2015 in creating Inclusv, a talent bank to identify, train, and place activists and operatives of color.[34] While that is a promising start, these kinds of efforts need to be taken to scale, which will require millions of dollars so that they can support thousands in the next generation of leaders, activists, and organizers.

Another approach is to elevate more women and people of color to at least the No. 2 and 3 positions of leadership in organizations. In this fashion, people gain the experience, exposure, and connections necessary to become heads of organizations themselves. When John Podesta was president of the Center for American Progress and Miles Rapoport was president of Demos, they modeled this behavior by supporting the leadership of Neera Tanden, who is Indian American, and Heather McGhee, who is African American, as key lieutenants (as chief operating officer and vice president of policy and outreach, respectively). Tanden and McGhee went on to become the heads of those large and respected organizations and now appear regularly on shows such as

Meet the Press, helping to shape the national political discourse and inform that dialogue with the views of women of color. Every progressive group should, at a minimum, be populating the positions below president or executive director with diverse talent. And political campaigns and the Democratic Party could go a long way in this direction by looking at the deputy positions in national, regional, and state campaign structures.

On the demand side, there are tangible steps that can be taken by those who really want to see change happen. It starts with commitment from the top, however. A 2014 report found that while 80 percent of funders of environmental organizations who were surveyed said they would like to see a diversity pipeline of talent, just 27 percent of the foundations were willing to fund such an endeavor.[35]

One step that can be taken by campaigns and organizations is to adopt the "Rooney Rule," which is followed by the National Football League (NFL). In the NFL, no general manager or head coach position can be filled unless at least one person of color has been interviewed for that job.[36] The Super Bowl rings on the fingers of Pittsburgh Steelers head coach Mike Tomlin, Baltimore Ravens general manager Ozzie Newsome, and former Indianapolis Colts coach Tony Dungy are proof that the Rooney Rule is no impediment to success.

In terms of setting a tone and example for the progressive movement, people in positions of impact and influence have myriad ways to use that influence to facilitate structural change. Freada Kapor Klein, a leading Silicon Valley investor and diversity champion, refuses to accept invitations to speak on panels that are all-White, and when she declines she tells conference organizers why. Jonathan Sposato, a Seattle entrepreneur and angel investor, publicly declared that he was going to invest only in companies that had at least one female founder.[37] Those are examples of using one's reputation and stature as capital in the struggle for social change.

ORGANIZATIONS

Community-based organizations that have deep roots and widespread respect among people of color can play pivotal roles in building

long-term political power. One of the leading examples of what is possible with long-term investment in civic engagement of voters of color
can be found with the organizations affiliated with California Calls,
a statewide network that grew out of the cutting-edge work done by
Los Angeles activist and organizer Anthony Thigpenn. Over the past
twenty-five years, Thigpenn has overseen the creation of a voter contact and mobilization operation that has grown from 50,000 voters to
500,000 in Los Angeles and served as the linchpin of electoral victories of progressive candidates of color for city council, state legislature,
and mayor. His approach consistently results in voters of color turning
out to vote in higher numbers than the rate of participation of voters
outside the reach of his program.

Another example can be found in San Diego, historically a home of
conservative politics, but demographic changes are altering its political
character. Alliance San Diego, led by Latina lawyer Andrea Guerrero,
has been a key driver of the increased voter participation of people of
color. A partner in Thigpenn's California Calls, the San Diego group
was able to increase voter turnout of the low-propensity voters by 11 percent in 2014, swelling voter participation by more than 5,000 voters.
With that expanded electorate, Democratic congressman Scott Peters
barely survived his reelection bid with a margin of 6,000 votes.

Thigpenn describes his approach as Integrated Voter Engagement
(IVE), and he has distilled the formula into the following elements:
(1) a multiyear strategy to increase the voter participation of communities and constituencies traditionally underrepresented in the electorate;
(2) engaging target voters year-round to build a relationship, educate on
issues, motivate to increase voter participation, and become involved
in advocacy and community organizing; (3) local, community-based
organizations (CBOs) that are rooted in communities embrace IVE
as an integrated part of their organizing strategy and ongoing work;
(4) development of grassroots leaders in communities as the primary
voter engagement organizers; (5) use of voter engagement technology
to increase the capacities of CBOs to reach a new scale of engaging
target constituencies; and (6) systematic tracking of engagement and
results through a living and growing voter database.[38]

Other areas across the country with growing numbers of people of color but insufficient organizational infrastructure cry out for long-term support along the lines of the IVE model. Investing in these kinds of anchor organizations in the next set of battleground states will be particularly beneficial over the coming decade.

PLACES

In determining where to invest in people and organizations, special attention needs to be paid to the geography of the New American Majority. Those states and regions at the epicenter of the demographic transformation need steady and sustained investment in leaders who are committed to their states, and in organizations that can harness and channel the energy of the emerging constituencies that are coming into their own.

The entire progressive movement should get ahead of the curve, accelerate the arrival of the future, and go all-in in the next set of battleground states: North Carolina, Georgia, and Arizona. Regarding Arizona, Obama campaign manager Jim Messina said in 2012, "It is going to be a swing state. The question is, whether we can get enough people registered to put it in play this year."[39] Messina was right to see the opportunity, but unfortunately opted against having the Obama re-election campaign contest the state (even a modest investment from Obama's billion-dollar campaign would have trained more activists, registered more voters, and added more people to the progressive database, hastening Arizona's transition to becoming a swing state).

Although Bill Clinton won Georgia in the 1992 presidential election, the state has been starved for resources ever since. Although in 2014 in Georgia Michelle Nunn's Senate campaign and Jason Carter's gubernatorial bid brought in a combined $24 million for Democrats,[40] as mentioned earlier, getting progressive donors to invest at scale in the kind of work that can yield results far into the future is still not happening. In an election cycle where the progressive side spent half a billion dollars (in 2014), $10 million should have been moved quickly to Georgia at least a year in advance of election day to support person-to-person voter contact work. Fortunately, Stacey Abrams has already laid a solid foundation with strategic and effective voter registration and leadership development programs in Georgia and across the South.[41] Going forward, that's the kind of investment that will hasten the political transformation of these new battleground states.

Building infrastructure, developing capacity, and supporting and training leaders are what we need to be doing now in these states. This type of investment by the 2016 Democratic nominee and her (or his) allies will produce the additional tactical benefit of forcing Republicans to expend resources in these places that they don't normally have to contest.

In addition to securing key Southern and Southwestern states, significant strategic progress can come through deep investments in the Blue parts of Red states. Texas is a perfect example of this. Conservatives have dominated statewide elections for the past two decades, but the state's largest cities are solidly Blue. Houston, with a population of 2.2 million people, is so Blue that it's elected a lesbian mayor. Twice. And without a whole lot of controversy. As discussed in Chapter 1, these "liberated zones" in Red states are potential places to pass progressive policies that can improve the lives of millions of people.

There is no excuse for conducting any campaign without a plan. Whether it's a $100 million campaign to help win a presidential race (or a $1 billion campaign, for that matter) or a volunteer advocacy effort to get a town council to put up a stop sign, we have the data, tools, knowledge, and experience to make sure our time, energy, and resources are being put to use to produce the maximum impact.

It is surprising how few of the best practices, transparency, and accountability demanded by investors in the for-profit world are insisted on in the political and social change space, despite the fact that those arenas are funded with dollars made through for-profit rigor and discipline (not that everything in the for-profit world is rigorous or disciplined, but that's a topic for another book). Minimally, political investors should want to get the most out of every dollar and every hour they invest. More fundamentally, the stakes are high, and the New American Majority is counting on progressive investors—small and large donors of time and money—to insist that Democrats and other progressive leaders and decision makers invest wisely to secure a permanent progressive majority and make this country more equitable and just.

Jesse Jackson used to say in 1984 that he was running a "poor campaign with a rich message," a message of social, economic, and racial justice. Today, the successors to the Rainbow Coalition and those who would seek to reach and rebuild a modern-day rainbow have millions to spend on campaigns. But having money—even having money and a plan—is insufficient. To win, one needs a rich message that resonates and inspires those who have experienced and still battle discrimination and injustice.

7

What Is Justice? Policy Priorities for the New American Majority

Poverty and violence didn't just randomly happen to this community. These issues are the result of a long history of systematic discrimination and abuse. . . . Given this history, we shouldn't be surprised at the challenges that kids in Indian Country are facing today. And we should never forget that we played a role in this. Make no mistake about it—we own this. And we can't just invest a million here and a million there, or come up with some five-year or ten-year plan and think we're going to make a real impact. This is truly about nation-building, and it will require fresh thinking and a massive infusion of resources over generations. That's right, not just years, but generations.[1]

—Michelle Obama, April 8, 2015, White House Convening
on Creating Opportunity for Native Youth

The house I grew up in is worth $178,000 today. It is located in the leafy suburbs of Cleveland Heights, Ohio, and has tripled in value during my lifetime. Three miles away, the house my maternal grandparents lived in is worth $36,000.[2] It is located in an inner-city neighborhood of Cleveland and has appreciated in value just $3,000 since the 1970s. As explained in Chapter 2, my parents were blocked from purchasing our home because they were Black, and it took a Herculean effort and significant legal sleight of hand to become the owners of the property. My family used the equity in that home to secure a second mortgage that gave us the funds to afford to send me to Hawken School, an expensive private school in the Cleveland suburbs where I gained the kind of education, test-taking skills, connections, and credentials that helped me get into Stanford University. Most people of

Median Family Wealth by Racial Group

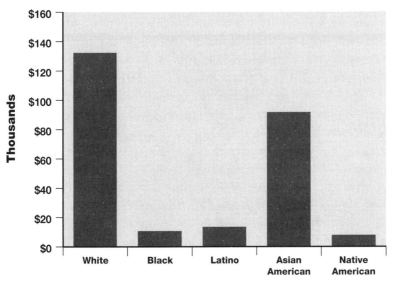

Figure 14. Source: Federal Reserve Bank of St. Louis, "The Demographics of Wealth," 2015, Insight Center for Community Economic Development, "Wealth Inequality and Racial Wealth Accumulation," 2007.

color in this country have not been as lucky as my family has been, and the realities of past and present racial discrimination are responsible for the profound inequality that is the moral imperative of this moment in history.

America has a gargantuan racial wealth gap, and that gap impacts nearly all public policy issues affecting the New American Majority. The median wealth, or net worth, of a White family in 2013 was $134,000, while the median wealth for a Black family was $11,000. Latino families have a net worth of $13,900, and Native American families have a net worth of $5,700.[3] For Asian American families that amount is $91,440, and much of that is attributable to the fact that 74 percent of all Asian American adults are immigrants, with many of them coming from the professional class of their home countries.[4] The extent of the disparity can be seen in Figure 14.

With Whites having such an overwhelming head start, it is nearly impossible for the groups of color to catch up. The historical average annual return on investments in the stock market is approximately 10 percent.[5] If the average White family invested their $134,000 in net assets in the stock market and received that 10 percent annual return, and the average Black family placed its $11,000 in investments that performed *twice as well* as the White family's, the Black family would still be behind even after 28 years of earning double on their investment.[6]

Today's racial wealth gap is a modern-day manifestation of the fact that America was built on land stolen from Native Americans and Mexicans and developed by the backbreaking labor of African Americans, Latinos, and Asian Americans. Given this reality, we all have to ask ourselves what is the right and just thing to do from a public policy standpoint to close this gap in a country that professes a belief in justice and equality? If progressives want to vastly improve the conditions in underserved and underdeveloped communities, capture the imagination of the New American Majority, and secure its lasting loyalty, then bigger and bolder policy solutions are required. Much bigger and much bolder.

ECONOMIC JUSTICE

Economic inequality is a defining issue of our time. The ultimate objective of all public policies should be to enable people to live their lives to their fullest potential, and that begins with the financial ability to meet one's basic needs.

In recent years, there has been increasing attention paid to the broad issue of economic inequality, but frequently the analysis doesn't go deep enough. It is critical to understand that there are three core dimensions of economic inequality. On one level, there is income inequality, or how much money people *make.* Income inequality has received the most attention in the form of campaigns to raise the minimum wage and highlight the pay disparity between CEOs and their employees. On a deeper, more radical level is wealth inequality, or how much money people *have.* Although there has been some rhetorical attention paid to income inequality in the early stages of the 2016 presidential race, less advocacy and organizing attention has been paid to disparities in net worth or assets, but the Occupy Wall Street movement's slogan, "We Are the 99%," began to highlight the reality of broad wealth inequality.

On an even deeper, truly revolutionary level is racial wealth inequality—the profound difference in net assets owned by people of different racial groups. Tackling the racial wealth gap in this country would be revolutionary because it requires grappling with the questions of *how* and *why* the enormous gap came to be, accepting and acknowledging the painful answers, and committing to investing time and money to do all that we can to bring about justice and fairness. As Michelle Obama said, it requires fresh thinking and a massive infusion of resources.

WHY DO WHITE PEOPLE HAVE ALL THE MONEY?

Joe Feagin, a White sociologist who has researched racism for forty years and written sixty books, succinctly summarized the context of contemporary economic inequality in a 2015 interview:

> Social science research is clear that white-black inequalities today are substantially the result of a majority of whites socially inheriting unjust enrichments (money, land, home equities, social capital, etc.) from numerous previous white generations— the majority of whom benefited from the racialized slavery system and/or the de jure (Jim Crow) and de facto overt racial oppression that followed slavery for nearly a century, indeed until the late 1960s.[7]

The origins of the racial wealth gap are as old as the history of White people in America. If you ask: "When has there *not* been a racial wealth gap in this country?" the picture starts to come into focus. A full and accurate recounting of our nation's history and its role in creating this gap is beyond the scope of this book, but most people looking honestly and objectively at early American history would have a hard time arguing that America's early wealth came from anywhere *but* stolen land worked by stolen people. English settlers arrived in 1607 as part of a privately financed profit-seeking venture, then launched attacks on the original inhabitants of the land, forcibly took control of the fertile soil, and shipped in enslaved Africans to pick crops that generated tremendous amounts of cash. That pretty much sums up the entire story of America's earliest wealth-creating activities.

The pattern did not stop in the 1600s. It continued on through the rise of slavery as a global economic engine, the betrayal of post–Civil War Reconstruction, which was designed to provide compensation to formerly enslaved people, and up through the resurgence of sharecropping and the rise of Jim Crow segregation in the twentieth century.[8]

Many of today's most profitable corporate enterprises have their roots in the blood and plunder of American history. Aetna, the largest health insurer in the United States, and New York Life, the largest mutual life insurance company in the country, made their first profits by issuing policies insuring slave owners from loss of their valuable "property." According to Tom Baker, director of the Insurance Law Center at the University of Connecticut School of Law, "It's not pleasant to talk about it today, to put it mildly, but slaves were insured just like any other thing that the farmers owned, that the slave owners owned."[9] ExxonMobil and Chevron are progeny of the Standard Oil Company, which was founded in 1870 on oil-rich land in Ohio less than a hundred years after the U.S. Army cleared the area for Whites to control that land by attacking and killing the indigenous inhabitants of the region in the Northwest Indian War in 1795.[10] Wells Fargo and Levi Strauss got their start during the Gold Rush era of the mid-1800s, which couldn't begin until California was violently seized from Mexico, and the Native Americans on the land were killed and driven out.

More recently, and almost erased from history, has been the role of the federal government—and many state and local governments— in creating and maintaining racial economic inequality in America. In the decades after the Great Depression, the federal government oversaw a massive investment of billions of dollars in expanding and elevating the middle class.

Few people realize the importance of the GI Bill, the massive federal program, formally called the Servicemen's Readjustment Act of 1944, which provided financial benefits to veterans returning from World War II and directly contributed to today's racial wealth gap. Ira

Katznelson explains in his book *When Affirmative Action Was White* that "no other New Deal initiative had as great an impact on changing the country." Developed to provide support and assistance to 16 million veterans returning from war, "it reached eight of ten men born during the 1920s" and still "qualifies as the most wide-ranging set of social benefits ever offered by the federal government in a single, comprehensive initiative." [11] Glenn Altschuler and Stuart Blumin note in their book *The GI Bill: A New Deal for Veterans* that "[t]he veteran cohort created by the war was huge, dwarfing in absolute numbers the demobilization of any other armed conflict in U.S. history." [12] In his book *When Dreams Came True: The GI Bill and the Making of Modern America*, Michael Bennett wrote, "After spending more than four years researching and writing this book, I feel I cannot overstate the value and meaning of the GI Bill." He described it as "a silent revolution that would first transform college campuses and then create a new suburban society. America was about to become a predominantly middle-class nation." [13]

Katznelson's book provides extensive detail about the specifics and workings of the bill. Among the most important provisions were the following:

> Between 1944 and 1971, federal spending for former soldiers in this "model welfare system" totaled over $95 billion. By 1948, 15 percent of the federal budget was devoted to the GI Bill. . . . With the help of the GI Bill, millions bought homes, attended college, started business ventures, and found jobs commensurate with their skills. Through these opportunities, and by advancing the momentum toward suburban living, mass consumption, and the creation of wealth and economic security, this legislation created middle-class America. No other instrument was nearly as important. [14]

In a nation of 140 million people when World War II ended, a program targeting 16 million veterans and 6 million volunteers reached "at least one-quarter of the population" in that it also benefited the spouses and children who shared the household of the recipients of the government support. [15] That bill essentially handed tens of billions of dollars a year to Americans for decades after World War II. There was just one problem with this big government program. While it "did create a more middle-class society, [it was] almost exclusively for whites. Written under southern auspices, the law was deliberately designed to accommodate Jim Crow." [16] A 1947 study by the American Veterans Committee concluded that it was "as though the GI Bill had been earmarked 'For White Veterans Only.' " [17] Job placement for GI Bill programs, for example, was run by White staff at U.S. Employment Services (USES), and White veterans learned radio repair, machine and electrical work, photography, carpentry, business and diesel engineering. Black veterans, on the other hand, were routed to fields such as dry cleaning and tailoring. [18] College tuition assistance was available through the bill, but many colleges and universities engaged in active and accepted racial discrimination in admissions. At Stanford University, for example, as recently as 1960, just three Black students were granted admission to the freshman class. [19]

Home ownership has been the principal wealth creator in America, and the GI Bill worked hand in hand with New Deal reforms to make it possible for millions of Americans to become homeowners, with all the wealth-creation benefits that that entailed. Berkeley Law professor Melissa Murray wrote, "Prior to World War II, home mortgages required a 50% down-payment with short repayment periods, making the prospect of home ownership impossible for all but the elite. The G.I. Bill broadened home ownership by permitting eligible veterans to borrow money for the purchase of homes, farms, and equipment without the security of a down-payment." [20]

As my own parents discovered when they tried to buy our home in Cleveland Heights, Ohio, in 1964, access to the "American Dream" of home ownership was frequently unavailable to people of color. During the Depression of the 1930s, the possibility of widespread defaults and foreclosures posed a profound risk to the entire banking system, and the federal government stepped in with a massive program that not only saved tens of thousands of homes from going into foreclosure, but also made homeownership—and wealth accumulation—possible for more than 35 million people from 1933 to 1978. [21] The establishment of the Home Owners' Loan Corporation (HOLC) and then the Federal

Housing Administration provided guarantees and down payment assistance that made home ownership possible at affordable rates. While this was great for those who benefited from the programs, the problem was that access to the federal gravy train was largely restricted to Whites.

The overriding concern of the bureaucrats at the HOLC and the FHA was preservation of property values, and one of the biggest threats to property values in their eyes was the presence of Black people. As Melvin Oliver and Thomas Shapiro describe in *Black Wealth/White Wealth*, those "[c]harged with the task of determining the 'useful or productive life of housing' methodically included in their procedures the evaluation of the racial composition or potential racial composition of the community." As a result, "communities that were changing racially or were already black were deemed undesirable and placed in the lowest category."[22]

The government created color-coded zones of which homes were most likely to appreciate or depreciate in value, and the ones in unfavorable areas were coded in red, giving birth to the term *redlining*. To implement those policies, the government developed an Underwriting Manual that stated, "If a neighborhood is to retain stability, it is necessary that properties shall continue to be occupied by the same social and racial classes." In order to foster such stability, the manual "further recommended that 'subdivision regulations and suitable restrictive covenants' are the best way to ensure such neighborhood stability."[23] This is how business was done in the 1930s and 1940s as the country was climbing out of the Depression and millions of veterans were returning home from World War II and buying homes with the support of government guarantees and loans.

Although these policies were outlawed in the 1950s, the practices were not. In 1991, the Federal Reserve conducted a study of 6.4 million loans made at 9,300 financial institutions and found widespread racial disparities in who was approved for mortgages and who was not. In fact, they found that a low-income White person was statistically more likely to be approved for a home loan than a middle-class African American.[24] The informal practice of exclusion extends to real estate agents as well. As recently as 2013, a national study conducted 8,000

undercover tests to glean information about the level of continued racial discrimination in housing and found that Black, Asian American,
and Latino testers were consistently shown or told about fewer units.
For example, White homebuyers were shown nearly 20 percent more
homes as equally qualified Black and Asian American homebuyers
were.[25]

The impact of these decades of discriminatory policies began to be
acknowledged after the protests of the police murder of Freddie Gray
in Baltimore in 2015. In a lead editorial, the *New York Times* attributed
the crisis facing the city to the "century-long assault that Baltimore's
blacks have endured at the hands of local, state and federal policy makers, all of whom worked to quarantine black residents in ghettos, making it difficult even for people of means to move into integrated areas
that offered better jobs, schools and lives for their children." It is a pattern, the *Times* was careful to note, that "happened in cities all over the
country."[26]

In addition to the generosity of the GI Bill and the practice of redlining in lending, regular old racial discrimination in employment also
played a big role in creating the country's wealth gap. Much of the leadership structure of corporate America was put in place during a time of
legalized racial discrimination in employment and hiring. Even today,
just 4 percent of the country's Fortune 500 CEOs are people of color
(as of 2014).[27] Centuries of racial preference for Whites (ending only
in 1964) helped establish the racial economic hierarchy that we have in
America today.

The bottom line is that, on average, White people have more wealth
today than people of color because they are beneficiaries of a long legacy of racial oppression, economic exploitation, and massive government programs that were reserved almost exclusively for Whites and
designed to give them assets and elevate them to the middle class.

TRANSFORMING THE TERMS OF DEBATE

Beyond the morality of the matter as motivation to act, there are also
significant strategic reasons to pursue an economic justice agenda.
Contemplating and addressing the question "What is justice?" will

give force and momentum to a compelling contemporary public policy agenda that can get Democrats and progressives off the defensive and frame future fights over the country's priorities. The notion of justice is so deeply embedded in the American value system that forty-five states have laws requiring students to recite the Pledge of Allegiance, which, of course, ends with the words "and justice for all." [28] But what does justice for all really look like?

Much of modern public policy is based on two profound myths: that America is a land of equal opportunity and that poverty is largely due to personal failing. Both undergird and constrain the current public policy debate. Challenging these myths by raising disruptive questions can turn the tables on the policy dialogue and expand the sense of what's possible to help move America closer to our professed values.

THE MYTH OF EQUAL OPPORTUNITY

The racial wealth gap makes a mockery of the cherished concept that America is a land of equal opportunity.

The very fact that the average White family has *12 times* more wealth than the average Black family, 10 times more than the average Latino family, and 23 times more than a Native American family almost by definition means that there is no equal opportunity for the children born into those respective families. In addition to the racial wealth gap, there is also a substantial racial *income* gap with the average White family earning $58,000 per year and the average Black family earning $34,000 per year and the average Latino family earning $41,000 (as of 2013).[29]

As the *State of Asian Americans and Pacific Islanders* report notes, "The story of income and poverty among Asian Americans and Pacific Islanders, or AAPIs, is a tale of contrasts," with some groups such as Indians and Filipinos having higher average incomes than the national average due to the "relatively high level of employer-based, high-skilled visas." At the other end of the spectrum are "Southeast Asian populations such as Cambodian, Hmong, and Laotian Americans—who predominantly came to the United States as refugees with limited educational attainment in their home countries—[and] have relatively high levels of poverty and low levels of household income."[30] An additional important variable behind the statistics of Asian American net worth, as detailed in the book *The Color of Wealth*, is that "Asians tend to live in the most expensive and therefore higher-wage parts of the U.S.—California, Hawaii and New York—and . . . Asian households tend to be bigger, with more earners, than white households." Adjusting for those variables, "[l]ooking at per capita income within any given state, white median incomes exceed that of Asians."[31]

Notwithstanding the statistical divergence reflecting the fact that many Asian Americans come from their country's professional classes, the fact remains that the average White child enjoys more advantageous life prospects than his peers of color. Consider the ways that an average White family with $134,000 in assets (the average net assets for White families)—and an annual income significantly greater than the average income of a Black or Latino family—stands to give their children a profoundly better head start in life. That family has a better chance than most Black and Latino families to provide their children with quality child care and early childhood education and to live in neighborhoods with schools with lower class sizes, cleaner classrooms, and more advanced digital tools. They can better afford the latest technology at home, giving their children an advantage in learning and mastering the tools of today and preparing them for the future. They are better able to expose their children to the world through travel. They are more likely to benefit from "legacy" admissions preferences at colleges that make it 45 percent easier for children of alumni to gain admission.[32] (Richard Kahlenberg, author of *Affirmative Action for Rich People*, has highlighted that legacy admissions are overwhelmingly and disproportionately White, concluding that alumni preferences are White preferences "and will continue that way far, far into the future.")[33] They are more likely to have "social capital" as well—relationships with economically successful professionals who can provide job opportunities, references, internships, etc. The asset and income advantages can make it easier for these children to grow up and take economic risks, such as taking unpaid internships that often allow entry into elite companies and institutions that subsequently hire from the pool of people they know. And that asset "safety net" can also make it possible to obtain family loans or take out bank loans to obtain seed capital to launch entrepreneurial ventures.

Since economic inequality provides privileges and pitfalls tied to skin color, and legalized racial discrimination only ended, at the earliest, in the mid-1960s, then every single person over forty-five years old has been either helped or hindered by the legacy of racism in America. If you were born before 1970, you were born into an unequal status quo, and that inequality directly flowed from the country's historic practices of racism and racial inequality. Nearly every person of color over forty-five started out behind. And, almost by definition, their children would have had to also be behind since they couldn't provide the same advantages as their White counterparts of a similar age.

With all the potential advantages—and many more—that the average White family stands to have, it's hard to argue that everyone has equal opportunity in America. The notion that we *do* have such equality is often used to argue against policy prescriptions, such as affirmative action, that seek to address and correct racial inequality. The good news is that the fact that this myth persists shows that most people do want America to be a place of equal opportunity. That shared value can be a starting point for discussing what we can do to genuinely provide such equality for everyone.

THE MYTH OF POVERTY AS A PERSONAL FAILING

The second pillar of public policy rooted in falsehoods is the myth that it's poor people's own fault that they are poor. The myth is that people are stuck in poverty because of personal shortcomings. It's a narrative that conservatives and liberals both perpetuate. Conservatives claim poor people lack the character, capacity, values, and habits to succeed, while liberals also say poor people lack the capacity, but that it's not really their fault, pointing to inferior schools in poor communities, for example, and insufficient job training. (The liberal focus on fewer skills and jobs has validity, but it misses the larger point of *why* those opportunities and conditions are unequal.)

The reality is that since the beginning of U.S. history people of color were *placed* in poverty as a group and *kept* in poverty by government-sanctioned and government-promoted policies (including frequent government *inaction* in the face of racial discrimination and violence by private actors working to "keep people of color in their place"). Conversely, Whites were lifted up, privileged, and protected *as a group.* With Whites now having such a significant head start, it is nearly impossible for most people of color to overcome the wealth gap on an individual basis (and please don't point to Oprah and the handful of other extremely wealthy people of color as evidence that the system is fair; individuals escaped slavery, too, but that doesn't mean slavery wasn't a problem).

We must change the narrative from one in which poverty is seen as an individual failing to one that connects modern-day poverty to more than four hundred years of systemic, intentional injustice against people of color as a group. Accepting the premise that Whites are in a privileged position because they have been favored as a group throughout our history while others have been held back as a group is the first step toward thinking about sweeping public policy solutions to address our racial wealth gap.

THE *LOGICAL* ANSWER TO "WHAT IS JUSTICE?"

Which brings us back to the question, "What is justice?" One could persuasively—and logically—argue that justice in the context of the history and conduct of the United States would entail the following:

- *Give back the land that was taken.* In criminal law, taking the property of another without consent is called theft, and the remedy for theft requires returning what was stolen. Logically, then, we should give back the land taken from Native Americans, then the land taken from Mexico, then the land taken from Black sharecroppers in the South, and also the land taken from Japanese Americans when they were rounded up and sent to internment camps in the 1940s.
- *Reparations for African Americans for the next 235 years.* Africans held in captivity generated much of America's wealth from 1620 until at least 1865, when the Civil War ended (the economic

exploitation of Black folks actually continued well beyond that, but let's stick with the simpler context of slavery for illustrative purposes). After 245 years of enslavement, African Americans received ten years of redress during the Reconstruction era. My great-grandparents and most other Black folks never received their "forty acres and a mule" promised by White political leaders. Reconstruction lasted only a decade before it was destroyed, so there are still 235 years of exploitation that remain unaddressed. Logically, every Black person who can trace their roots to enslaved people is entitled to reparations, as heirs of those who were enslaved and never compensated. A reparations program fulfilling that obligation would take us to the year 2250. Some have estimated that the modern-day value of forty acres and a mule for every freed slave would be $6.4 trillion.[34] It is worth noting that there is precedent for this: in 1988 the United States finally paid some reparations to Japanese Americans who were placed in internment camps during World War II. The Civil Liberties Act of 1988 provided financial redress of $20,000 for each surviving detainee, totaling $1.2 billion.[35]

In 2014, Ta-Nehisi Coates wrote a seminal and eloquent article for the *Atlantic* titled "The Case for Reparations." Coates highlights the fact that

[h]aving been enslaved for 250 years, black people were not left to their own devices [after the Civil War]. They were terrorized. In the Deep South, a second slavery ruled. In the North, legislatures, mayors, civic associations, banks, and citizens all colluded to pin black people into ghettos, where they were overcrowded, overcharged, and undereducated. Businesses discriminated against them, awarding them the worst jobs and the worst wages. Police brutalized them in the streets. . . . Now we have half-stepped away from our long centuries of despoilment, promising, "Never again." But still we are haunted. It is as though we have run up a credit-card bill and, having pledged to charge no more, remain befuddled that the balance does not

disappear. The effects of that balance, interest accruing daily, are all around us.[36]

I don't expect these things—returning of land and reparations—to happen anytime soon, but if they sound outrageous, then by comparison, other policy proposals to correct injustice—making massive investments in public education, enacting comprehensive immigration reform, establishing universal voter registration, ending mass incarceration, adopting "Polluter Pays" taxes nationwide, and imposing a wealth tax on the richest 1 percent—should seem modest by comparison.

EDUCATION

Education has long offered the promise of a better life, and an even better one for the next generation. As such it holds a special place in the hearts and minds of disadvantaged populations around the world. In this country, people of color have always fought for access to quality education. Many of the seminal struggles of the civil rights movement involved the quest for educational justice: for example, the Little Rock, Arkansas, school desegregation standoff in 1957; the Chicano Walkouts in East Los Angeles in 1968; and the Third World strikes at San Francisco State University and other campuses across the country in 1969 all bore testament to the centrality of quality education as a cause worth struggling and sacrificing for.

Despite high hopes and passionate battles over the years, many American children continue to languish in inferior and ineffective schools, and the majority of them are children of color. Stanford professor Linda Darling-Hammond, one of the country's foremost education reform experts, describes this situation as one where we have " 'apartheid schools'—schools serving exclusively students of color in low-income communities."[37] An educational equity lawsuit in San Francisco graphically portrayed the conditions in one such school as an example of the specific problem of inferior facilities:

Luther Burbank [Middle School] is infested with vermin and roaches and students routinely see mice in their classrooms.

One dead rodent has remained, decomposing, in a corner of the gymnasium since the beginning of the school year. The school library is rarely open, has no librarian, and has not recently been updated. The school no longer offers any art classes for budgetary reasons. . . . Two of the three bathrooms at Luther Burbank are locked all day, every day. . . . Students have urinated or defecated on themselves at school because they could not get into an unlocked bathroom. . . . When the bathrooms are not locked, they often lack toilet paper, soap, and paper towels, and the toilets frequently are clogged and overflowing. . . .[38]

As shockingly bad as some of the conditions in our schools are, perhaps the most important inequality between schools is in teacher quality. Abundant evidence shows the significant difference that well-trained and effective teachers can make in a student's education; we are failing to provide all schools with qualified teachers and the gap between schools and districts is once again a racial one. As Darling-Hammond concluded, "By every measure of qualifications—certification, subject-matter background, pedagogical training, selectivity of college attended, test score, or experience—less-qualified teachers are found in schools serving greater numbers of low-income and minority students."[39]

The dichotomy between progressives' deep and wide passion for quality education, on the one hand, and materially deficient public schools—largely in communities of color—on the other, creates the conditions for a genuine, fervent movement for change among New American Majority voters.

Progressives must be careful, however, not to be outflanked on this issue by conservatives. The hunger for improvement in education is real, and people who are desperate for change will entertain all sorts of solutions from all corners. For example, in the past several years many people of color have pinned their hopes on high-visibility solutions—such as school vouchers or charter schools. However, in many cases these "solutions" are ideologically inspired and educationally ineffective. They have been Band-Aids at best and rackets at worst wrapped in pseudo-radical rhetoric of "disruption" promoted by "reformers." Most of these "reforms" have not been able to provide evidence of actually improving the education system and quality of education.[40]

The New American Majority has the political power to make high-quality public education for all a true national priority. We can make sure we build and maintain first-rate educational facilities where teachers are well trained and well paid, and students from all racial and economic backgrounds receive cutting-edge instruction and support to unleash their intellectual curiosity and develop the skills necessary for success in life in the twenty-first century. There can be no disputing the fact that far too many children have been relegated to inferior and inadequate schools for no other reason than being born into poverty. What we do—or don't do—about this injustice will speak volumes about who we are as a society and a people.

COMPREHENSIVE IMMIGRATION REFORM

Progressives are often too apologetic when it comes to advocating for immigration reform, frequently accepting the narrative that many people are here "illegally." As discussed in Chapter 3, America has a long and explicitly racist history on this issue. Between stealing land from the Native Americans (making the early English settlers and America's founders the original illegal immigrants), codifying racism into the "free White persons" restriction of the first naturalization law, passing the Chinese Exclusion Act, and establishing a racially restrictive national immigration quota system in the 1920s that continues to influence the modern policy debate, conservatives are the ones who should be apologizing.

An effective and pro-active approach to immigration reform should encompass at least four core components. First, yes, provide amnesty to everyone who is here and undocumented. The 2014 Senate Immigration Reform Bill essentially addressed this challenge, providing a solution and security to those living in fear of deportation and disruption to their families and their lives. The ten-year path to citizenship is too long, however, and progressive advocates should be pressing for a much shorter time span of months, not years. These 11 million undocumented people are part of the American family, and it's time to set them on a course to becoming citizens. We should especially expedite the process to keep families together. More than 4 million people have applied to be reunited with their families, and humanity, compassion, and family values should dictate immediate—and favorable—action on these applications. Second, progressives need to make large-scale naturalization of the 9 million documented immigrants who can become citizens quickly a top priority. This will expand the constituency of those who understand the immigrant experience. Also, lowering the $680 naturalization fee would be a strategic and smart focus for immigration reform advocacy. The progressive movement spends more than $1 billion a year on politics and advocacy, so why not establish a scholarship fund to offset the cost of the naturalization fees? If a pool of large foundations such as the Gates Foundation, the Ford Foundation, the Open Society Foundation, and others, along with billionaires who care about immigration (paging Mark Zuckerberg) each put up $10 million a year for ten years, they could cover half the fee for naturalization for nearly 3 million people over the next decade.

After addressing those who are here, reforms should focus on the issue of future immigration. Two additional changes can help in this regard. First, we need to reconfigure the current system for allocation of visas. Right now, every country in the world gets the same number of slots, whether that country's population is one thousand people or 1 billion people. As Columbia University professor Mae Ngai outlined in a 2013 *New York Times* op-ed, our visa system "stipulates that no country may have more than 7 percent of the total each year," resulting in an annual per-country limit of 25,620 visas. The result of this system is that "it is easy to immigrate here from, say, Belgium or New Zealand, but there are long waits—sometimes decades—for applicants from China, India, Mexico and the Philippines." Ngai proposed consideration of an alternative proposal that was floated, but not adopted, in the 1960s. This new system "would have given 20 percent of the visas to refugees; 32 percent to countries in proportion to the size of their populations (recognizing need); and 48 percent to countries in proportion to their amount of emigration in the last 15 years (supporting family unification and existing ties in immigrant communities in the United States)."[41]

Ultimately, we need to step back and look at the root causes of why people are coming here in the first place. As Oralia Maceda, an immigrant mother from Oaxaca, Mexico, asked, why would senators spend $50 billion on more border walls yet show no interest in why people leave home to cross them?[42] Mexico's economy has suffered profoundly in the wake of the North American Free Trade Agreement (NAFTA), and those economic problems contribute to the desperation of Mexican workers seeking to provide for their families. Maceda is part of the Binational Front of Indigenous Organizations, a group that seeks to renegotiate NAFTA to end the causes of displacement. There is successful international precedent for this approach in Europe, where the members of the European Union provided economic assistance to the poorer countries to strengthen the overall union while working to reduce the incentive for immigration to more prosperous countries. Former U.S. assistant attorney general Bill Hing has called for the creation of a North American Union consisting of Canada, the United States, and Mexico, and this union could work in partnership "to develop a new vision of their relationships and their borders." Such a vision "needs to be formed with an understanding of the social, economic, and political strategic needs of the region, as well as those of each nation."[43]

Politically, immigration reform is a winning strategy for Democrats and other progressives. It's one of those issues that affect people so deeply and emotionally that families who benefit from laws allowing undocumented immigrants to come out of the shadows will most likely have lasting loyalty to the champions of those laws for decades to come. By supporting progressive immigration reform, Democrats have a unique generational opportunity to imprint their identity deep into the communities of immigrant families who will grow by millions in coming years.

In November 2014, when President Obama announced the executive action designed to protect millions of undocumented immigrants, people across the country gathered in church basements and community halls to watch the speech together. Tears flowed and people hugged as the president spoke directly to millions, offering them hope, dignity, and safety, saying, "You can come out of the shadows." Those who had been living in the shadows—and the people who love them—will not soon forget this action. Although Obama's executive action was temporarily blocked in the courts, those seeking to succeed him in the White House would be wise to champion the same cause. In the words of Janet Murguía, president of the National Council of La Raza, "A bright line will soon emerge between those who seek to preserve a status quo, which serves no one except those who profit from a broken system, and those who are working in good faith to reach compromise and deliver a solution the country desperately needs. . . . This bright line will be burnt indelibly in the minds of Latino voters."[44] As the 2016 season intensified in 2015, many Republicans escalated their anti-immigrant rhetoric, but as the November general election approaches, some presidential candidates will attempt to blur the differences between the parties on immigration with talk of things such as immigrants having a "legal status" (as Jeb Bush has said). Progressives must make it absolutely clear that they are the ones who will continue to fight for an efficient pathway to full citizenship, and that they are on the solution side of the bright line that burns in the minds of all voters who care about immigration reform. Slavery was a "legal status" too, and nothing less than a fast path to citizenship should be acceptable.

DEMOCRACY

There is no more fundamental act of belonging to one's community and country than the act of voting and partaking in self-governance. Democracy is obviously central to the American self-image, and an aggressive voter inclusion program can simultaneously marginalize those seeking to restrict the franchise and expand the ranks of New American Majority voters participating in elections.

The combination of the yearning among people of color to belong and participate in their democracy, the mathematical advantages of bringing more people of color into the political process, and the ever-increasing numbers of eligible voters of color should make fighting for a democracy-expanding policy agenda a top progressive priority. Furthermore, this is a situation where Blue cities in Red states can make strategic progress by increasing the number of people of color in their cities who vote, thereby shrinking the gap of what's required to win statewide. In Texas, for example, Democrats lose state elections by 600,000 to 900,000 votes, but hundreds of thousands of eligible, nonvoting people of color live in the Democratic cities of Houston and San Antonio. This approach could also be applied in Georgia, Arizona, and Nevada, where maximizing the New American Majority turnout in Atlanta, Phoenix, and Las Vegas, for example, can accelerate statewide political transformation of those states.

Because the opponents of progress have worked so hard to disenfranchise people of color, voting rights advocates have understandably been on the defensive for years. In order to make the breakthroughs required to change the political balance of power, it is necessary to take the offensive. After California Common Cause, PowerPAC.org, and many other groups worked together successfully in 2012 to get California to adopt online voter registration, 800,000 people registered to vote within six weeks.[45] Those new voters helped Democrats win a two-thirds majority in the state legislature. These types of forward-looking, institutional, and transformative changes should infuse the democracy reform agenda in the twenty-first century. In theory, online voter registration should appeal to conservatives since studies have shown that it is extremely cost-effective and lowers the cost of government. In California, implementing online voter registration resulted in $2 million in savings.[46]

Even in the case of fighting voter ID laws (see Chapter 8), one of the biggest current battles under way, we need to think outside the box. Ashindi Maxton, a social justice strategist and organizer, helped the Service Employees International Union lead the fight against Pennsylvania's proposed voter ID laws in 2012. After spending six weeks coordinating data collection and locating witnesses for the lawsuits that successfully challenged the law in the courts, Maxton concluded that it may be more cost-effective and impactful to run programs to help people get IDs than to engage in protracted and expensive fights to overturn the laws themselves. That is the kind of fresh thinking that the movement needs.

One of the most promising democracy reforms is automatic voter registration. In 2013, Representatives John Lewis, Steny Hoyer, James Clyburn, John Conyers, and Robert Brady and Senator Kirsten

Gillibrand introduced the Voter Empowerment Act. Among some of its key provisions:

- Electronic registration for all consenting citizens when they interact with a wide range of government agencies.
- Making registration portable, keeping voters on the rolls even when they move.
- Fail-safe procedures to ensure that eligible voters whose information is not on the rolls or not up to date can correct the information online or at the polls.
- Offering states federal funding to make necessary technological upgrades to improve voting systems.[47]

In 2015, Oregon showed what's possible in this regard when it became the first state to pass a law automatically registering all eligible state residents to vote unless they affirmatively opted *out* of being registered.[48]

It's a sad reality that fifty years after passage of the Voting Rights Act we're still defending that law and others like it from attacks by the right wing. We must be wary, however, of falling into the trap of fighting yesterday's battles. It is possible to leapfrog the opposition, dramatically expand democracy, and cement the power of the New American Majority by thinking outside the box and proposing bold, proactive solutions.

CRIMINAL JUSTICE REFORM AND PUBLIC SAFETY

An unarmed Black person was shot and killed by the police every nine days during the first half of 2015.[49] Unarmed. Nationwide Black Lives Matter protests over the past couple of years in response to the police killings of unarmed African Americans Michael Brown in Ferguson, Missouri; Eric Garner in New York City; Tamir Rice in Cleveland; Freddie Gray in Baltimore; Samuel DuBose in Cincinnati; to the police custody death of Sandra Bland in Waller County, Texas; and to similar incidents elsewhere have revealed just how widespread and visceral feelings of frustration and anger over police brutality are in America's communities of color.

Police murders of unarmed people of color are not isolated incidents. There have been more than seventy-six such killings since
1999.[50] ProPublica and the *Guardian* have now created databases cata-
loging these killings since the FBI and police departments have refused
to track the data. These high-profile cases involving shootings and
other violent acts are just the most visible manifestations of what many
call the "prison industrial complex." America arrests and puts in cages
more people than any other country in the world. No other nation even
comes close to America's propensity for locking up its inhabitants.[51]

The protests of the past couple of years have lifted up some immediate policy prescriptions, such as creating community-based police
accountability boards, requiring police officers to wear body cameras,
developing accurate reporting and data collection of police shootings
in order to identify and address the actual extent of the problem, and
taking the review of police shootings out of the closed-door proceed-
ings of secret grand juries.[52] In August 2015, California became the
first state in the country to adopt such a law.[53]

At the same time, we cannot ignore the fact that many people live
with fear of violence and being victimized, including by people in their
own community; they fear for their safety and that of their families
and neighbors. Crime and violence are all-too-prevalent realities in
many communities.[54] When children can't sleep at night because of
gunshots, they can't learn as well in school in the morning. When local
small businesspeople try to develop their businesses, it's significantly
more difficult if they have to worry about being robbed on a regular basis. A progressive policy platform must acknowledge and address this
reality as well.

Fortunately, from a policy-coherence standpoint, solutions to our
crime and safety crisis are closely connected to the imperatives to advance economic justice and educational excellence. Lack of good jobs
and economic opportunity result in a larger pool of people who may
fall into criminal behavior or lifestyles. The failures of underfunded,
ineffective, and uncaring public schools push too many young people
out of the education system and into the school-to-prison pipeline. An
estimated 80 percent of people in prison are high school dropouts.[55]

In addition to providing better economic opportunities and

education, public safety can be enhanced by improving the way we treat offenders and by seeing them as human beings who have made mistakes and are capable of redemption. For those who do choose the wrong path, there are now ample examples of programs and approaches to reclaim those lives and bring them back into society as constructive and caring citizens. In Newark, New Jersey, in 2009, then-mayor Cory Booker developed a reentry program for ex-offenders that helped find jobs for two thousand people coming out of jail or prison. The participants in the system had a recidivism rate that was half the rate for the average state parolee.[56] Offering college-level education in prisons has been shown to bring recidivism rates close to zero.

As a political matter, the fact that more than 2 million people are locked up creates a potentially large criminal justice reform constituency consisting of the family and friends of incarcerated individuals.[57] Most people in jail or prison have a sibling, child, parent, friend, or neighbor. If each incarcerated person motivated three friends or family members to vote, that would create a voting bloc of 6 million people. If each of those friends or family members donated $10 to a political action committee, that could add up to $60 million in political donations, which would make it the third-largest political action committee in the country.[58]

The leaders who highlight the need for a systemic overhaul and then champion these changes will strike a chord with and solidify the support of the people in the communities most devastated by our current broken law enforcement and incarceration complex. The events in Baltimore after the murder of Freddie Gray showed what can happen when a strong grassroots movement is in sync with increased civic engagement and voter participation. In 2014, Marilyn Mosby, an African American attorney, defeated her White opponent to become the state's attorney, and her sense of accountability to the community—as opposed to just the police—led her to move quickly in investigating Gray's death and then bringing murder charges against the officers who were involved. That swift application of justice highlights how the pieces of the progressive agenda are most powerful when they work together.

We should harbor no illusions about how difficult it will be to address crime and punishment in America. The mass incarceration complex is so large, so longstanding, and so well funded—and society's racialized fears are so prevalent—that overhauling the system will require truly radical and far-reaching changes. Michelle Alexander highlighted the scale and scope of the needed reforms in her book *The New Jim Crow*:

> If we hope to end this system of control, we cannot be satisfied with a handful of reforms. All of the financial incentives granted to law enforcement to arrest poor black and brown people for drug offenses must be revoked. Federal grant money for drug enforcement must end; drug forfeiture laws must be stripped from the books; racial profiling must be eradicated; the concentration of drug busts in poor communities of color must cease; and the transfer of military equipment and aid to local law enforcement agencies waging the drug war must come to a screeching halt. And that's just for starters.[59]

Changes of this order of magnitude will not occur quickly or easily, but the invigorated movement for criminal justice reform has begun to change the context and tone of the conversation. The mayor of a major American city told me in 2015 that he noticed that judges were being more fair and careful in the wake of the nationwide Black Lives Matter protests. Reform is now on the agenda. Nationally, all the leading Democratic candidates for president saw the importance of developing specific policy platforms to address criminal justice and racial inequality in mid-2015.

ENVIRONMENTAL EQUITY AND JUSTICE

There are no toxic waste sites in Beverly Hills. Twenty miles away, however, in South Gate, California, sits the Cooper Drum site, where toxic chemicals were used to recondition steel drums from 1941 until 2003.[60] Approximately 95 percent of the residents in South Gate are Latino.[61] The majority of people who live within two miles of a toxic waste site are people of color.[62] The South Gate situation is but one example of hundreds across the country, affecting millions of people.

Land use decisions are essentially political in nature and reflect the political balance of power in a given region. That is why there are no toxic waste sites in Beverly Hills and why communities of color bear the disproportionate brunt of chemical dumping in America. In fact, the California Waste Management Board actually commissioned a study to determine which communities were least likely to resist waste facilities being built in their neighborhoods.[63] In the years after the study, the only three trash incinerators built in California were in communities of color. Where dangerous chemicals exist, health problems frequently follow. In a very real and material sense, environmental equity and justice issues are fundamental to the health and well-being of the country's communities of color. A twenty-first-century social justice public policy agenda, then, must have environmental justice and equity high on its list of priorities.

The robust and well-funded environmental movement in America is too often detached from the immediate concerns of people of color. The typical image of an environmentalist is usually of an educated, White progressive, a "tree hugger" or "hippie" type who shops organic, recycles, enjoys hiking in nature, wears Birkenstocks, drives a hybrid car (if he or she drives at all), and occasionally joins rallies against oil and chemical companies. But many people of color are also "environmentalists" in that even if they don't share anything in common with the typical image of environmentalists they worry about industries polluting the air their families breathe, toxic chemicals leaking into their drinking water, particulate matter (or soot) from heavy-duty truck routes running through their neighborhoods, and the absence of clean and safe parks for their children to play in.

Climate change, renewable energy, and the Keystone Pipeline are critical issues to address for the country and the planet. These important issues, however, are too often portrayed in ways that are abstract and disconnected from the immediate concerns of many people of color. As a result, the entire environmental movement will suffer and struggle from lack of majority support. As civil rights and environmental leader Van Jones likes to say, "If Blacks and Browns don't vote, Greens don't win."

Fortunately, there are exciting examples of ways to synthesize community-of-color concerns with the mainstream environmental movement in promising and powerful combinations. Creative policy solutions can address "Triple Bottom Line" results that make meaningful improvements in outcomes for people, profits, and the planet. Green jobs programs address structural environmental challenges such as the need for more renewable energy while also putting people to work and improving economic opportunities in hard-hit communities. The city of Portland, Oregon, for example, partnered with the innovative environmental justice organization Green for All in 2009 to develop Clean Energy Works Portland, a program launched with $18 million in federal Recovery Act funds (also known as the 2009 "Stimulus") to retrofit homes and make them more energy efficient while giving contracts to local businesses and jobs to local residents. In its first five years, the program upgraded 4,500 homes, stimulated $90 million in spending, and supported 500 construction jobs. In addition, they have developed a sustainable revenue model built on modest monthly payments from homeowners, who pay the equivalent of the savings on their energy bill so that their net energy costs don't increase.[64]

The growing awareness of and commitment to addressing climate change also presents opportunities to prepare for climate disruption by strengthening infrastructure in ways that benefit communities. As described by the Environmental Protection Agency, "green infrastructure"—as opposed to "gray infrastructure" of concrete buildings—consists of things such as rain gardens, green roofs, and conservation of tracts of open land. Intelligently designed, this kind of infrastructure "can enhance community resiliency by increasing water supplies, reducing flooding, combatting urban heat island effect, and improving water quality."[65]

Polluter Pays and Invest programs offer an especially exciting example of the potential of bridging the priorities of the environmental movement with the needs of communities of color and low-income neighborhoods. While politically challenging because of industry opposition, these types of initiatives offer tremendous possibilities to make a meaningful difference in the lives of underserved communities. In California in 2012, environmental leaders such as Vien Truong, now executive director of Green for All, worked with Latino legislative leader Kevin de León to pass a measure that required 25 percent of "cap and trade" revenues—nearly $300 million in California—to be directed to disadvantaged communities, creating a model that could be replicated across the country.[66] Examples of the uses of the funds include affordable housing, subsidized public transportation, trees for concrete jungles, and electrifying trucks and buses to reduce pollution emissions.

THE JUSTICE AND EQUALITY FUND: THE 1 PERCENT SOLUTION

In his last book, *Where Do We Go from Here?*, Martin Luther King showed how to tackle the biggest public policy challenges. Not content with half measures and incrementalism, Dr. King called for the outright abolition of poverty, noting that "We are likely to find that the problems of housing and education, instead of preceding the elimination of poverty, will themselves be affected if poverty is first abolished."[67] King called for a "guaranteed income . . . pegged to the median income of society . . . [that would] automatically increase as the total social income grows." In that light, we can see that the current progressive attention to raising the minimum wage, while necessary and positive, is still much more modest than what we can and should be fighting for.

For a sense of how far the scale of current proposals are from what's needed, consider that the White House's "My Brother's Keeper" initiative, launched by President Obama in 2014, aims to direct $300 million per year (most of it from foundations and private sector sources) to empower boys and young men of color.[68] By contrast, as mentioned earlier, the GI Bill spent many billions a year (converted to 2014 dollars) throughout the mid-twentieth century to help a group of millions of Americans identified as needing assistance. My Brother's Keeper's annual funding commitment is just a tiny fraction of what was spent on the GI Bill.

True justice will require solutions matching the scale of the problem. To that end, I would like to propose that the United States create a Justice and Equality Fund. This fund, modeled on the GI Bill, would invest $500 billion a year (indexed to increase with inflation) in wealth-building opportunities such as home purchase and housing assistance, higher education, job training, and construction and entrepreneurship.

The initiative would be funded by taxing the assets—not just the income—of the wealthiest 1 percent of Americans. The current tax code taxes only annual *income*, not the underlying wealth people hold, and it's that wealth that generates the income for most rich people (in the form of interest, dividends, and capital appreciation of investments). The top 1 percent in America—households whose average net worth is $13.8 million—hold more wealth than the bottom 90 percent combined—approximately $26 trillion.[69] If we were to institute an annual wealth tax of just 2 percent on the assets of the country's wealthiest 1 percent, that could generate $500 billion per year for the nation. With an average return in the stock market of 10 percent per year (annualized since inception), a 2 percent tax would not *decrease* anyone's net worth at all; it would simply slow the rate at which the wealthiest 1 percent of Americans' assets grew.

With this Justice and Equality Fund, we could finally address the wealth inequality crisis and other persistent economic crises. Experts estimate that a $22.5 billion initiative focused on "giving rental assistance to everyone whose income is at or below 30 percent of area median income (AMI), or between $13,650 for a single person to $19,500 for a family of four, through a reformed voucher program" would essentially "end homelessness for the vast majority of those experiencing it."[70] Think about that for a moment. By asking just those families with at least $14 million in assets to pay a 2 percent wealth tax, we could end homelessness and *still* have $477 billion per year to invest in other equity and growth programs.

The possibilities of what could be possible are far-reaching. We could use this tax revenue to make zero-interest down payment loans available to anyone who wants to buy a house and to guarantee the underlying mortgage. This would enable people who didn't come from families that could leave them an inheritance via real estate or other assets to jump on the wealth-creation train. The Justice and Equality Fund could also replicate the role of the GI Bill in expanding access to higher education for millions of people. President Obama already offered a bold and inspiring plan in January 2015 to make community college in America tuition-free.[71] But why can't we also provide truly affordable university education and zero-percent interest student loans? Why can't we expand the student loan forgiveness programs to include loans held by teachers, those in STEM careers, public interest lawyers, military volunteers, and a much broader range of health care professionals?

The benefits from the Justice and Equality Fund would also provide a dramatic boost to the overall economy. For example, we'd need to build more schools and colleges and hire more teachers to provide all students with equal high-quality public education. In addition, entrepreneurship would flourish with start-ups reflecting and serving the full diversity of our nation's population. The 2009 economic stimulus package injected nearly $800 billion into the economy, and studies have shown that that investment resulted in the creation of nearly 3 million jobs and a reduction in unemployment by 1.5 percent.[72]

WHAT ABOUT WHITES?

A bold social and economic justice policy agenda will also significantly benefit White Americans, just as health care reform did. Before the first Affordable Care Act open enrollment period in 2013, 22.4 percent of African Americans and 41.8 percent of Latinos were uninsured. Since 2013, there has been a 9.2 percent drop in the number of African Americans who are uninsured, resulting in 2.3 million individuals gaining coverage. In that same time, Latinos have seen a 12.3 percent drop in the uninsured rate, with 4.2 million individuals gaining coverage.[73] While African Americans and Latinos have seen greater declines in uninsured rates, Whites have benefited the most in terms of the sheer number of people who now have access to health insurance. Of the over 46 million Americans who were previously uninsured, approximately 21 million were White.[74] Since the implementation of the Affordable Care Act, that number has dropped by 5.3 percent, resulting in 6.6 million White Americans receiving coverage. The situation is similar with poverty and economic inequality. While 27.2 percent

(10.9 million) of African Americans and 26.6 percent (13.6 million) of Latinos live in poverty, more White Americans live in poverty (18.9 million).[75] An aggressive antipoverty agenda will truly lift the economic boats of all racial groups.

As we saw with the Occupy movement, drawing attention to the profound economic inequality in America can capture the attention and imagination of many White people as well. A plan and program to address economic inequality in America can both benefit and attract a multiracial coalition of "the 99%" who are working to make this country more fair and equal.

A bold social justice agenda is the key to bringing forward and bringing out the best in progressive Whites. Progressive people are not simply motivated by material self-interest; there is a value and benefit to living in a more just and equal society and having a sense of meaning and purpose in one's life. Given this moment in time, a strong social justice agenda could help progressive Whites who often find themselves asking "What is justice?" to answer that question with decisive, nondefensive, bold action.

THE WAY TO WIN: YES, PEOPLE WILL VOTE FOR THIS STUFF

Championing economic justice is more than moral and just. It's also the way to win elections. In a changing population where people of color are nearly 40 percent of the country and White allies and advocates of justice make up another quarter of the country's population, speaking boldly and unapologetically to the causes of inequality has proven to be good and smart politics.

Ironically, progressive leaders and influencers are doing exactly the wrong thing by going after small goals. Politics and policy are inextricably intertwined. People of color vote in lower numbers because many of them feel that most of the U.S. public policy agenda has little relevance to their lives.

The political power of fighting for economic justice and its potential became clear in Obama's 2008 campaign when he specifically addressed "the wealth and income gap" in his campaign speeches, grabbing the attention of voters everywhere.[76] Elizabeth Warren's 2012

U.S. Senate campaign galvanized support from progressives across the country, enabling her to raise more money from small donors than any other non-presidential candidate in the country that year.[77] In their endorsement of her Senate bid, the *New York Times* noted her willingness to call for higher taxes and wrote, "Ms. Warren talks about the nation's growing income inequality in a way that channels the force of the Occupy Wall Street movement but makes it palatable and understandable to a far wider swath of voters. She is provocative and assertive in her critique of corporate power and the well-paid lobbyists who protect it in Washington, and eloquent in her defense of an eroding middle class."[78] In 2013, New York City mayor Bill de Blasio's "tale of two cities" message about the disparity in wealth among the city's residents catapulted him from fourth in the polls during his mayoral campaign into a commanding lead and a landslide victory. In 2014, even in Red states such as Arkansas, Alaska, and South Dakota, where Democratic senators ultimately went down in defeat, ballot measures to raise the minimum wage still won majority support at the polls. Throughout 2015, Bernie Sanders drew tens of thousands of people to his rallies where he decried inequality and declared that, "When people have no work, when kids have no food, when people have no health insurance, that's where we should be."

Grappling with the question "What is justice?" will not only be good for America's soul; it can also move us closer to the kind of society whose deeds match its words. In the process, we can build popular support for a progressive public policy agenda that will honor the country's highest and best values while also making a tangible and meaningful difference in the daily lives of the American people.

Attacking and forcibly removing Native Americans from America's fertile fields, enslaving and economically exploiting Africans in America, launching war against Mexico so Texas could continue to practice slavery, encouraging Chinese immigration to build an economically valuable railroad but then explicitly excluding Chinese from becoming citizens, and racially restricting access to mortgage loans in economically expanding neighborhoods were not unfortunate aberrations carried out by a few rogue officials and bad actors, the likes of which we don't see anymore. These were the official public policies of the United States of America.

Although justice has long been delayed, those who bore the brunt of those attacks now have the numbers to serve as the cornerstone of a New American Majority. With those numbers, with that majority, we have the opportunity—indeed the obligation—to make new public policies. Policies rooted in justice and dedicated to the proposition that all people are indeed created equal.

8

Conservatives Can Count

The first law of politics is that you have to learn how to count.
      —Willie L. Brown, former Speaker of the California Assembly, after
defeating an attempt to unseat him from his position as Speaker in 1988

*The Republican Party must focus its efforts to earn new supporters and
voters in the following demographic communities: Hispanic, Asian and Pacific Islanders, African Americans, Indian Americans, Native Americans,
women, and youth. This priority needs to be a continual effort that affects
every facet of our Party's activities, including our messaging, strategy, outreach, and budget.*
      —Republican Party, *Growth and Opportunity Project*, March 17, 2013[1]

Democrats have rarely had to fight for the votes of people of color,
but that luxury is coming to an end. For the past several decades,
when conservative leaders could form a majority by wooing enough
White swing voters, Republicans have pursued a political strategy that
catered to the fears and resentments of Whites worried about the demographic changes that have resulted in today's New American Majority. In the wake of the 1960s' reforms that increased the number
of people of color in this country, conservatives have used coded and
not-so-coded racial appeals to secure enough solid support from White
voters to make Republicans competitive. Their language has been calculated and effective, featuring such phrases as "law and order" (favored by Richard Nixon to signal the need for cracking down on crime,
which conservative Whites read as code for cracking down on Black

people), "welfare queens" (famously used by Reagan to portray single Black mothers as lazy opportunists taking advantage of government handouts), and "illegal immigrants" (today's inflammatory code word for undocumented Latinos, suggesting hordes of dark-skinned immigrants streaming across the border—to take away jobs and undermine the American way of life). While effective in appealing to conservative Whites and many White swing voters, this approach has driven most people of color further into the arms of Democrats, who had to do little to earn that support. But now the math has changed—and many Republicans can count.

Conservatives are keenly aware of the political potential of the growing population of color and they're actively working both to slow its influence and shift its partisan preferences. These Republican-led efforts are well funded, widespread, and increasingly impactful. Over the past decade, the conservative playbook has had two broad strategies for countering the demographic revolution—suppression and seduction. Suppression has mainly appeared in the form of voter ID laws and other obstacles to voting, and litigation seeking to secure damaging legal precedents that undermine the reforms instituted after the passage of the 1965 Voting Rights Act. Seduction takes the form of promoting candidates of color for high-profile positions, conducting race-specific outreach, and funneling millions of dollars to groups targeting people of color.

Conservatives are moving so deliberately that their efforts pose a very real risk to the prospects of consolidating a lasting multiracial progressive majority in America. Progressives have a small and shrinking window to secure the support of the New American Majority. If they fail to act quickly, an unprecedented opportunity will be lost.

DENIAL OF DEMOCRACY: VOTER SUPPRESSION

Conservative efforts to restrict voting rights of people of color stretch back to the founding of this country. From the Founding Fathers' reserving the right to vote to White male property holders to the violence and terrorism accompanying the obliteration of post–Civil War

Reconstruction reforms to twentieth-century Jim Crow barriers and attacks on voting rights activists in places like Selma, a long litany of actions has excluded people of color from participating in America's democracy and democratic process (raising the question: can we even properly use the word "democracy" to describe a country where not everyone can participate?). Undeterred by the Voting Rights Act's elimination of legalized, explicit racial discrimination in elections, conservative assaults on measures that make it easier to vote have continued unabated for the past fifty years. As reporter Jim Rutenberg's ten-thousand-word *New York Times Magazine* analysis, "A Dream Undone: Inside the 50-Year Campaign to Roll Back the Voting Rights Act," concluded in 2015, there is "a little-known part of the American civil rights story [that] involves a largely Republican countermovement of ideologues and partisan operatives who, from the moment the Voting Rights Act became law, methodically set out to undercut or dismantle its most important requirements."[2]

Most progressive attention in recent years has focused on fighting two main forms of voter suppression: creating voter ID laws and eliminating laws that make it easier to vote. Voter ID laws require government-issued photo identification. A 2011 study by the Brennan Center for Law and Justice found that 21 million American adult citizens (11 percent) do not possess a government-issued ID.[3] Conservatives justify their support for these laws by saying they are necessary to fight voter fraud, but an independent study of allegations of voter fraud over fourteen years identified just 31 cases of fraud out of *1 billion* votes that were cast in elections during that period.[4] The real motive behind these measures was inadvertently revealed in 2012 when Mike Turzai, Republican majority leader of the Pennsylvania House of Representatives, slipped up in a speech at the Republican state committee meeting by saying that the state's voter identification law was "gonna allow Governor Romney to win Pennsylvania."[5] (That law was blocked by the courts in 2012 and Obama won the state by 287,865 votes, with more than 900,000 of his votes coming from people of color.)[6]

Conservatives' second suppression strategy has been to eliminate laws that previously made it easier to vote. Over the past decade, several states instituted prodemocracy laws that enacted measures such as same-day voter registration, early voting, and weekend voting, among other reforms. In 2008 Ohio law permitted counties to allow voting on Sundays.[7] Cleveland lawyers Subodh Chandra, Alli Harper, and others, for example, ran a "Souls to the Polls" program that picked up Black voters at churches on Sunday and took them to the Board of Elections to cast their ballots. When Republicans recaptured control of Ohio's top offices in 2010, they promptly repealed the law that made Sunday voting possible. Ohio was not alone. According to the Brennan Center report, in 2011, just months after Republicans won sweeping victories across the country in 2010, "At least thirteen states introduced bills to end highly popular Election Day and same-day voter registration, limit voter registration mobilization efforts, and reduce other registration opportunities."[8]

The U.S. Supreme Court joined this antidemocracy parade in 2013 by gutting a key part of the Voting Rights Act in its decision in *Shelby County v. Holder*. As part of the Voting Rights Act, counties with a history of racial discrimination were required to be monitored by the federal government and they had to receive approval from the Justice Department before they could implement changes in their voting procedures.[9] The *Shelby* decision eliminated both safeguards, effectively returning control of the electoral henhouse to the fox in key states that, not coincidentally, have large numbers of people of color. Freed from federal oversight, four Southern states—Texas, Alabama, Mississippi, and North Carolina—immediately passed additional restrictive voting measures just days after the decision came down.[10]

The map in Figure 15 illustrates the extent of efforts to roll back democracy in 2011 as state after state introduced legislation that erected additional obstacles to voting. (Nearly all the old Confederate states passed these new restrictions into law.)

Conservative leaders in the country didn't just wake up one day and decide to erect roadblocks to democratic participation. These laws were carefully considered and methodically developed in think tanks over a number of years. One key vehicle for carrying out the antidemocratic agenda is the American Legislative Exchange Council (ALEC),

Voting Law Changes in 2011

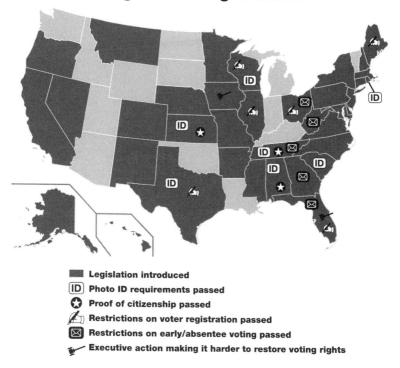

Legislation introduced
[ID] Photo ID requirements passed
⭐ Proof of citizenship passed
🖊 Restrictions on voter registration passed
✉ Restrictions on early/absentee voting passed
⚒ Executive action making it harder to restore voting rights

Figure 15. Source: Brennan Center for Justice, "Voting Law Changes in 2012," 2011.

a nonprofit organization funded by conservative donors and corporations that works with state legislators to quickly draft and disseminate legislation to conservative politicians across the country. According to one national study, 62 photo ID bills were introduced in 37 states in 2011 and 2012, and more than half those bills were sponsored by ALEC.[11] The suppression efforts have been effective.[12] A 2014 study by the U.S. Government Accountability Office found that voter ID laws were responsible for a 2–3 percent drop in voter turnout in elections from 2008 to 2012, more than enough to decide a close race.[13] In fact, Obama's margin of victory in Florida, Virginia, and Ohio in 2012 was 3 percent or less in each of those states.

SEDUCTION: COURTING COMMUNITIES OF COLOR

Meanwhile, over the seven years following Obama's election, Republicans have done a much better job than Democrats in identifying and backing candidates of color. Since 2008, most of the people of color elected to statewide office outside of California and Hawaii (two of the earliest majority-minority states) have been Republicans.[14] Since 2010, Republican people of color have won races for the U.S. Senate in Florida (Marco Rubio), Texas (Ted Cruz), and South Carolina (Tim Scott). New Mexico's Susana Martinez and Nevada's Brian Sandoval—both Latinos—won state gubernatorial elections in 2010. In 2014 Maryland elected an African American Republican, Boyd Rutherford, to the lieutenant governor's office. In the House of Representatives, two Black Republicans—Mia Love in Utah and Will Hurd in Texas—won elections in 2014. As of Fall 2015, the 2016 presidential field was a virtual right-wing rainbow coalition including two Latinos (Rubio and Cruz), an Asian American (Louisiana governor Piyush "Bobby" Jindal), and an African American (neurosurgeon Ben Carson).

Democrats, by contrast, perhaps thinking their work was done after successfully seating America's first Black president, have not kept pace. Outside of California and Hawaii, Democrats can point only to four candidates of color elevated to statewide offices since 2008—New Jersey senator Cory Booker, New Mexico attorney general Hector Balderas, former Delaware treasurer Chip Flowers, and Rhode Island secretary of state Nellie Gorbea (the first Latina elected statewide in all of New England).

The lack of urgency on the part of top Democratic leaders in addressing this problem was revealed in early 2015 after Maryland senator Barbara Mikulski announced she would not seek reelection in 2016. Maryland is one of the Blackest states in America: 30 percent of its population is Black, and African Americans accounted for fully 37 percent of the state's Democratic voters in 2008.[15] Presented with the opportunity to support either a strong Black candidate (Congresswoman Donna Edwards) or stay neutral by not endorsing anyone, the top Democrat in the Senate, Minority Leader Harry Reid, rushed to throw his support behind a White male candidate, Congressman Chris

Van Hollen, this despite the fact that there has only been one Black woman *ever* elected to the Senate in U.S. history (Illinois's Carol Moseley Braun in 1992).[16] In stark contrast to the Democrats' approach, Republicans actively addressed their diversity deficiency in 2013 by plucking African American Tim Scott, a first-term congressman, from obscurity and placing him in a vacated South Carolina U.S. Senate seat, giving him a huge head start in his successful race for that seat in 2014.

In 2016, Democrats will have a chance to diversify their ranks in the U.S. Senate significantly as a record number of women of color are running strong campaigns for the seats in Maryland (Donna Edwards), Illinois (Tammy Duckworth and Andrea Zopp), Nevada (Catherine Cortez Masto), and California (Kamala Harris).

In addition to promoting candidates of color, over the past several years Republicans have deliberately and effectively reached out to voters of color in ways that Democrats could stand to learn from. In many ways, George W. Bush pioneered these efforts in 2004 when he courted Latinos with a very effective ad called *"Nos Conocemos"* (We Know Each Other).[17] The ad noted that much of the land in the Southwest used to belong to Mexico, acknowledged that displaced Mexicans "suffered discrimination and injustice," and made specific mention of Cubans, Puerto Ricans, and South and Central Americans as part of the "40 million Latinos in the United States."

Bush's respectful messaging to Latinos stands in contrast to the historic reluctance of Democrats to do much, if any, explicit outreach to this group. John Kerry, for example, spent less money targeting Latinos in his 2004 presidential campaign against Bush than Al Gore did in 2000, despite the fact that Kerry had $200 million *more* to spend than Gore did. (Gore spent $48 million on his entire presidential campaign; Kerry spent $235 million.)[18] Put another way, of the nearly $200 million in additional funding Kerry received, not one cent was spent targeting Latinos. Had Kerry received 127,000 additional votes in the heavily Latino states of Colorado, New Mexico, and Nevada, he would have defeated Bush and won the White House.

After winning the 2000 election (or, more accurately, winning the *Bush v. Gore* case in the Supreme Court), Bush and Karl Rove shrewdly rolled out their "faith-based initiative" in 2002 in another move to win over people of color. The initiative moved significant sums of money into Black churches across the country in hopes of winning over some Black voters in time for Bush's 2004 reelection. Furthermore, despite strong anti-immigrant sentiments among many Republicans and other conservatives during his tenure, Bush was a champion of immigration reform, calling for, among other things, a path to citizenship.[19] This kind of cultural competence helped Bush receive 44 percent of the Latino vote in 2004, a modern-day record for a Republican presidential candidate.

If George W. Bush was on the right track when it came to trying to show Latinos that he cared about them, his younger brother Jeb is poised to make an even greater impression. Jeb, former governor of Florida and 2016 Republican presidential candidate, is married to a Mexican woman, Columba. He holds a degree in Latin American studies and is fluent in Spanish. He is the father of three adult children, whom his father, George H. W. Bush, once referred to publicly as "the little brown ones." Democrats should not lose sight of the fact that one of "the little brown ones," thirty-nine-year-old George P. Bush, grew up to become a lawyer, won statewide elected office in Texas in 2014, and has his sights set on even higher office (running for president is, after all, the Bush family business). As a candidate for president, Jeb has promoted a policy agenda sympathetic to Latinos with (qualified) support for immigration reform. When he was elected governor in 1998, Jeb won an impressive 61 percent of the Latino vote.[20] After entering the gauntlet of the Republican primaries in 2015, Jeb backed away from his previous support for a path to citizenship and started embracing the offensive phrase "anchor baby" (although he later claimed that he was referring to Asian anchor babies, as if that somehow made it okay). Should Jeb make it through the primaries and become the Republican nominee for president, his knowledge of and connection to the Latino community would make him a formidable contender for the White House and a serious threat to the electoral math that makes the New American Majority possible.

Texas governor Republican Greg Abbott, like Jeb Bush, made good political use of being married to a Mexican woman in his successful campaign in 2014. In campaign appearances before Latinos, Abbott repeatedly talked about how his wife, Cecilia, would be the first Mexican American first lady of Texas. Furthermore, Abbott aggressively campaigned in the Rio Grande Valley, which is near the Mexican border and has a large population of Mexican Americans.[21] On election day, Abbott won 44 percent of the Latino vote (significantly higher than the 31 percent and 38 percent of Texas Latinos who voted Republican in 2006 and 2010).[22]

New Jersey governor Republican Chris Christie took a page from the Bush/Rove playbook and actively courted Black church leaders in advance of his 2013 reelection campaign.[23] Regarding Latinos, one of Christie's top advisors said in an interview: "I think that as a party what we have done wrong is that we only talk to Hispanics in an election year, instead of doing it all the time."[24] Christie, who was described by the same advisor as someone who "built inroads into the Latino community for the past 11 years going back to his days as a U.S. attorney," supported a version of the Dream Act by providing in-state tuition to undocumented immigrants. (It was a watered-down version of the act but still helped some people and sent a strong signal to the Latino community.) Christie reaped the fruits of that labor on election night in 2013 when he racked up 21 percent of the Black vote—nearly three times the percentage of Black votes that McCain won in New Jersey in 2008—and an impressive 51 percent of the Latino vote, more than doubling McCain's percentage.[25] If those percentages were earned by a Republican presidential candidate nationwide they would be deadly to the prospects of a Democratic nominee.

Not to be outdone in the Republican courtship of voters of color, Kentucky Republican senator (and 2016 presidential candidate) Rand Paul boldly ventured where few politicians of either party had gone before—namely, to the scene of intense racial conflict. In August 2014, during the height of protests in Ferguson, Missouri, following the police murder of eighteen-year-old unarmed African American Michael Brown, Paul went to Ferguson to meet with Black community leaders. "Anyone who thinks that race does not still, even if inadvertently, skew the application of criminal justice in this country is just not paying close enough attention," he wrote in an op-ed piece in *Time*.[26] His show of outreach and concern was more than that of any other White politician—Democrat or Republican—during that time. Furthermore, Paul partnered with New Jersey Democratic senator Cory Booker on criminal justice reform measures in 2014. Paul has outlined how Republicans could win one-third of the Black vote in 2016 by emphasizing an agenda of criminal justice reform, school choice, and economic empowerment.[27] His issue set is not far off the mark.

CONSERVATIVE DONORS INVEST IN COMMUNITIES OF COLOR

While many leading Republican politicians are reaching out to and speaking up for communities of color, conservative moneymen are following suit. Since 2011, billionaire brothers David and Charles Koch and their allies have put nearly $10 million into a Latino-focused 501(c)4 advocacy organization called the Libre Initiative.[28] On its website, Libre describes itself as "a nonpartisan, nonprofit grassroots organization that advances the principles and values of economic freedom to empower the U.S. Hispanic community." It also touts its work advancing the Koch brothers' beliefs: "constitutionally limited government, property rights, rule of law, sound money supply, and free enterprise." Although the group is ostensibly nonpartisan, it spent hundreds of thousands of dollars in 2014 attacking four Democratic incumbent Congress members, three of whom were defeated.[29] Understanding the geographic trends of recent demographic shifts, Libre (and by extension, the Koch operation) has concentrated its efforts in the heavily Latino states of Texas, Florida, Colorado, Nevada, and Arizona.[30]

Libre isn't the only conservative effort to court Latinos. In 2011, Jeb Bush helped launch the Hispanic Leadership Network, characterized as an organization that works to "help Republicans and conservatives listen to the Hispanic community and, in the process, figure out how to win more of their votes."[31] Its initial conference attracted six hundred Latino leaders and activists from across the country. The grouping, which describes itself as "the largest network of Hispanic advocates in the country," is part of the $22-million-per-year conservative "action tank," the American Action Network.[32]

Further evidence of moving money to appeal to voters of color came in the 2012 election cycle when the Republican State Leadership Committee (RSLC) committed to spend $3 million as part of its "Future Majority Project" to identify and support new GOP Latino candidates and women for state office.[33] About 125 new Republican Latino candidates and 185 new women candidates were identified. More than $5 million was spent to elect 84 people and grow the state-level Republican Hispanic caucus.[34] The RSLC then established a Future Majority Caucus, led by New Mexico governor Susana Martinez and Nevada governor Brian Sandoval along with a board of "ten rising stars" from state legislatures across the country.[35] The group's plans for 2016 were described as "aiming to recruit 250 new candidates to run for state-level office, get 50 of them elected or appointed, and see 10 minority elected officials enter leadership in states around the country, on a $7 million budget, including women."[36]

REPUBLICAN PARTY "AUTOPSY"—GENUINE SELF-REFLECTION

In 2013, Republicans issued a report on their "Growth and Opportunity Project," a hundred-page "autopsy" of the GOP's electoral failures released in the wake of the 2012 election. The report provides a road map for how the GOP can win more voters and elections. The clear answer: woo voters of color. "Many minorities wrongly think that Republicans do not like them or want them in the country," it says. "The nation's demographic changes add to the urgency of recognizing how precarious our position has become. . . . If we want ethnic minority voters to support Republicans, we have to engage them and show our sincerity. . . . Our Party has an incredible opportunity on our hands, but we must seize it enthusiastically."[37]

The Republican autopsy is startling in its specificity and candor. It recognizes that GOP messages need to become "non-inflammatory and inclusive to all." (In other words: "You can't call someone ugly and expect them to go to the prom with you," as former House majority leader and Tea Party leader Dick Armey told the report drafters on the Party's relations with Latinos.)[38]

The Democratic Party, for its part, commissioned a similar study after the devastating 2014 elections, but its preliminary report, a slender nine-page document, was described by the *Washington Post* as "largely political pablum."[39]

Because the Republican manifesto provides a detailed deep dive into what progressives are also up against, namely how to mobilize more voters of color, it's worth examining their report at length. In fact, Democrats would be wise to adopt many of the recommendations for themselves.

In order to make inroads with voters of color, the Republican report recommends the following:

- Formation of a new Growth and Opportunity Inclusion Council "to expand and diversify the base of the state party."
- Engaging people of color throughout the year (not just "every four years . . . inclusion efforts can no longer be lip service").
- More people of color field staff, communications directors, political directors, and committee members.
- Increasing people of color staff and candidates ("and at the staff level, the personnel should be visible and involved in senior political and budget decisions and not be limited to demographic outreach").
- Developing best practices of candidates successful with voters of color.
- Building ongoing relationships with ethnic media.
- Designing a surrogate program to train and prepare ethnic conservatives to talk in national and local media.
- Establishing a training program available to all Republican candidates that would educate them on the particular culture, aspirations, positions on issues, contributions to the country, etc., of various racial and ethnic communities.
- Hiring a faith-based outreach director to focus on engaging faith-based organizations and communities.

Nor does the report settle for broad-brush recommendations. Displaying a meaningful measure of cultural competence, it offers proposals and ideas for specific racial and ethnic groups. These include the following:

For Latinos:
- "We must embrace and champion comprehensive immigration reform. If we do not, our Party's appeal will continue to shrink to its core constituencies only."
- Develop an extensive network of Hispanic and other demographic groups' political operatives that can help provide continuity for Republican political candidates around the country.

For Latinos and Asian Americans:
- Introducing new citizens to the Republican Party after naturalization ceremonies.

For African Americans:
- Establish a presence in Black communities and with groups like the NAACP, engage with historically Black colleges and universities, and develop a national database of Black leaders.

The Republican report shows that conservatives realize they need a comprehensive and coordinated response to the browning of America. The Party's actions—and those of the Koch brothers and other conservative donors—prove that the recommendations are not simply empty rhetoric. A meaningful segment of the conservative movement is dead serious about contesting for the votes of people of color. Progressives and Democrats should be plenty worried.

At the same time as conservatives are reaching out to people of color, they do have to perform a racial high-wire act. On the one hand they have to win over more voters of color, but on the other hand, they need to deal with the fact that much of the enthusiasm for conservative candidates comes from White voters who fear the implications of a Brown America. Roughly 20–25 percent of the Republican base consists of White voters susceptible to racial demagoguery, and those voters are angry and eager to support a leader who will stand up and fight for the way America used to be. Shortly after Donald Trump made his controversial anti-immigration comments in mid-2015 describing Mexican immigrants as "rapists" who were "bringing drugs and bringing crime" to America, he surged to the top of the polls for the Republican presidential nomination, polling as high as 24 percent.[40]

Republicans have historically tried to thread this needle through the use of coded messages to signal their solidarity with aggrieved Whites. In his book *Dog Whistle Politics*, Berkeley Law professor Ian Haney-López documents this phenomenon by writing, "In general, using a dog whistle simply means speaking in code to a target audience. Politicians routinely do this, seeking to surreptitiously communicate support to small groups of impassioned voters whose commitments are not broadly embraced by the body politic."[41] While not blatant enough to elicit outrage about racially charged comments, Haney-López goes on to explain, the coded language elicits "predictable responses among those who immediately hear the racial undertones of references to the undeserving poor, illegal aliens, and sharia law."[42]

In such fashion, Republicans have historically worked to appeal to the substantial portion of their base that is fearful of and hostile to people of color and have tried to do so in a way that would go largely unnoticed by people of color and White swing voters. But when Donald Trump entered the race for the Republican nomination in 2015, he was playing a whole different game and tore up the dog-whistle script in favor of his preferred bullhorn style and prime-time platforms, where all the world could see and hear his outrageous and inflammatory statements that appealed to the base in a much more open and raw way. Republicans like their racial appeals more coded and quiet than that.

Further complicating the balancing act is the reality that leading conservative commentators and writers also frequently see no need to use dog whistles. Influential conservative writer Ann Coulter gave voice to the nativist wing of the Republican Party in her provocatively titled, bestselling book *Adios America: The Left's Plan to Turn Our Country into a Third-World Hellhole*. Interestingly, Coulter also shows that she has studied history and done the math when she writes, "Liberals had tried convincing Americans to vote for them, but that kept ending badly. Except for Lyndon Johnson's aberrational 1964 landslide, Democrats have not been able to get a majority of white people to vote for them in any presidential election since 1948. Their only hope was to bring in new voters . . . from the Third World." [43]

The success Republicans have had with these George Wallace–like appeals has worked to their great advantage at the local level in House of Representative districts that are overwhelmingly White and conservative. As the writer Ron Brownstein observed in 2015, "Republicans have consolidated a commanding advantage in districts where whites exceed their share of the national population—especially in those places where fewer whites than the national average hold at least a four-year college degree." [44] Comfortable in their largely White districts, the hard-liners in the House have had little incentive to support the drive to broaden the Party's appeal.

The difficulty of this dance could be seen in the debate over the Confederate flag after the murder of nine Black church members at Emanuel AME Church in Charleston, South Carolina, by a White supremacist who had been photographed proudly displaying the Confederate flag. Some Republican presidential candidates, such as Jeb Bush, recognized the danger to their "brand" and publicly called for the removal of the flag from the grounds of South Carolina's state capitol. Southern Republicans in the House of Representatives, however, tried to block a bill in Congress that would have removed Confederate symbols from public lands across the country. These irreconcilable positions create an opening for Democrats that needs to be aggressively exploited while they are still, for now, the preferred party among people of color.

But the window of opportunity won't remain open for long, and it could close as soon as the Republicans settle on a 2016 nominee for president, especially if that person is a candidate such as Jeb Bush or Marco Rubio who can plausibly appeal to Latino voters. These Republican overtures are particularly dangerous to Democrats because the Democratic shortcomings in cultural competence have been masked by the historical partisan preferences of voters of color. Democrats now confront the unfamiliar challenge of having to actually contend for the votes of people of color. Conservatives can count, and the battle is being joined. Demography is not destiny, and it's clear that Republicans are actively trying to turn the tide in their favor.

CONCLUSION

From Fear to Hope

As California has reluctantly faced the prospect of becoming the first state in the continental United States to have a majority of people of color, white Californians have increasingly mirrored the fears and anxieties of the dominant culture that these ethnic minorities, darker-skinned immigrants and refugees will engulf them in an inevitable tide of unfamiliar and undesirable values and mores, that they will dilute or destroy the traditional American middle-class way of life.[1]

—Jewelle Taylor Gibbs and Teiahsha Bankhead, *Preserving Privilege*

We gon' be alright.

—Kendrick Lamar, "Alright"

When they shot the tear gas canisters at us, I turned and ran in the opposite direction. When one of my fellow protestors threw a rock that shattered the rear window of a police car, my friend and mentor Kim Geron turned to me and said, "You're not at Stanford anymore." It was 1986, and I had traveled with a delegation of Stanford students to Watsonville, California, to march in solidarity with the one thousand cannery workers, mainly Latinas, who had gone out on strike against the Watsonville Canning Company to protest the reduction in their wages from $6.66 an hour to $4.75 an hour.[2]

In addition to the simple morality of the matter, we were drawn to this particular struggle because we knew that Watsonville was on the cutting edge of larger social change. The *Los Angeles Times* captured what was at stake in an article that said, "The strike also has become a

CONCLUSION   165

rallying point for the Bay Area labor movement and minority activists. Most of the members of Local 912 are Latino women and a third of them are single mothers. They are pitted against a white-owned company and a town that is more than half Latino, but whose mayor, fire and police chiefs and City Council are all white."³ Three years after the strike, the workers had elected one of their advisors, Oscar Rios, as the first Latino mayor of Watsonville. A couple of years after that, Latinos had been elected to a majority of the positions in the Watsonville city council.

Watsonville, like California, and now like America, went through wrenching social changes as its population became increasingly diverse. The then-elected leaders of the town called out the police because of their fear of the Brown women leading the strike. I'll never forget the image of a phalanx of heavily armed police officers standing guard in front of an empty cannery while thousands of people rallied outside the concrete structure, and I wondered just whom the police were there to serve.

What California has shown is that these kinds of demographic changes often produce widespread fear. In California in the 1990s, politicians and others fomented the fear by promoting divisive ballot measures to increase incarceration, eliminate bilingual education, and outlaw affirmative action. As authors Jewelle Taylor Gibbs and Teiahsha Bankhead noted, "Politicians and power brokers who were ambivalent about the emerging majority of people of color and unwilling to accept its inevitability launched a series of initiatives that would effectively turn back the clock on the socioeconomic progress of minorities and immigrants in the state by undermining their civil rights, eroding their civil liberties, and restricting their access to educational, employment, and entrepreneurial opportunities."⁴

But the demographic tide in California was indeed irreversible, and the anti-immigrant backlash galvanized the growing Latino population to become more involved in politics. Whereas Latinos comprised 7 percent of the state's voters in 1992, that number had doubled to 14 percent by the year 2000. Simultaneously, the Asian American population in the Pacific Rim state grew significantly in the 1990s and early 2000s, increasing by more than 50 percent between 1990 and 2000.

Despite the fears and anxieties about the implications of these changes, what has actually emerged is a more hopeful and promising picture of a society moving toward greater justice and equality. Politically, California has been transformed from the political home and launching pad of Ronald Reagan to a state so reliably Blue that Democrats now control all statewide elected offices, and Obama twice won 60 percent of the vote, defeating his opponents by 23 percent.

The demographic revolution that has brought about a political transformation has also opened the door to a new public policy era. California is now a national leader on environmental issues, having passed model legislation reducing greenhouse gas emissions and instituting "Polluter Pays" provisions that will move hundreds of millions of dollars into low-income communities. In the realm of criminal justice policy, progressive criminal justice reform ballot measures have been passed, and in 2015 the state became the first in the nation to ban the use of secretive grand juries in investigating police shootings. Laws establishing online voter registration, felon reenfranchisement, and the possibility of adopting automatic registration make the state a compelling example of what's possible in terms of expanding democracy and civic participation. Immigration reform advocates succeeded in 2014 in passing legislation that makes it possible for 200,000 immigrants to get driver's licenses even if they are otherwise undocumented. After years of cutting taxes, the state's voters adopted a measure to make the rich pay their fair share and more properly fund schools. Much more is possible, and the state is limited only by the imagination of its leaders, not by the politics of moderate voters.

California has shown that rather than being something to fear, the demographic revolution can actually mark the beginning of a hopeful and exciting era of positive and progressive change. If we correctly respond to the demands of the day, we gon' be alright.

In order to realize the potential of this moment, we must embrace and invest in the power of the New American Majority. Ironically, the fear of the population changes also extends to progressives. While many conservatives fear the fact of a new, Browner, society, too many progressives fear that the fears of conservatives will cause them to lose elections.

As I've tried to document in this book, the demographic tidal wave that washed over California during the past few decades also spread across the entire country, culminating in the election of Barack Obama as president of the United States in 2008. Since the seminal civil rights struggles of 1965 that resulted in the passage of the Voting Rights Act and the Immigration and Nationality Act, the number of people of color in America has more than quadrupled, and the vast majority of them are voting for Democrats. The modern-day New American Majority consists of progressive people of color, who are now 23 percent of all the eligible voters in the country, and progressive Whites, who account for 28 percent of the eligible voters. This 51 percent majority has elected and reelected an African American president, is poised to elect America's first female president, and has the power and potential to reshape politics, policies, and priorities all across the country for decades to come.

And yet, many of the nation's leading political reporters, Democratic pollsters, and elected officials remain skeptical about the existence of a New American Majority anchored in the country's communities of color. After so many years of focusing on and chasing after White swing voters, many cannot conceptualize or comprehend a reality in which White people are not the most important voters to prioritize.

What is perhaps most surprising is the number of people in influential positions in national politics who can't count. We saw this in the criticism of Hillary Clinton's campaign strategy in 2015. The early months of her effort featured strong statements about immigration reform, economic inequality, mass incarceration, marriage equality, voter suppression, and the persistence of racism—all critical and important issues to people of color and progressive Whites. By staking out such policy positions, Clinton was sending a clear signal that she was enthusiastically and unapologetically casting her lot with the country's changing demographics.

The *New York Times*, however, prominently featured a lengthy critique of Clinton's strategy that displayed an inability to do arithmetic and research and also perpetuated the anachronistic understanding of who comprises the modern-day electorate. The *Times* piece, by leading national political reporters Jonathan Martin and Maggie Haberman, looked at Clinton's policy proposals and concluded that "her left-leaning policy stances" suggested that she "appears to be dispensing with the nationwide electoral strategy that won her husband two terms in the White House and brought white working-class voters and great stretches of what is now red-state America back to Democrats." Martin and Haberman then went on to draw a contrast between Bill Clinton's supposed success with White working-class voters and Barack Obama's "far narrower path to the presidency."[5] But Martin and Haberman's math doesn't add up. Barack Obama actually won the support of *more* White voters than Bill Clinton did (43 percent for Obama in 2008 versus 39 percent for Clinton in 1992). And White voters didn't come back to Democrats in 1992 and vote for Bill Clinton, they went to Ross Perot's third-party candidacy, which siphoned off millions of Whites who usually vote Republican. (George H. W. Bush got just 41 percent of the White vote in 1992, compared to the 60 percent he received in 1988 when Perot was not in the race.) Their factually flawed analysis was picked up and amplified by the rest of the media echo chamber, which repeated the mantra about Hillary's risky leftward lurch.

A similarly surprising example of bad math can be found in the conclusions drawn about why Democrats lost control of the House of Representatives in 2010. Obama's former chief strategist David Axelrod writes in his memoir that after passing health care reform in 2010, "[Obama's] standing with moderate, swing voters had taken a hit . . . he had ignited a blazing grassroots opposition that would cost him his House majority and bedevil him for the remainder of his presidency."[6] Top Democratic Senate leader Chuck Schumer similarly blamed the Party's misfortunes in 2010 and 2014 on the fact that it championed health care reform, saying, "We put all of our focus on the wrong problem—health care reform. . . . Republicans and the anti-government Tea Party filled that vacuum and . . . falsely convinced the electorate that government couldn't work anywhere."[7] But some fairly simple mathematical calculations prove that Democrats lost the House—and then the Senate four years later—because Democratic voters, particularly people of color, did not turn out to the polls. The notion that "the voters" recoiled against the Democrats is simply a myth.

And even prominent pollsters—who make their living adding up numbers—are still conducting their calculations and making their recommendations as if Obama's election never occurred. Stan Greenberg's warning that Democrats can't win unless they "run much stronger with White working-class and downscale voters" is directly contradicted by the fact that Obama won reelection with 5 million fewer White votes than he received in his initial election in 2008.

It's beyond worrisome when the top leaders and political consultants in the country are reaching conclusions and developing plans based on faulty data and bad math.

With all the attention focused on technological firepower and data-driven analytics and metrics, the existence of a New American Majority really should be common knowledge by now for anyone who knows how to use a spreadsheet. And the resistance to recognizing the dawning of a new demographic day continues to come from the kinds of people whom Andy Young called smart-ass White boys with big budgets and small stockpiles of cultural competence. Their determination to continue pursuing the shrinking sector of the electorate made up of White swing voters is not only mathematically unsound, it's also incredibly fiscally irresponsible. Millions of dollars are being spent on a losing strategy at a time when we need to be investing tens, if not hundreds, of millions of dollars in organizing and strengthening the New American Majority.

The absolute top priority for the progressive movement and progressive politics must be expanding the participation of and securing the lasting loyalty of this majority. That means moving large amounts of money to voter registration, door-to-door organizing, and culturally compelling communications. It means strengthening organizations and nurturing leaders who come from and can speak to the communities who make up the New American Majority. It means turning the growing analytics engine of the progressive movement to the critical questions of how to engage America's communities of color and their progressive White allies. The progressive problem in Texas, for example, will ultimately only be solved by a comprehensive campaign to change attitudes and behavior about voting among that state's Latino population. If Latinos in Texas can be moved to dramatically increase their civic engagement, then that will alter the politics of a state that is an anchor of the conservative coalition. But bringing about that behavioral change requires a sustained and sophisticated effort led by people with deep knowledge of Latino history and culture.

It's not just math that demands attention; it's also sociology and psychology, because we have to come to terms with the enduring centrality and significance of race in American life. Far from being postracial, this is still a country where race matters, and building an electoral majority requires getting comfortable with the political imperative of embracing race. Many people are understandably uncomfortable talking about racial issues and, not unrelated to that fact, many folks are also ignorant about the histories and cultures of the various racial groups in America. Constructing a political majority on the cornerstones of the country's communities of color requires great cultural competence and expertise. Accordingly, organizations and leaders throughout the progressive movement must hire, promote, and empower large numbers of people from the communities upon which the New American Majority rests. Given the dominance and predominance of Whites in the leadership of the movement, progressive Whites need to humble themselves and educate themselves about the realities of the lives of people of color.

People of color also need to learn about groups other than their own, including progressive Whites, and they need to prepare themselves for the responsibility of leadership by learning the skills and developing the habits required to bring about meaningful social change. I'm sure that Harriet Tubman had to deal with people who wanted to sleep in late and cut their walks short during the days of the Underground Railroad, but those who made it to freedom got up early in the morning and had the discipline to cover many miles during difficult days and nights.

The reality of the political landscape we face is that racism is real, and inequality is widespread. In order to inspire the New American Majority and meaningfully make their lives better, we need bold policy proposals and political platforms that speak specifically to racial injustice and economic inequality. By asking, "What is justice?" and then answering that question with proposals that could drive hundreds of billions of dollars toward finally and fully addressing the country's most intractable problems, progressives can upend the national public policy conversation, retake the intellectual initiative about the changes America truly needs, and actually move down the road to creating a more just and fair society. This agenda should infuse the activities of every progressive elected official and the campaign platforms of every progressive political campaign.

"It's hard to tell time by revolutionary clocks," African American historian Lerone Bennett Jr. wrote in a 1969 essay in *Ebony* magazine. He went on to observe, "We have a mandate from history, a mandate from the living, the dead, and the unborn, to make this moment count by using the time and resources history has given." [8]

These are indeed revolutionary times, and it is in fact hard to get one's bearings. But we do have a mandate, and we must get it right. Our mandate flows from those who walked the Trail of Tears, dreaming and hoping that the lives of their children and grandchildren would be better. We inherit the legacy and the obligation of carrying on the struggle for which Jimmie Lee Jackson gave his life so that people of all races could vote. We can draw courage to lift up our own voices from the example of William Lloyd Garrison, who launched his nineteenth-century abolitionist newsletter with the words "Urge me not to use moderation in a cause like the present. I am in earnest—I will not equivocate—I will not excuse—I will not retreat a single inch—AND I WILL BE HEARD." [9] We have the opportunity to honor the sacrifice and courage of those who risked their lives laying the tracks of America's railroads in order to make enough money to support their families back home in Asia. We have a charge to continue the work of Dolores Huerta and Cesar Chavez and all the farmworkers who went on strike to demand dignity and economic fairness. Those who endured and stood strong against racial violence and hate crimes—as recently as modern-day anti-Arab and anti-Muslim attacks—did so with the hope that the country would eventually, as Rev. Jackson would say, move from racial battleground to economic common ground and moral higher ground.

When Martin Luther King accepted the Nobel Peace Prize in 1964, he offered a concise vision of a better world, saying, "I have the audacity to believe in a world where peoples everywhere can have three meals a day for their bodies, education and culture for their minds, and dignity, equality and freedom for their spirits."[10] Four years later, on the day before he was killed, he had a premonition of his death and said in his last speech ever, "I may not get there with you, but we as a people will get to the Promised Land."[11]

Martin didn't make it, but we are still here, and it is for us, the living, to press forward on the journey to the promised land. The promised land is a place of greater justice, equality, and hope. A place where no one is barred from achieving her or his fullest potential because of the color of one's skin. A place where everyone does have nourishment and education and culture and dignity. To get there will require profound political change, considerable personal courage, and tireless organizing and advocacy. Because of the work of those who have gone before us, we have, for the first time in U.S. history, a mathematical majority with the power and potential to foster true justice and equality in America. We have a moment where we can make history and leave a better world for those who will come after us. We are the New American Majority, and the legacy we leave is up to us.

ACKNOWLEDGMENTS

The phrase "It takes a village" is both overused and, in the case of this work, inadequate to describe what it took to birth this book. I very consciously saw this project as a collective endeavor and labored to create something of value to the broader movement for justice and equality in America. Appropriately, many, many people in that movement contributed great collective knowledge, insight, and assistance. Let the thank-yous begin!

Before getting to those who helped contribute to the content of the book, I must first acknowledge the parents of the process. There are a few people without whom this book would not even exist.

First and foremost, there is Sharline Chiang, my book editor, coach, and now friend. Trying to weave together an exploration of America's racial history, a contemporary look at the country's communities of color, and a controversial critique of modern progressive politics is no small feat. To guide me on this journey required someone who loved language, words, and writing and also had deep cultural competence, knowledge, and insight. It's not an easy combination to find, and I have been exceedingly fortunate to have Sharline's partnership. (And I am glad our relationship survived her seemingly constant demands that "you need more examples to better illustrate this point.")

Elmaz Abinader introduced me to Sharline, and for that I will be forever grateful. Elmaz also encouraged me at a critical juncture and gave me a real confidence boost by telling me, "We need this book." Aimee Allison introduced me to Elmaz and also planted the seed that I should write a book. Her personal support and professional partnership are both deeply appreciated. Subodh Chandra and Meena Morey Chandra encouraged me to speak at the City Club of Cleveland (my hometown) in 2014 and then worked their connections to make it happen. I didn't believe people like me could speak at the City Club (my dad had heard two speeches there in his life—by Martin Luther King and Bobby Kennedy). Dan Moulthrop's generous invitation to speak, the warm response to my remarks, and then C-SPAN's rebroadcast of the speech on MLK weekend gave me the confidence that maybe I did have something to say.

When Julie Martinez Ortega and I were housemates at Stanford back in the 1980s marching in protests together and dancing to MC Hammer at Casa Zapata, I had no idea she even liked numbers, let alone that she'd grow up to get a PhD and become one of the country's preeminent data geeks. Julie put in many hours making spreadsheets, crunching numbers, taking my calls, and overseeing the quantitative analysis in the book.

Throughout this process, I have felt the warm embrace and encouraging words of the extended social justice family. Unfortunately, there are too many people to list by name, but there are a few I must highlight. I am profoundly grateful to Andy Wong and Lisa Le for a lifetime of political partnership and personal friendship as we fought the fights that became the experiences and knowledge base that informed this work. Kathy Coll has been a writing partner, Facebook friend, research resource (I promise to return your books), and Sherpa through academia, pointing me to exactly the right sources. Lisa Garcia Bedolla met with me early, shared her book proposals so I could see the format, and always quickly answered my random questions. Ashindi Maxton, Anathea Chino, Judy Wu, Felicia Wong, Vivian Chang, and Vien Truong all were kind enough to share their considerable knowledge regarding their respective areas of expertise. Very early in the process, Mike Lux spent significant time sharing his book-writing experience and painting a helpful picture of the road ahead. It was my good fortune that Julie Lythcott-Haims published her book months before mine and was willing to share lessons-learned and provide moral support. My executive coach, Viveka Chen, both helped me get my life organized to write this and also served as a consistent cheerleader.

Dr. Laura Lara-Brady is not only a brilliant data goddess with an extremely bright future, but a fearless and friendly researcher able to turn around projects on a moment's notice.

My comrades from back in the day were exceedingly gracious in letting me use their family stories to illustrate the lives and journeys of the New American Majority. Colin Cloud Hampson, Dave Brown, Julie

Martinez Ortega, and Lisa Le took time out to share their stories and edit pertinent sections of early drafts.

The staff, board, and team at PowerPAC+ provided critical research assistance and logistical support during the entire twenty months of this process, and I thank them for their contributions: Kirk Clay (the spreadsheet wizard and happy warrior), Johanna Silva, Sophie Rane, Edil De Los Reyes, Shirley Burke, and Ronni McCoy. Amy Chen rose to the occasion in the crush of the final deadlines to provide fast, cheerful, and valuable graphics assistance that contributed mightily to the quality of the images in the book.

The editing team was ably assisted by Michael Tayag, Lauren Harrison (who also did excellent copyediting and proofreading), Amir Rabiyah, and Jasmine Evans, who put in long hours and went the extra mile to ferret out far-flung facts. Lauren and Jasmine also tamed the unruly beast of endless endnotes and proper formatting in timely fashion. Jocelyn Truitt did an especially noteworthy job of copyediting and proofreading on a tight timeline. Kimberly Hu, graphic designer by day and my yoga teacher at night, did an early design of the words of the title that helped us arrive at the ultimate cover design, and she provided regular tips on graphics and overall moral support after our yoga sessions.

I am indebted to Diane Wachtell and Marc Favreau of The New Press. Not only did they believe that this first-time author had something worth publishing and offer critical interest and encouragement at an early stage, but they lent their considerable editorial expertise to helping refine and improve the finished product. I am proud to partner with them to try to change the conventional wisdom of progressive political strategy.

Neera Tanden, John Podesta, Daniella Gibbs Léger, and the Center for American Progress have been staunch supporters, good friends, and trailblazers on many of these issues. I am honored to serve as a CAP Fellow and grateful for their partnership.

I am also grateful to all my Facebook friends who clicked Like or wrote comments on my near-daily check-ins from Philz Coffee. Those digital expressions of support really did keep my spirits up and momentum going. And a special shout-out to the Facebook "nerd crew" who quickly responded to my crowdsourced questions about obscure topics. And of course, I must thank the fine folks at Philz Coffee's Berry Street, DeHaro, and Dogpatch locations for fueling the creative process in their high-energy, friendly, multicultural stores. Kayla, Marley, Abby, Sandi, Leanne, Damian, Chenea, thanks so much for your hospitality. "Large Ecstatic, medium-medium!"

Lastly, I am forever grateful to my actual family. From my parents to my late uncle Raymond Cochran (Renzi), one of the first Black writers on the White House beat, who helped me become a writer, to my aunts Janis Cochran and Mildred Talbot and my uncle Lumumba Akabule (slave name, Lonnie Turner), and my brothers, Jimmy and Jeff, my family has lifted me up in more ways than I can count. There's nothing like unconditional love. I am also extremely appreciative of Susan's side of the family—Herb, Marion, Jim, and Gretchen—for consistent moral support, encouragement, advice, assistance, and tolerance of my antisocial behavior (even by my standards) during this process.

To the next generations of the family, I am inspired by your energy, enthusiasm, and optimism, and I hope that this book is helpful to you as inheritors of the legacy of struggle for justice described in these pages. Chris, Courtney, Africa, Jordan, Jarrod, Christian, Dierra, Leah, and Elijah, we have high hopes for your futures and deep faith in your potential.

The work involved in writing a book has a significant impact on the lives of those closest to you. I have been extraordinarily blessed to have a life partner who has shown exceeding patience, flexibility, understanding, accommodation, and support during the nearly two years I worked on this book. Susan was not just tolerant, but actively engaged in listening to my stories, cheering me on and offering very, very valuable feedback and constructive comments on the content itself (once I could bring myself to let her look at the manuscript). Embarking on this sojourn of becoming an author is just the latest adventure I have pursued over the past twenty-five years, and I have had the extraordinary privilege of being joined on all these escapades by a truly amazing woman who shares my passion for justice. I can hardly wait to see what change we can create over the next twenty-five.

APPENDIX A

Math and Methodology

Ah, the appendix. The numbers. The math. The fields of play where data geeks and data-geek wannabes go to roam. Welcome. Let's dive right in.

In this appendix, I'll walk through the underlying data sets used in the calculations for chapter 1, "51 Percent (and Growing Every Day): The New American Majority" and I'll explain the methodology used to arrive at the conclusions in the book. I have been blessed in my life to know people with the rare combination of deep cultural competence and an affinity for numbers, spreadsheets, and all things data, and I owe a deep debt of gratitude to Dr. Julie Martinez Ortega, JD, PhD, president and co-founder of the American Majority Project Research Institute, and Dr. Laura Lara-Brady, PhD, for many hours of number-crunching, and double- and triple-checking my math.

METHODOLOGY

The New American Majority analysis involves combining official government population data and exit poll data, and then carrying out some straightforward calculations on these numbers. Included in this government data was the Census Bureau's American Community Survey (ACS). The Census Bureau describes the ACS as "an ongoing survey that provides vital information on a yearly basis about our nation and its people. Information from the survey generates data that help determine how more than $400 billion in federal and state funds are distributed each year." The key point is that the ACS collects data on an ongoing monthly basis throughout the years between the decennial census. The Census Bureau regularly releases data within approximately two years of its collection. The ACS uses as its base the most recent decennial census. That census information is then supplemented with the ACS's ongoing surveys. This combination of decennial and more current survey data is then used to create estimates about how the population has grown and changed since the most recent decennial census.

Researchers and policy makers who want to conduct work with smaller, harder-to-survey populations can use data aggregated over multiple years in order to increase the accuracy of their estimates. The ACS provides three-year and five-year aggregated data files for such work. In addition, special tabulations and reports are released by the ACS. One of those special tabulations, the Citizen Voting Age Population (CVAP) Special Tabulation from the 2009–2013 5-Year American Community Survey, provides pertinent data on race and ethnicity about the voting-age population and those eligible to vote at the national and state levels. This data set served as the core body of information upon which many of the analyses in this book are based.

Grouping data on eligible voters into race and ethnic groups is fraught with methodological and theoretical challenges. Government data sources tend to be inconsistent with regard to creating race and ethnicity categories and oftentimes either don't collect or fail to provide information that enables researchers to align data from various sources. One example of this involves the government's decision to place individuals who indicate that they have a mixture of both African American and White ancestry into the "other race" category, or to place them into a "mixed race" category, alongside people with Asian American and Latino ancestry. I have chosen to include people who indicated on census surveys and exit polls that they are African American and White into the African American category. Likewise, I have included those individuals who indicated that they are Asian American or Pacific Islander American and White into the Asian American category. Just as President Obama is mixed-race Black and White, he is thought of (and treated) as our first Black president. The treatment afforded to our president largely tracks with how other mixed African American and White people are treated, so that's the rationale for proceeding in this fashion.

Data on each race and ethnic group's preference for Democrats (my proxy for "progressive") are based on the 2012 National Election Pool

Exit Poll, conducted by Edison Research.[1] Exit polls are the only data that exist that measure political *behavior*—as opposed to just political opinions—across all demographic groups in response to the exact same "product" (that is, candidate for president). In their book *Exit Polls*, political science professors Samuel Best and Brian Krueger have said that "the exit polls are unmatched as a tool for describing the voting population [because] they contact actual voters immediately after they depart polling locations across the nation." This sets them apart from "standard public opinion polls, such as the American National Election Study or Gallup Poll [which] do not capture respondents as they depart the voting booth [and] these standard surveys often fail to correctly identify voters from nonvoters."[2] The professors note that additional advantages of exit polls include the methodological benefit that "respondents self-administer the questionnaire and record their own responses, rather than requiring interviewers to read them the questions," and the sample size benefit in that "national exit polls collect completed questionnaires from far greater numbers of respondents than telephone surveys," usually five times more responses than typical telephone polls.[3] Noted Brookings Institution demographer William Frey also uses exit polls and census data in his book *Diversity Explosion* and in his other analyses of the role of voters of color in affecting electoral outcomes.[4]

In the most recent federal election cycles, a consortium of news agencies commissioned the exit poll. The *New York Times* described the exit polls as follows:

> The Election Day polls were based on questionnaires completed by voters as they left voting stations throughout the country on Tuesday, supplemented by telephone interviews with absentee and early voters. The polls were conducted by Edison Research of Somerville, N.J., for the National Election Pool, a consortium of ABC News, Associated Press, CBS News, CNN, Fox News and NBC News. The national results are based on voters in 350 randomly chosen precincts across the United States, and include absentee voters and early voters interviewed by telephone.

And now for the methodology behind my calculation of the New American Majority estimates. In a nutshell, I multiplied the share of each racial or ethnic group that voted for Obama by the total number of eligible voters of that group to arrive at the number of progressive eligible voters of that race.

Let's look at Latinos to see how this works in practice. The ACS shows that there were 22,620,810 Latino eligible voters in America as of 2013. The exit poll found that 71 percent of Latino voters cast their vote for Obama in 2012. I then multiplied 22,620,810 by 71 percent to get 16,060,775, the number of progressive Latino eligible voters in the country. That calculation was then repeated for African Americans, Whites, Asian Americans, and "Other" eligible voters. The exit poll does not segment out any other racial groups and uses the category of "Other" as a catchall. Since that's the data we're stuck with, I use the share of the vote for Obama that the exit poll assigns to "Other" for Native Americans and Arab Americans.

Having determined the number of progressive people of each racial or ethnic group, I then added all those numbers together to arrive at the figure of 110,591,848 progressive people in the voting-eligible population, or 50.83 percent of all eligible voters in the United States.

It is important to note that these numbers only relate to the Citizen Voting Age Population and *not* to the total U.S. population. The share that people of color comprise in the total population is larger than the share in the voting-eligible pool, and this is the case for two reasons. First, young people, especially those under the age of eighteen, comprise a much larger share of the total people of color population than of the White total population. As these young people of color age into the adult population, they are making the voting-eligible population even larger and more diverse. Second, a significant number of people of color in America are not yet citizens (hence, the fierce flashpoint battle over immigration reform and offering a pathway to citizenship).

Since the population is getting more diverse every hour of every day, I calculated projections that looked at how the eligible voter pool will become more diverse as each cohort of seventeen-year-olds turns eighteen. The underlying data set in Tables F and G list out the racial breakdown of each age group from one-year-olds to ninety-five-year-olds and then adds that grouping to the eligible voter ranks, applies the proxy percentages of 39 percent for Whites and 80.5 percent for people of color and recalculates the total NAM percentage for each year until 2028.

Lastly, in terms of how this plays out in the states, the above approach of taking the eligible voter population figures and multiplying them by the Obama percentage was replicated for all fifty states. In that way, we identified thirty-three states that either currently have or will soon have a progressive majority based on population growth trends. Here I had to rely solely on 2008 numbers since the 2012 Exit Poll departed from past practice and did not poll in all fifty states, focusing instead on just thirty-one states. Obama's overall percentage of White voters declined by 4 from 2008 to 2012, but his Latino percentage increased by 4 percent, and his Asian American percentage increased by 9 percent. And, as is the case nationally, the population of all the states has become more diverse since the 2013 ACS data was published, so that also balances out the mathematical impact of the decline in Obama's White support in 2012. At the end of the day, 2008 data is what we have, so it's what we used for the specific states, with the aforementioned caveats.

THE TABLES AND CALCULATIONS

And with that explanation, let's turn to the tables of the actual data.

Table A shows the figures for each racial group in the total population, what percentage of the total population each racial group comprises, the Citizen Voting Age Population (CVAP) total number for each racial group, what percentage of the CVAP each racial group comprises, and what percentage of that racial group's population is currently eligible to vote.

Table B has the 51 percent calculation for the New American Majority. It shows how each racial group voted in the 2012 presidential election by percentage (the proxy for "progressive" voters) and then applies that percentage to the number of eligible voters in each racial group. The table also shows what percentage each group of voters (progressive Whites, non-progressive Whites, etc.) comprise of the total of all eligible voters.

Table C takes the same data as in Table A and collapses Latinos, Blacks, Asian Americans, and Others into one "People of Color" row.

Table D takes the same data as in Table B and also collapses Latinos, African Americans, Asian Pacific Islanders, and Others into one "People of Color" row.

Table E shows the ranking of the fifty states and the District of Columbia by the percentage that the New American Majority comprises of the eligible voter population.

Tables F and G show the number of Whites and people of color by age cohort (all White seventeen-year-olds, eighteen-year-olds, etc.) and estimates of how their aging into the voting population (over eighteen years old) affects the composition of the New American Majority. Table F has the aggregate population growth for Whites and people of color—and the corresponding New American Majority percentage—projected out through 2028, and Table G has the underlying data for Table F = the racial composition of Whites and People of Color by each age cohort.

Okay, that's it! If that hasn't been enough fun for you, I'd love to continue the conversation online. Feel free to find me on social media (on Facebook or on Twitter @StevePtweets), or visit and reach out via the website www.democracyincolor.org.

TABLE A

	Total Pop.	% of Total Pop	CVAP	% of CVAP	% of Group Elig to Vote
White	197,529,430	63%	155,319,725	71%	79%
Black	40,375,600	13%	27,449,780	13%	68%
Latino	51,786,590	17%	22,620,810	10%	44%
Asian American	17,256,405	6%	9,065,515	4%	53%
Other	4,588,565	1%	3,121,135	1%	68%
Total	311,536,590		217,576,965		

TABLE B

	2012 Obama Share	# Prog Elig Voters	% of all Elig Voters	# Non-Prog Elig Voters	% of all Elig Voters	Total Votes
White	39%	60,574,693	28%	94,745,032	44%	
Black	93%	25,528,295	12%	1,921,485	1%	
Latino	71%	16,060,775	7%	6,560,035	3%	
Asian American	73%	6,617,826	3%	2,447,689	1%	
Other	58%	1,810,258	1%	1,310,877	1%	
Total		110,591,848	50.8%	106,985,118	49%	217,576,966

TABLE C

	Total Pop.	% of Total Pop	CVAP	% of CVAP	% of Group Elig to Vote
White	197,529,430	63%	155,319,725	71.39%	79%
People of Color	114,007,160	37%	62,257,240	28.61%	55%
Total	311,536,590		217,576,965		

TABLE D

	# Prog Elig Voters	% of all Elig Voters	# Non-Prog Elig Voters	% of all Elig Voters	Total Votes
Total	110,591,848	50.83%	106,985,118	49.2%	
White	60,574,693	27.84%	94,745,032	44%	
People of Color	50,017,155	22.99%	12,240,085	6%	
Total					217,576,965

TABLE E

State	Total CVAP	Progressive People of Color	NAM (Progressive POC + Prog Whites)	% Electorate new majority (Total NAM Share/CVAP)	Electoral votes
District of Columbia	462,895	258,666.30	422,316.40	91.2%	3
Hawaii	848,115	410,175.96	600,925.96	70.9%	4
Vermont	484,405	11,325.05	325,756.05	67.2%	3
Delaware	659,350	166,765.20	424,575.05	64.4%	3
Maryland	4,062,310	1,384,113.60	2,608,331.41	64.2%	10
California	23,110,250	8,403,618.83	14,781,755.77	64.0%	55
Massachusetts	4,721,115	631,143.95	3,003,539.97	63.6%	11
New York	13,222,635	3,719,013.30	8,385,702.89	63.4%	29
Rhode Island	762,580	87,505.95	476,096.98	62.4%	4
Illinois	8,838,355	2,110,718.55	5,378,077.33	60.8%	20
New Jersey	5,929,975	1,615,284.78	3,598,208.37	60.7%	14
Oregon	2,725,215	222,113.90	1,643,544.05	60.3%	7
Washington	4,666,435	588,913.45	2,781,119.89	59.6%	12
Maine	1,027,235	19,432.65	612,213.36	59.6%	4
Michigan	7,230,480	1,236,084.91	4,295,718.02	59.4%	16
Connecticut	2,533,175	433,545.30	1,476,337.57	58.3%	7
Wisconsin	4,190,650	356,974.50	2,401,474.50	57.3%	10
Nevada	1,758,635	451,231.00	991,084.06	56.4%	6
New Mexico	1,300,055	433,664.79	728,577.65	56.0%	5
Minnesota	3,825,240	289,899.85	2,143,347.32	56.0%	10
New Hampshire	999,330	31,138.30	558,508.91	55.9%	4
Pennsylvania	9,596,015	1,355,097.45	5,255,267.15	54.8%	20
Colorado	3,558,070	506,526.21	1,945,748.15	54.7%	9
Iowa	2,246,740	111,857.41	1,207,376.44	53.7%	6
Ohio	8,588,585	1,183,873.69	4,608,165.32	53.7%	18
Florida	13,322,495	3,317,867.96	7,125,842.96	53.5%	29
Virginia	5,762,780	1,392,218.98	3,009,265.34	52.2%	13
Indiana	4,705,615	521,701.70	2,381,492.61	50.6%	11
North Carolina	6,806,255	1,660,453.00	3,416,779.52	50.2%	15
Georgia	6,740,345	2,340,565.55	3,322,461.11	49.3%	16
Missouri	4,425,385	567,522.15	2,168,952.45	49.0%	10
Montana	717,025	19,035.30	339,363.39	47.3%	3
Arizona	4,156,610	754,831.62	1,960,884.15	47.2%	11
South Carolina	3,441,520	992,089.05	1,616,077.23	47.0%	9
Texas	16,056,960	5,082,017.85	7,455,790.27	46.4%	38
Kansas	1,994,365	215,089.35	912,703.49	45.8%	6
Tennessee	4,699,175	817,573.40	2,146,466.91	45.7%	11
North Dakota	498,635	13,199.05	221,573.17	44.4%	3
West Virginia	1,440,860	59,858.75	633,819.01	44.0%	5
Nebraska	1,298,850	104,701.35	569,173.44	43.8%	5
Mississippi	2,171,975	795,544.85	945,166.52	43.5%	6
South Dakota	559,960	15,460.60	243,589.67	43.5%	3
Arkansas	2,107,725	358,878.55	881,885.69	41.8%	6
Louisiana	3,321,200	1,066,507.30	1,373,405.15	41.4%	8
Kentucky	3,237,690	276,736.47	1,338,063.75	41.3%	8
Alaska	424,325	51,655.95	171,333.14	40.4%	3
Oklahoma	2,421,565	307,394.20	902,742.45	37.3%	7
Idaho	1,079,825	63,209.45	396,583.53	36.7%	4
Alabama	3,533,855	941,045.31	1,288,344.82	36.5%	9
Utah	1,771,260	138,113.35	641,665.21	36.2%	6
Wyoming	411,710	25,126.35	148,189.21	36.0%	3

TABLE F

TOTAL CVAP ALL	White ALL	People of Color ALL	Of All Electorate White	Of All Electorate People of Color	NAM White	NAM People of Color	NAM	Year
279,426,330	187,465,596	91,960,734	67.1%	32.9%	26.2%	26.5%	52.7%	2028
276,794,736	186,449,178	90,345,558	67.4%	32.6%	26.3%	26.3%	52.5%	2027
273,800,375	185,258,860	88,541,515	67.7%	32.3%	26.4%	26.0%	52.4%	2026
270,592,290	183,938,374	86,653,916	68.0%	32.0%	26.5%	25.8%	52.3%	2025
267,282,273	182,517,358	84,764,915	68.3%	31.7%	26.6%	25.5%	52.2%	2024
263,968,689	181,049,522	82,919,167	68.6%	31.4%	26.7%	25.3%	52.0%	2023
260,569,396	179,477,833	81,091,563	68.9%	31.1%	26.9%	25.1%	51.9%	2022
257,061,296	177,722,922	79,338,374	69.1%	30.9%	27.0%	24.8%	51.8%	2021
253,301,144	175,772,893	77,528,251	69.4%	30.6%	27.1%	24.6%	51.7%	2020
249,396,609	173,672,540	75,724,069	69.6%	30.4%	27.2%	24.4%	51.6%	2019
245,741,816	171,741,627	74,000,189	69.9%	30.1%	27.3%	24.2%	51.5%	2018
242,373,204	170,059,271	72,313,933	70.2%	29.8%	27.4%	24.0%	51.4%	2017
239,042,380	168,373,864	70,668,516	70.4%	29.6%	27.5%	23.8%	51.3%	2016
235,067,628	166,099,622	68,968,006	70.7%	29.3%	27.6%	23.6%	51.2%	2015

TABLE G

Age	2013	2016	White	People of Color	TOTAL	Age	2013	2016	White	People of Color	TOTAL
<1			1,900,981	1,784,954	3,685,935	48	51	54	3,030,219	1,157,018	4,187,237
1	4	7	2,005,499	1,948,834	3,954,333	49	52	55	3,116,744	1,118,980	4,235,724
2	5	8	2,091,096	2,030,707	4,121,803	50	53	56	3,258,210	1,215,244	4,473,454
3	6	9	2,111,269	1,998,879	4,110,148	51	54	57	3,054,369	1,055,812	4,110,181
4	7	10	2,068,904	1,945,971	4,014,875	52	55	58	3,121,309	1,042,259	4,163,568
5	8	11	2,124,566	1,917,426	4,041,992	53	56	59	3,090,976	1,006,779	4,097,755
6	9	12	2,150,757	1,812,123	3,962,880	54	57	60	3,014,030	992,422	4,006,452
7	10	13	2,142,560	1,836,479	3,979,039	55	58	61	3,033,766	988,886	4,022,652
8	11	14	2,144,089	1,808,217	3,952,306	56	59	62	2,906,573	891,799	3,798,372
9	12	15	2,205,752	1,796,598	4,002,350	57	60	63	2,866,190	863,128	3,729,318
10	13	16	2,250,269	1,783,341	4,033,610	58	61	64	2,777,500	809,599	3,587,099
11	14	17	2,218,913	1,725,526	3,944,439	59	62	65	2,678,677	805,861	3,484,538
12	15	18	2,316,341	1,701,447	4,017,788	60	63	66	2,733,600	850,761	3,584,361
13	16	19	2,245,724	1,704,319	3,950,043	61	64	67	2,591,268	728,432	3,319,700
14	17	20	2,277,388	1,690,867	3,968,255	62	65	68	2,640,448	718,757	3,359,205
15	18	21	2,342,489	1,661,911	4,004,400	63	66	69	2,752,753	664,367	3,417,120
16	19	22	2,373,844	1,716,446	4,090,290	64	67	70	2,119,159	572,227	2,691,386
17	20	23	2,383,432	1,698,850	4,082,282	65	68	71	2,043,582	552,163	2,595,745
18	21	24	2,576,268	1,852,791	4,429,059	66	69	72	2,004,428	493,433	2,497,861
19	22	25	2,470,308	1,671,448	4,141,756	67	70	73	2,062,875	482,682	2,545,557
20	23	26	2,680,591	1,701,857	4,382,448	68	71	74	1,831,039	452,055	2,283,094
21	24	27	2,567,257	1,573,505	4,140,762	69	72	75	1,655,865	425,724	2,081,589
22	25	28	2,419,610	1,416,895	3,836,505	70	73	76	1,617,581	427,306	2,044,887
23	26	29	2,287,312	1,362,025	3,649,337	71	74	77	1,491,992	359,816	1,851,808
24	27	30	2,326,469	1,281,733	3,608,202	72	75	78	1,444,380	363,453	1,807,833
25	28	31	2,460,496	1,335,472	3,795,968	73	76	79	1,372,235	335,887	1,708,122
26	29	32	2,322,033	1,259,759	3,581,792	74	77	80	1,287,975	307,693	1,595,668
27	30	33	2,394,896	1,235,364	3,630,260	75	78	81	1,274,735	299,063	1,573,798
28	31	34	2,378,687	1,228,556	3,607,243	76	79	82	1,178,293	268,375	1,446,668
29	32	35	2,336,803	1,188,056	3,524,859	77	80	83	1,124,719	248,208	1,372,927
30	33	36	2,426,137	1,282,905	3,709,042	78	81	84	1,102,058	243,093	1,345,151
31	34	37	2,228,653	1,162,050	3,390,703	79	82	85	1,072,940	217,923	1,290,863
32	35	38	2,240,974	1,128,660	3,369,634	80	83	86	1,083,251	212,859	1,296,110
33	36	39	2,158,111	1,101,296	3,259,407	81	84	87	977,224	188,236	1,165,460
34	37	40	2,117,705	1,085,827	3,203,532	82	85	88	945,482	178,173	1,123,655
35	38	41	2,275,250	1,164,150	3,439,400	83	86	89	884,563	169,778	1,054,341
36	39	42	2,132,179	1,100,223	3,232,402	84	87	90	815,181	144,791	959,972
37	40	43	2,207,510	1,119,942	3,327,452	85	88	91	770,610	143,108	913,718
38	41	44	2,390,771	1,154,324	3,545,095	86	89	92	690,253	109,878	800,131
39	42	45	2,602,499	1,186,172	3,788,671	87	90	93	601,068	100,223	701,291
40	43	46	2,747,917	1,264,131	4,012,048	88	91	94	552,877	89,822	642,699
41	44	47	2,494,854	1,115,405	3,610,259	89	92	95	395,846	58,934	454,780
42	45	48	2,492,280	1,135,028	3,627,308	90	93	96	192,531	26,356	218,887
43	46	49	2,566,046	1,110,286	3,676,332	91	94	97	43,736	4,035	47,771
44	47	50	2,627,348	1,131,471	3,758,819	92	95	98	274,839	72,718	347,557
45	48	51	2,924,230	1,207,377	4,131,607	93	96	99	567,913	97,085	664,998
46	49	52	2,898,096	1,146,837	4,044,933	94	97	100	533,506	80,109	613,615
47	50	53	3,003,988	1,155,821	4,159,809	95	98	101	42,099	937	43,036

APPENDIX B

What's in a Name?

People feel passionately about their names and the names of their groups; I know I do. This appendix explains the thinking behind the language choices I made in writing this book. In terms of the title and subsequent usage, by "Brown" I mean "people of color." In terms of terminology regarding specific groups of color, the reasoning is below.

BLACK/AFRICAN AMERICAN

The word "Black" is capitalized throughout this book when referring to people of African descent. Standard journalistic practice, for some strange reason, is to use a lowercase *b* for "black" but to capitalize "African American" even though both terms refer to the same group of people. Lori Tharps, a professor at Temple University, gave voice to the frustration and anger that many of us feel about this practice in her 2014 essay in the *New York Times*, "The Case for Black with a Capital B." She wrote: "[t]he New York Times and Associated Press stylebooks continue to insist on black with a lowercase b. Ironically, The Associated Press also decrees that the proper names of 'nationalities, peoples, races, tribes' should be capitalized. What are Black people, then?"[1] I use the words "African American" and "Black" interchangeably, depending on what sounds better to my ear in a particular sentence or paragraph.

HISPANIC/LATINO

Great confusion surrounds the racial and ethnic terminology choices used to refer to people known as Hispanics or Latinos. The term "Hispanic" means "of or relating to a Spanish-speaking people or culture" and derives from the Latin word *Hispania*, for "Spain." It is, fundamentally, a language-oriented, not geography-oriented, frame of reference to describe a people. The term "Latino," on the other hand, emphasizes geography and refers to a "native or inhabitant of Latin America." It is meant to describe descendants of the countries of Latin America. The census added the term "Latino" during Bill Clinton's administration in 2000.[2]

For the purpose of this book, I use the term "Latinos" for two reasons. First, it's the term many progressive Latinos use. (Interestingly, President Obama referred to Supreme Court justice Sonia Sotomayor as a "Hispanic" judge, but she describes herself as "Latina" and famously made the remark about the need for more "wise Latinas.") Also, I feel, referring to geographic origin is a more accurate way to understand the experience of a group of people and their history than the language they share. Spaniards, for example, are Hispanics but they are not Latinos.

ASIAN AMERICAN/ASIAN PACIFIC ISLANDER

The nomenclature regarding the term "Asian Americans" is less confusing than it is for "Latinos/Hispanics," although it also has its own, somewhat complex history. At the most elemental level, Asian Americans are Americans whose ancestry originates from countries in Asia. The census defines an Asian American as "a person having origins in any of the original peoples of the Far East, Southeast Asia, or the Indian subcontinent, including, for example, Cambodia, China, India, Japan, Korea, Malaysia, Pakistan, the Philippine Islands, Thailand, and Vietnam."

As I address in chapter 2, there is growing sentiment for Pacific Islander Americans to be identified and treated distinctly, but many Asian American leaders and activists still use Asian American or Asian American/Pacific Islander (AAPI) or Asian Pacific Americans (APA). I don't feel it's appropriate for me, as someone outside that community, to weigh in on this debate, and from what I can tell from the outside, it appears that the conversation has not reached resolution around nomenclature. Consequently, I refer to this group simply as Asian Americans because that's the phrase that most of the Asian American activists and leaders I came of age with use most commonly.

NATIVE AMERICAN/INDIAN AND ALASKA NATIVE

How to describe the descendants of America's indigenous inhabitants is complicated by the fact that although we now have a racial group frame of reference, the people who were here when the English ships first arrived considered themselves distinct nations. In her book *An Indigenous Peoples' History of the United States*, Roxanne Dunbar-Ortiz explains: "Native peoples were colonized and deposed of their territories as distinct peoples—hundreds of nations—not as a racial or ethnic group."[3] As for terminology, Dunbar-Ortiz says, "I use 'Indigenous,' 'Indian,' and 'Native' interchangeably. . . . Indigenous individuals and peoples in North America on the whole do not consider 'Indian' a slur."

When I started this book, I frankly did not know that "Indian" was acceptable as a term. I wrote my early drafts exclusively using the phrase "Native American." Along the way, reading, listening, and learning, I came to understand that "Indian" was acceptable. But since I'd already committed to "Native American"—and since that term is also acceptable—I stuck with it.

The Census Bureau, which has had a complicated and inconsistent history when it comes to counting Native Americans and other people of color, uses a shared category of "American Indian and Alaska Native." Since Alaska Natives are also indigenous people, when I use the term "Native American" I also intend for it to refer to Alaska Natives.

WHITE/white

When it comes to the descendants of Europe, I am frankly more ambivalent about capitalizing "White." The writer Touré capitalizes "Black" and uses lower case for "white," explaining, "I don't believe that whiteness merits the same treatment. Most American whites think of themselves as Italian-American or Jewish or otherwise." In many ways, the equivalent of "Latino," "Asian American," and "African American" is not "White," but, rather, "Irish American," "Italian American," "Anglo American," etc. But, as covered in chapter 3, the idea of Whites as a distinct group on this continent is deeply embedded in American history, law, and culture. Given this reality, I have gone ahead and capitalized "White" throughout the book.

DEMOCRATS/PROGRESSIVES

Lastly, I use the words "Democrats" and "progressives" frequently throughout the book.

When mentioning "Democrats" I'm referring to people who are either registered Democrats or generally vote for the Democratic candidate. When I refer to the Democratic Party, I mean the official national entities that control and direct the hundreds of millions of dollars spent trying to elect Democratic candidates. Those entities are the Democratic National Committee (DNC), the Democratic Congressional Campaign Committee (DCCC), the Democratic Senatorial Campaign Committee (DSCC), the Democratic Governors Association (DGA), and the Democratic Legislative Campaign Committee (DLCC). At times, when referring to "Democrats," I mean the leadership of the Democratic Party (as distinguished from Democratic voters), and I hope the usage is clear in the context in which I'm using the word.

The term "progressive" relates to the broader movement for social change, justice, and equality in America. It consists of activists, organizations, and advocates. Many are members of the Democratic Party, but there is not 100 percent overlap (some are Green Party members, some are independent).

Any attempt to define "progressive" is obviously an exercise fraught with peril. Since this is a book about politics and winning elections, a very basic proxy for a progressive is a person who voted for Barack Obama in 2012 (with the emphasis on 2012 and not 2008, when, it could be argued, many people who don't necessarily regularly vote for Democrats may have been caught up in the excitement of making history). By 2012, after the glow of electing the first Black president had faded, and everyone could see that Obama had created an $800 billion economic stimulus package, passed the Affordable Care Act, wound down the war in Iraq, signed women's equality legislation (the Lily Ledbetter Act), and took executive action to protect "the Dreamers" (undocumented young immigrants), his policy priorities were clear. I think it's fair to call those who voted for four more years of that "progressive." Furthermore, 5 million fewer Whites voted for Obama in 2012 than cast ballots for him in 2008, so I see the 2012 voters as the more "hard-core" progressives.

Lastly, when including quotes that reference a racial group, I have left the writer's original punctuation in place.

APPENDIX C

Recommended Reading

The histories and sojourns of each racial group in America are fascinating, complex, and far, far beyond the scope of this book. Fortunately, serious scholars have already done that work. I highly recommend adding the following works to your library if you wish to deepen your understanding of the New American Majority:

Latino Politics, by Lisa Garcia Bedolla
A New History of Asian America, by Shelley Sang-Hee Lee
An Indigenous Peoples' History of the United States,
    by Roxanne Dunbar-Ortiz
Arab Americans: A History, by Gregory Orfalea
African Americans: A Concise History, by Darlene Clark Hine
A People's History of the United States, by Howard Zinn

There is also a growing array of excellent online resources that provide greater depth and insight into the New American Majority. Among some of the best are the following:

- The States of Change website, part of a collaboration between the Center for American Progress, the American Enterprise Institute, and William Frey of the Brookings Institute, has extensive data and interactive tools showing past, present, and future demographic shifts in each state. https://www.americanprogress .org/issues/progressive-movement/report/2015/02/24/107261 /states-of-change/
- Fwd.us, an immigration reform organization, used the data from States of Change to create an easy-to-use tool at its page "The Republican Road to the White House" that lets users experiment with changing the partisan vote share of each racial

group to see how that change would affect the outcome in presidential elections. http://www.fwd.us/gopfuture

- PolicyLink, the national equity-focused research and action institute, has created a National Equity Atlas that aggregates data for tracking, measuring, and making the economic and policy argument for inclusive growth. http://nationalequityatlas.org/
- The Women Donors Network has created the Reflective Democracy Campaign, a project that has built a database that identifies the race and gender of 42,000 elected officials in the country, and their online tool enables you to examine how reflective a city or state's elected officials are compared to the composition of the population. http://wholeads.us/

Links to all of the above resources as well as much of the underlying data used in the preceding chapters can be found at Democracy in Color, the online portal created as a companion to this book. www.democracyincolor.org

NOTES

INTRODUCTION

1. "Barack Obama's Caucus Speech," *New York Times*, January 3, 2008, www.ny times.com/2008/01/03/us/politics/03obama-transcript.html (accessed August 21, 2015).

2. Taylor Branch, *At Canaan's Edge: America in the King Years, 1965–68* (New York: Simon & Schuster, 2006), Chapter 30, "Requiem."

3. Sandra L. Colby and Jennifer M. Ortman, "Projections of the Size and Composition of the U.S. Population: 2014 to 2060," U.S. Census Bureau, March 2015, https://www.census.gov/content/dam/Census/library/publications/2015/demo/p25-1143.pdf (accessed August 24, 2015).

4. Christopher Hamner, "Booth's Reason for Assassination," http://teachinghistory .org/history-content/ask-a-historian/24242 (accessed August 21, 2015).

CHAPTER 1: 51 PERCENT (AND GROWING EVERY DAY): THE NEW AMERICAN MAJORITY

1. See Taylor Branch, *Pillar of Fire: America in the King Years 1963–65* (New York: Simon & Schuster, 1998), Chapter 40, "Saigon, Audobon, and Selma," and Taylor Branch, *At Canaan's Edge: America in the King Years 1965–1968* (New York: Simon & Schuster, 2006), Chapter 2, "Scouts."

2. Dennis Hevesi, "Rev. James E. Orange, 65, Aide to Dr. King, Dies," *New York Times*, February 22, 2008, www.nytimes.com/2008/02/22/us/22orange.html (accessed August 21, 2015).

3. Branch, *At Canaan's Edge.*

4. See Lyndon Johnson, "President Johnson's Special Message to the Congress: The American Promise," LBJ Presidential Library, 1965, www.lbjlibrary.org/lyndon -baines-johnson/speeches-films/president-johnsons-special-message-to-the-congress -the-american-promise (accessed August 21, 2015).

5. See Branch, *At Canaan's Edge*, Chapter 11, "Half-Inch Hailstones."

6. See Appendix for current figures and for 1965 see U.S. Census Bureau, Resident Population plus Armed Forces Overseas—Estimates by Age, Sex, and Race: July 1, 1965, U.S. Census Bureau, Population Division Internet, October 1, 2004, www.census .gov/popest/data/national/asrh/pre-1980/tables/PE-11-1965.pdf (accessed August 21, 2015).

7. Jim Rutenberg, "A Dream Undone: Inside the 50-Year Campaign to Roll Back the Voting Rights Act," *New York Times Magazine*, July 29, 2015, www.nytimes.com/2015 /07/29/magazine/voting-rights-act-dream-undone.html (accessed August 21, 2015).

8. Tova Andrea Wang, "The Politics of Voter Suppression: Defending and Expanding Americans' Right to Vote," *Demos*, August 18, 2012, www.demos.org/publication /politics-voter-suppression-defending-and-expanding-americans-right-vote (accessed August 21, 2015).

9. Michael J. Pitts, "The Voting Rights Act and the Era of Maintenance," *Alabama Law Review*, March 12, 2008, http://papers.ssrn.com/sol3/papers.cfm?abstract_id =1105115 (accessed August 21, 2015).

10. Barack Obama, "Remarks by the President at the 50th Anniversary of the Selma to Montgomery Marches," White House, March 7, 2015, www.whitehouse.gov/the-press -office/2015/03/07/remarks-president-50th-anniversary-selma-montgomery-marches (accessed August 21, 2015).

11. "How Groups Voted in 2012," Roper Center, University of Connecticut, www .ropercenter.uconn.edu/polls/us-elections/how-groups-voted/how-groups-voted-2012 (accessed August 21, 2015).

12. Eileen J. Leamon and Jason Bucelato for the Federal Election Commission, "Federal Elections 2012: Election Results for the U.S. President, the U.S. Senate and the U.S. House of Representatives," Federal Election Commission, July 2013, www.fec .gov/pubrec/fe2012/federalelections2012.pdf (accessed August 21, 2015).

13. U.S. Census Bureau, "Voting Age Population by Citizenship and Race (CVAP)," 2009–2013 5-Year American Community Survey, 2014, http://www.census.gov/rdo /data/voting_age_population_by_citizenship_and_race_cvap.html (accessed August 25, 2015).

14. See Appendix A for detailed discussion of the math and methodology.

15. The U.S. Census Bureau maintains a population clock on its website that provides continuously updated information about U.S. births, deaths, and immigration. Sometimes the number for the frequency of births varies slightly, www.census.gov /popclock (accessed August 21, 2015).

16. U.S. Census Bureau, "Most Children Under Age 1 Are Minorities, Census Bureau Reports," May 17, 2012, www.census.gov/newsroom/releases/archives/population /cb12-90.html (accessed August 21, 2015).

17. U.S Census Bureau, "U.S. and World Population Clock," International Database, www.census.gov/popclock (accessed August 21, 2015).

18. U.S. Census Bureau, "Resident Population plus Armed Forces Overseas—Estimates by Age, Sex, and Race: July 1, 1949," U.S. Census Bureau, Population Division Internet, October 1, 2004, https://www.census.gov/popest/data/national/asrh /pre-1980/tables/PE-11-1949.pdf (accessed September 23, 2015). The White population was 89.6 percent in 1949 and dropped to 89.3 percent in 1950, so at the beginning of 1950, it was likely 90 percent White, rounding up.

19. U.S. Centers for Disease Control and Prevention, "Number of Deaths and Percent Distribution by Specified Hispanic Origin and Race for Non-Hispanic Population: United States and Each State, 1999–2007," National Vital Statistics System, last

updated November 12, 2009, www.cdc.gov/nchs/nvss/mortality/gmwkh10.htm (accessed August 21, 2015).

20. U.S. Census Bureau, "U.S. and World Population Clock." Also, the CDC report in Footnote 19 has the precise number of U.S. deaths in 2007 (2,423,712), and, of those, 80 percent (1,939,606) were White.

21. See U.S. Department of Homeland Security, *2013 Yearbook of Immigration Statistics*, U.S. Department of Homeland Security, Office of Immigration Statistics, August 2014, www.dhs.gov/sites/default/files/publications/ois_yb_2013_0.pdf (accessed August 21, 2015). Also, for statistics on undocumented immigrants, see, "Profile of the Unauthorized Population: United States," Migration Policy Institute, www.migrationpolicy.org /data/unauthorized-immigrant-population/state/US (accessed August 21, 2015).

22. U.S. Census Bureau, "U.S. and World Population Clock."

23. In recognition and opposition to this fact, Texas officials have been denying birth certificates to parents who are suspected of being undocumented. Immigration lawyers filed suit in May 2015 to challenge the practice. For more information, see Melissa del Bosque, "Children of Immigrants Denied Citizenship," *Observer*, July 13, 2015, www.texasobserver.org/children-of-immigrants-denied-citizenship (accessed August 21, 2015).

24. U.S. Census Bureau, "2009–2013 5-Year American Community Survey," 2014. See Appendix A: Math and Methodology for racial composition of each age group.

25. See U.S. Department of Homeland Security, *2013 Yearbook of Immigration Statistics*, U.S. Department of Homeland Security, Office of Immigration Statistics, August 2014, www.dhs.gov/sites/default/files/publications/ois_yb_2013_0.pdf (accessed August 21, 2015).

26. See Appendix A: Math and Methodology.

27. Ibid.

28. The District of Columbia has three electoral votes but no voting members in Congress (a matter that should be high on the reform agenda in a country founded on the principle of no taxation without representation), so that is why there are 33 states where the New American Majority can elect presidents, but just 32 that elect voting members of Congress.

29. William H. Frey, *Diversity Explosion: How New Racial Demographics Are Remaking America* (Washington, D.C.: Brookings Institution Press, 2014).

30. Patrick Oakford, "The Changing Face of America's Electorate: Political Implications of Shifting Demographics," January 6, 2015, Center for American Progress, www.scribd.com/doc/251769181/The-Changing-Face-of-America-s-Electorate (accessed August 21, 2015).

31. Ronald Brownstein, "American's New Electorate: How rising minority populations can reshape U.S. politics and carry Obama to victory in 2012," *Atlantic*, April 1, 2011, www.theatlantic.com/politics/archive/2011/04/americas-new-electorate/73317 (accessed August 21, 2015).

32. Adam C. Smith, "Democrats Grow Coy about Courting the South," *St. Petersburg Times*, February 1, 2004, www.sptimes.com/2004/02/01/Worldandnation/Democrats _grow_coy_ab.shtml (accessed August 21, 2015).

33. "Historical Presidential Election Information by State," 270 to Win, www.270 towin.com/states (accessed August 21, 2015).

34. National Election Pool exit poll conducted by Edison Research, "Election Day Exit Poll," November 5, 2008, accessed via Election 2012, *New York Times*, http://elections .nytimes.com/2012/results/president/exit-polls (accessed August 23, 2015).

35. Mark Joseph Stern, "How the Right Was Won," *Slate Book Review*, November 3, 2014, www.slate.com/articles/arts/books/2014/11/winning_marriage_by_marc_solo mon_reviewed.html (accessed August 21, 2015).

36. See Ballotpedia.org for states with Democratic governor and Democratic control of the state legislature. Also see "Annual Estimates of the Resident Population: April 1, 2010 to July 1, 2014," U.S. Census Bureau, Population Division.

37. "USA States in Profile," StatsAmerica, www.statsamerica.org/profiles/sip_index .html (accessed August 21, 2015).

38. Charlie Saginaw, "The Unexpected Blue in Texas," *Huffington Post*, August 15, 2013, http://www.huffingtonpost.com/charlie-saginaw/the-unexpected-places-whe_b _3759449.html (accessed August 25, 2015). And see U.S. Census Bureau, "American Community Survey."

39. Branch, *Pillar of Fire*, Epilogue.

CHAPTER 2: MEET THE NEW AMERICAN MAJORITY

1. Isabel Wilkerson, *The Warmth of Other Suns* (New York: Vintage Books, 2010), Part One: The Great Migration 1915–1970.

2. Lynette Clemetson, "Hispanics Now Largest Minority, Census Shows," *New York Times*, January 22, 2003, www.nytimes.com/2003/01/22/us/hispanics-now-largest -minority-census-shows.html (accessed August 21, 2015).

3. There are entire agencies within the federal government dedicated to pinpointing various population statistics. Among these agencies one finds slight discrepancies in the population data reported, most of which is attributable to the use of different methodologies by the various agencies. Here I provide the most commonly cited population statistics. At times, they differ slightly from other numbers provided in this book. However, the variation among the numbers are not so great that they impact my underlying arguments about the relative size and social significance of a New American Majority.

4. Carmen K. Sisson, "Why African Americans are moving back to the South," *Christian Science Monitor*, March 16, 2014, www.csmonitor.com/USA/Society/2014/0316 /Why-African-Americans-are-moving-back-to-the-South (accessed August 21, 2015).

5. See "Election Polls—Presidential Vote by Group," Gallup, www.gallup.com/poll /139880/election-polls-presidential-vote-groups.aspx (accessed August 21, 2015). And

see "National Election Day Exit Polls," Roper Center of the University of Connecticut, www.ropercenter.uconn.edu/polls/us-elections/exit-polls/ (accessed August 21, 2015).

6. U.S. Census Bureau, Current Population Survey, November 2012; Table 4b. Reported Voting and Registration, by Sex, Race and Hispanic Origin, for States: November 2012, U.S. Department of Commerce, May 2013, https://www.census.gov/hhes /www/socdemo/voting/publications/p20/2012/tables.html (accessed August 24, 2015).

7. See "National Election Day Exit Polls," Roper Center of the University of Connecticut.

8. National Election Pool, "Profile of the Primary Voters," *New York Times*, 2008, http://politics.nytimes.com/election-guide/2008/results/votes/index.html (accessed August 25, 2015).

9. U.S. Census Bureau, Current Population Survey, November 2012; Table 4b.

10. In this chapter, I use the census figures most commonly reported in the media about the size of the respective racial groups, but as these numbers are often based on projections they may differ slightly from the figures in Appendix A: Math and Methodology. The variations do not affect the underlying calculations about the size and composition of the New American Majority, and, in fact, the popularly cited numbers are actually larger than the data used for my calculations.

11. See Mark Hugo Lopez and Daniel Dockterman, "U.S. Hispanic Country of Origin Counts for Nation, Top 30 Metropolitan Areas," Pew Research Center Hispanic, May 26, 2011, www.pewhispanic.org/2011/05/26/us-hispanic-country-of-origin -counts-for-nation-top-30-metropolitan-areas/ (accessed August 21, 2015). Also see Sharon R. Ennis, Merarys Rios-Vargas, and Nora G. Albert, "The Hispanic Population: 2010," U.S. Census Bureau, May 1, 2011, www.census.gov/prod/cen2010/briefs /c2010br-04.pdf (accessed August 21, 2015).

12. U.S. Census Bureau, Current Population Survey, November 2012; Table 4b.

13. Randolph B. Campbell, *An Empire for Slavery: The Peculiar Institution in Texas, 1821–1865* (Baton Rouge: Louisiana State University Press, 1989).

14. Library of Congress, "The Treaty of Guadalupe Hidalgo," Library of Congress, Hispanic Reading Room, www.loc.gov/rr/hispanic/ghtreaty (accessed August 21, 2015).

15. Sharon R. Ennis, Merarys Rios-Vargas, and Nora G. Albert, "The Hispanic Population: 2010," U.S. Census Bureau, May 1, 2011, www.census.gov/prod/cen2010/briefs /c2010br-04.pdf (accessed August 18, 2014).

16. Puerto Ricans born on the island are U.S. citizens, but their citizenship flows from an act of Congress, not the U.S. Constitution. This means that a hostile Congress (and a compliant president) could actually revoke the citizenship of all Puerto Ricans. Although they are essentially U.S. citizens, Puerto Rico itself does not get to vote for a U.S. president, and residents of Puerto Rico lack voting representation in Congress (relegated to the same kind of "visitor's pass" afforded to residents of the District of Columbia wherein there is a congressional representative who can physically show up but

not vote). Puerto Ricans who move to or live in a formal state of the United States can vote for federal officers. For more details, Lisa García Bedolla's *Latino Politics* provides a thorough and informative description of the history and situation of Puerto Ricans.

17. D'Vera Cohn, Eileen Patten, and Mark Hugo Lopez, "Puerto Rican Population Declines on Island, Grows on Mainland," Pew Research Center, Hispanic Trends, July 2014, www.pewhispanic.org/files/2014/08/2014-08-11_Puerto-Rico-Final.pdf (accessed August 21, 2015).

18. Anna Brown and Eileen Patten, "Hispanics of Cuban Origin in the United States, 2011," Pew Research Center, 2013, www.pewhispanic.org/2013/06/19/hispanics-of-cuban-origin-in-the-united-states-2011 (accessed August 21, 2015).

19. Mark Hugo Lopez and Jens Manuel Krogstad, "As Cuban American Demographics Change, so Do Views of Cuba," Pew Research Center, December 23, 2014, www.pewresearch.org/fact-tank/2014/12/23/as-cuban-american-demographics-change-so-do-views-of-cuba/ (accessed August 21, 2015).

20. See U.S. Census Bureau, Current Population Survey, November 2012; Table 4b. There is some minor discrepancy between the number of people determined by the Census Bureau to have voted and the number indicated by looking at the exit polls.

21. See Department of Homeland Security, *2013 Yearbook of Immigration Statistics*, Office of Immigration Statistics, August 2014, www.dhs.gov/sites/default/files/publications/ois_yb_2013_0.pdf (accessed August 21, 2015).

22. U.S. Census Bureau, Current Population Survey, November 2012; Table 4b.

23. Ana Gonzalez-Barrera, Mark Hugo Lopez, Jeffrey S. Passel, and Paul Taylor, "The Path Not Taken: Recent Trends in Naturalization, 2000–2011," Pew Research Center: Hispanic Trends, February 4, 2013, www.pewhispanic.org/2013/02/04/ii-recent-trends-in-naturalization-2000-2011-2 (accessed August 21, 2015).

24. "How Groups Voted," Roper Center of the University of Connecticut, www.ropercenter.uconn.edu/polls/us-elections/how-groups-voted (accessed August 17, 2015).

25. "A Deep Dive into Party Affiliation," Pew Research Center, April 7, 2015, www.people-press.org/2015/04/07/a-deep-dive-into-party-affiliation (accessed August 21, 2015).

26. U.S. Census Bureau, Current Population Survey, November 2012; Table 4b.

27. "How Groups Voted," Roper Center of the University of Connecticut.

28. U.S. Census Bureau, Current Population Survey, November 2012; Table 4b.

29. Ibid.

30. Mark Hugo Lopez, "In 2014, Latinos will surpass whites as largest racial/ethnic group in California," Pew Research Center, 2014, www.pewresearch.org/fact-tank/2014/01/24/in-2014-latinos-will-surpass-whites-as-largest-racialethnic-group-in-california (accessed August 21, 2015).

31. Karthick Ramakrishnan and Farah Z. Ahmad, "Language Diversity and English Proficiency: Part of the 'State of Asian Americans and Pacific Islanders' Series,"

Center for American Progress, May 27, 2014, www.americanprogress.org/wp-content /uploads/2014/04/AAPI-LanguageAccess1.pdf (accessed August 21, 2015).

32. "The Rise of Asian Americans," Pew Research Center: Social and Demographic Trends, www.pewsocialtrends.org/asianamericans-graphics (accessed August 15, 2015).

33. Citizen Voting Age Population Special Tabulation from the 2009–2013 5-Year American Community Survey, U.S. Census Bureau.

34. "The Rise of Asian Americans," Pew Research Center.

35. Elizabeth M. Hoeffel, Sonya Rastogi, Myoung Ouk Kim, and Hasan Shahid, "The Asian Population: 2010," U.S. Census Bureau, March 2012, www.census.gov /prod/cen2010/briefs/c2010br-11.pdf (accessed August 21, 2015).

36. Shelley Sang-Hee Lee, *A New History of Asian America* (New York: Routledge, 2014), Chapter 13.

37. Davianna McGregor and Edmund Moy, "Native Hawaiians and Pacific Islander Americans," 2003, Asian-Nation: The Landscape of Asian America, www.asian-nation .org/hawaiian-pacific.shtml (accessed August 21, 2015).

38. Lindsay Hixson, Bradford B. Hepler, and Myoung Ouk Kim, "The Native Hawaiian and Other Pacific Islander Population: 2010," U.S. Census Bureau, May 2012, www.census.gov/prod/cen2010/briefs/c2010br-12.pdf (accessed August 21, 2015).

39. Ibid.

40. McGregor and Moy, "Native Hawaiians and Pacific Islander Americans."

41. The number of Asian American voters was calculated by using exit poll estimates of what percentage of all voters consisted of Asian Americans.

42. "The Rise of Asian Americans," Pew Research Center, http://www.pewsocial trends.org/2012/06/19/chapter-6-political-and-civic-life/ (accessed October 8, 2015).

43. "How Groups Voted," Roper Center of the University of Connecticut.

44. Ibid.

45. Roxanne Dunbar-Ortiz, *An Indigenous Peoples' History of the United States* (Boston: Beacon Press, 2014), Chapter 5, "The Birth of a Nation."

46. The Indian Reorganization Act of 1934 is controversial among some Native Americans. Dunbar says in her book, "For those Native nations, the majority, that did accept the Indian Reorganization Act, a negative consequence was that English-speaking Native elites, often aligned with Christian denominations, signed on to the law and formed authoritarian governments that enriched a few families and undermined communal traditions and traditional forms of governance, a problem that persists. However, the IRA did end allotment and set a precedent for acknowledging Indigenous self-determination and recognizing collective and cultural rights, a legal reality that made it difficult for those who sought to undo the incipient empowerment of Indigenous peoples in the 1950s."

47. Dunbar-Ortiz, *An Indigenous Peoples' History of the United States*, Chapter 1, "Follow the Corn."

48. Richard T. Schaefer (editor), *Encyclopedia of Race, Ethnicity, and Society* (Thousand Oaks, CA: Sage Publications, Inc., 2008), 46.

49. Tina Norris, Paula L. Vines, and Elizabeth M. Hoeffel, "The American Indian and Alaska Native Population: 2010," U.S. Census Bureau, January 2012, www.census .gov/prod/cen2010/briefs/c2010br-10.pdf (accessed August 21, 2015).

50. "Voting Rights and Citizenship: Native Americans and Chinese Get the Vote," City University of New York, www1.cuny.edu/portal_ur/content/voting_cal/americans _chinese.html (accessed August 21, 2015).

51. Unfortunately, we don't have figures on how many are registered to vote because the census doesn't collect voter registration numbers for Native Americans. This is something the census should look into changing. Also unfortunately, most political surveys, including exit polls, don't include enough Native Americans for a statistically accurate picture of their partisan voting preferences. See Citizen Voting Age Population Special Tabulation from the 2009–2013 5-Year American Community Survey, United States Census Bureau. For more information on Native American voters see Tova Wang, "Ensuring Access to the Ballot for American Indians & Alaska Natives: New Solutions to Strengthen American Democracy," *Demos*, 2012, www.demos.org /sites/default/files/publications/IHS%20Report-Demos.pdf (accessed August 21, 2015). Also see "What Matters Most in 2008 and Beyond: What Matters Most to American Indians and Alaska Natives," National Education Association, 2008, www.nea.org /assets/docs/HE/votingfocus08.pdf (accessed August 21, 2015).

52. "Official Election Results for United States Senate 2012," Federal Election Commission, 2012, http://www.fec.gov/pubrec/fe2012/2012congresults.pdf (accessed October 8, 2015).

53. Walter Isaacson, *Steve Jobs* (New York: Simon & Schuster, 2013), 3–4.

54. "Facts about Arabs and the Arab World," American-Arab Anti-Discrimination Committee, November 29, 2009, www.adc.org/2009/11/facts-about-arabs-and-the -arab-world (accessed August 21, 2015). Also see "Is Iran an Arab Country?," *Slate*, October 3, 2001, www.slate.com/articles/news_and_politics/explainer/2001/10/is_iran _an_arab_country.html (accessed August 21, 2015).

55. Dan Murphy, "What is an Islamist?," *Christian Science Monitor*, August 13, 2012, www.csmonitor.com/World/Middle-East/2012/0813/What-is-an-Islamist (accessed August 21, 2015).

56. See "World's Muslim Population," About.com, http://islam.about.com/od/mus limcountries/a/population.htm (accessed August 21, 2015). Also see "Arab, People," *Encyclopaedia Britannica*, www.britannica.com/topic/Arab (accessed August 21, 2015).

57. Todd Hertz, "Are Most Arab Americans Christian?," *Christianity Today*, March 1, 2003, www.christianitytoday.com/ct/2003/marchweb-only/3-24-22.0.html (accessed August 21, 2015).

58. See Gregory Ofalea, *The Arab Americans: A History* (Ithaca, NY: Olive Branch Press, 2006), 190. Also see "Muslim Americans: No Signs of Growth in Alienation

or Support for Extremism," Pew Research Center: U.S. Politics and Policy, August 30, 2011, www.people-press.org/2011/08/30/muslim-americans-no-signs-of-growth-in -alienation-or-support-for-extremism (accessed August 21, 2015).

59. See Heather Brown, Emily Guskin, and Amy Mitchell, "Arab-American Population Growth," Pew Research Center: Journalism & Media, November 28, 2012, www .journalism.org/2012/11/28/arabamerican-population-growth (accessed August 21, 2015). Also see "Demographics," Arab American Institute, www.aaiusa.org/demo graphics (accessed August 21, 2015).

60. G. Patricia de la Cruz and Angela Brittingham, "The Arab Population: 2000," U.S. Census Bureau, December 2003, www.census.gov/prod/2003pubs/c2kbr-23.pdf (accessed August 21, 2015).

61. See Jens Manuel Krogstad, "Census Bureau Explores New Middle East/North Africa Ethnic Category," Pew Research Center, March 24, 2014, www.pewresearch.org /fact-tank/2014/03/24/census-bureau-explores-new-middle-eastnorth-africa-ethnic -category (accessed August 21, 2015). Also see "Demographics," Arab American Institute, http://www.aaiusa.org/demographics (accessed October 8, 2015).

62. Maryam Asi and Daniel Beaulieu, "Arab Households in the United States: 2006–2010," U.S. Department of Commerce Economics and Statistics Administration, May 2013, www.census.gov/prod/2013pubs/acsbr10-20.pdf (accessed July 1, 2015).

63. "Is Iran an Arab Country?," *Slate*, October 3, 2001, www.slate.com/articles /news_and_politics/explainer/2001/10/is_iran_an_arab_country.html (accessed August 21, 2015).

64. Iranian American activists are engaged in an ongoing effort to work with the Census Bureau to improve its reporting on Iranian Americans. See the Public Affairs Alliance of Iranian Americans, "Frequently Asked Questions and Answers U.S. Census & Proposed MENA Category," http://www.paaia.org/CMS/frequently-asked -questions-and-answers—us-census-proposed-mena-category.aspx (accessed August 25, 2015). To view the census data that is available see U.S. Census Bureau, "Table 52. Population by Selected Ancestry Group and Region: 2009," 2009, http://www .census.gov/compendia/statab/2012/tables/12s0052.pdf (accessed August 25, 2015).

65. "Arab American Voters 2014: Their Identity and Political Concerns," Arab American Institute, November 25, 2014, www.aaiusa.org/arab-american-voters-2014-their -identity-and-political-concerns (accessed August 21, 2015).

66. Simone Sebastian, "School Board to Vote on Defying Exit Exam Law," *San Francisco Chronicle*, April 5, 2006, www.sfgate.com/education/article/School-board-to-vote -on-defying-exit-exam-law-2500665.php (accessed July 1, 2015).

67. "Conservatives Launch TV Attack Ad on Dean," *Washington Times*, January 5, 2004, www.washingtontimes.com/news/2004/jan/5/20040105-103754-1355r (accessed August 21, 2015).

68. See Appendix A: Math and Methodology, Table E.

69. See Appendix A.

70. "Election Polls—Vote by Groups, 1960–1964," Gallup Poll, www.gallup.com /poll/9454/election-polls-vote-groups-19601964.aspx (accessed July 1, 2015).

71. "National Election Day Exit Polls," Roper Center of the University of Connecticut, www.ropercenter.uconn.edu/polls/us-elections/exit-polls (accessed August 21, 2015).

72. "How Groups Voted in 2012," Roper Center of the University of Connecticut.

73. "Beyond Red vs. Blue: The Political Typology," Pew Research Center: U.S. Politics & Policy, June 26, 2014, www.people-press.org/2014/06/26/the-political-typology -beyond-red-vs-blue (accessed August 21, 2015).

74. To arrive at the 37 percent figure, I performed the following calculations: The study consisted of 10,013 people. The study refers to "the Left" as "Next Generation Left," "Faith and Family Left," and "Solid Liberals." Appendix 1 of the report shows that Next Generation Left respondents made up 12 percent of the total respondents, the Faith and Family Left group was 15 percent of the total, and Solid Liberals were also 15 percent. Page 92 of the study has responses broken out by racial group, and that table shows that Whites were 68 percent of Next Generation Left, 41 percent of Faith and Family Left, and 69 percent of Solid Liberals. With that baseline data set, I multiplied the share of adults who fell within one of the eight groups by 10,013 (the total number of participants in the study) to get the number of adults in that typology. I then multiplied the White percentage of that typology by the total number of adults to determine the number of Whites who were within that group. Then I added up the raw number of Whites for all three Left typologies to get the number 2,466, which is 37 percent of the total number of White respondents. Also, I used "Adult" and not "Registered Voters," as my emphasis throughout the book has been on those eligible to vote, not necessarily just those already registered.

CHAPTER 3: BLINDED BY THE WHITE

1. James Baldwin, "The White Man's Guilt," *Ebony*, 20:10 (1965), 176.

2. Isabel Wilkerson, "Our Racial Moment of Truth," *New York Times*, July 18, 2015, www.nytimes.com/2015/07/19/opinion/sunday/our-racial-moment-of-truth.html (accessed August 16, 2015).

3. Emma Brown, "Texas officials: Schools should teach that slavery was 'side issue' in Civil War," *Washington Post*, July 5, 2015, www.washingtonpost.com/local/education /150-years-later-schools-are-still-a-battlefield-for-interpreting-civil-war/2015/07/05/ e8fbd57e-2001-11e5-bf41-c23f5d3face1_story.html (accessed August 21, 2015).

4. Lyndsey Layton, "Conservatives Convinced College Board to Rewrite American History," *Washington Post*, July 30, 2015, www.washingtonpost.com/local/education /college-board-rewrites-american-history/2015/07/30/cadadd4c-36d1-11e5-b673-1dfoo 5aofb28_story.html (accessed August 21, 2015).

5. *Dred Scott v. Sandford*, 60 U.S. 393, 407 (1857).

6. Cynthia Roldan, " 'New Day in South Carolina': House Votes to Take Down Confederate Flag," *Post and Courier*, July 8, 2015, www.postandcourier.com/article/20150708/PC1603/150709494 (accessed August 21, 2015).

7. Richard Fausset and Alan Blinder, "Oratory on Confederate Flag in South Carolina Legislature Shows Deep Divisions," *New York Times*, July 8, 2015, www.nytimes.com/2015/07/09/us/confederate-flag-debate-south-carolina-house.html (accessed August 21, 2015).

8. A. Leon Higginbotham, *In the Matter of Color: Race and the American Legal Process: The Colonial Period* (Oxford: Oxford University Press, 1978), 167.

9. "The Preamble to the *South Carolina Slave Code of 1712*," in *Statutes at Large of South Carolina*, vol. 7 (Columbia, SC: A. H. Pemberton State Printer, 1840), 352.

10. U.S. Constitution Article IV, Section 2, Clause 3: "No Person held to Service or Labour in one State, under the Laws thereof, escaping into another, shall, in Consequence of any Law or Regulation therein, be discharged from such Service or Labour, but shall be delivered up on Claim of the Party to whom such Service or Labour may be due."

11. Dr. Cartwright, "Diseases and Peculiarities of the Negro Race," from *De Bow's Review, Southern and Western States*, vol. 11, New Orleans, 1851, PBS, *Africans in America*, PBS.org, www.pbs.org/wgbh/aia/part4/4h3106t.html (accessed August 21, 2015).

12. U.S. Supreme Court, *Johnson & Graham's Lessee v. M'Intosh*, 1823, https://supreme.justia.com/cases/federal/us/21/543/case.html (accessed August 21, 2015).

13. "Indian Removal Act," Library of Congress, www.loc.gov/rr/program/bib/ourdocs/Indian.html (accessed August 21, 2015).

14. Crawford, quoted in *New World Encyclopedia*, says "at least 82,000 men served as regular or guerrilla troops; of these approximately 14,700 were reported as killed or wounded. . . . Civilian losses are even harder to approximate." For more information, see Mark Crawford, David Stephen Heidler, and Jeanne T. Heidler, *Encyclopedia of the Mexican American War* (Santa Barbara, CA: ABC-CLIO, 1999), 68. Also see Tom Gray, "Teaching with Documents: The Treaty of Guadalupe Hidalgo," National Archives, www.archives.gov/education/lessons/guadalupe-hidalgo (accessed August 21, 2015).

15. "Native Americans in the Gold Rush," PBS, *The American Experience: The Gold Rush*, PBS.org, www.pbs.org/wgbh/amex/goldrush/sfeature/natives_03.html (accessed August 21, 2015). For present-time value of 1852 dollars see Consumer Price Index (Estimate) 1800, Federal Reserve Bank of Minneapolis, www.minneapolisfed.org/community/teaching-aids/cpi-calculator-information/consumer-price-index-1800 (accessed August 21, 2015).

16. *Plessy v. Ferguson*, 163 U.S. 537, 550, 552 (1896).

17. The Court's actual holding is, "We conclude that, in the field of *public education*, the doctrine of 'separate but equal' has no place. Separate *educational facilities* are inherently unequal" (emphasis added). See *Brown v. Board of Education of Topeka*, 347 US 483, 495 (1954).

18. Immigration Naturalization Act of 1790, Chapter 3, Section 1, http://library.uwb.edu/guides/usimmigration/1%20stat%20103.pdf (accessed August 21, 2015).

19. *Dred Scott v. Sandford*, 60 U.S. 393, 420 (1857).

20. *Takao Ozawa v. United States*, 260 U.S. 178 (1922). Also see *United States v. Bhagat Singh Thind*, 261 U.S. 204 (1923).

21. "Chinese Exclusion Act (1882)," Our Documents, www.ourdocuments.gov/doc.php?flash=true&doc=47 (accessed August 21, 2015).

22. "The Immigration Act of 1924 (The Johnson-Reed Act)," U.S. Department of State, Office of the Historian, https://history.state.gov/milestones/1921-1936/immigration-act (accessed August 21, 2015).

23. Joseph A. Hill, "The Problem of Determining the National Origin of the American People," address at the Social Science Conference, Hanover, NH (August 25, 1926), 7, file 17, box 2, Quota Board Papers." Quoted in Mae M. Ngai, *Impossible Subjects: Illegal Aliens and the Making of Modern America* (Princeton, NJ: Princeton University Press, 2004), Chapter 1, "The Johnson-Reed Act of 1924 and the Reconstruction of Race in Immigration Law."

24. Ngai, *Impossible Subjects*, Introduction.

25. *The Daily Show*, "Barack Obama Pt. 1," Comedy Central, April 21, 2008, http://thedailyshow.cc.com/videos/supb9b/barack-obama-pt—1 (accessed August 21, 2015).

26. Lynn Langton, Michael Planty, and Nathan Sandholtz, "Hate Crime Victimization, 2003–2011," U.S. Department of Justice, Office of Justice Programs, Bureau of Justice Statistics, March 21, 2013, www.bjs.gov/index.cfm?ty=pbdetail&iid=4614 (accessed August 21, 2015).

27. E. Ann Carson, "Prisoners in 2013," U.S. Department of Justice, Office of Justice Programs, Bureau of Justice Statistics, September 30, 2014, www.bjs.gov/content/pub/pdf/p13.pdf (accessed August 21, 2015).

28. Big Bill Broonzy, "Black, Brown, and White," YouTube, www.youtube.com/watch?v=koc1coZsTLA (accessed August 21, 2015).

29. Rachel D. Godsil, Linda R. Tropp, Phillip Atiba Goff, and john a. powell, "Addressing Implicit Bias, Racial Anxiety, and Stereotype Threat in Education and Health Care," *The Science of Equality*, Volume 1, November 2014, 3.

30. john a. powell, "How Implicit Bias and Structural Racialization Can Move Us Toward Social and Personal Healing," *Pathways to Racial Healing and Equity in the American South*, 40, http://clintonschool.uasys.edu/wp-content/uploads/2013/12/Clinton-School-Compendium-2013.pdf (accessed August 31, 2015). For more on implicit bias, the Kirwan Institute for the Study of Race and Ethnicity, the Perception Institute, the Haas Institute for a Fair and Inclusive Society, and the Center for Social Inclusion have excellent collections of articles, essays, and books on the topic.

31. Wilkerson, "Our Racial Moment of Truth."

32. Marianne Bertrand and Sendhil Mullainathan, "Are Emily and Greg More Employable than Lakisha and Jamal? A Field Experiment on Labor Market Discrimination,"

National Bureau of Economic Research, July 2003, www.nber.org/papers/w9873.pdf (accessed August 21, 2015).

33. Claire Zillman, "Microsoft's New CEO: One Minority Exec in a Sea of White," *Fortune*, February 4, 2014, http://fortune.com/2014/02/04/microsofts-new-ceo-one -minority-exec-in-a-sea-of-white (accessed August 21, 2015).

34. The data is based on 185 investments in Internet companies in the first half of 2010. See "Venture Capital Human Capital Report," CB Insights, August 3, 2010, www .cbinsights.com/blog/venture-capital-human-capital-report (accessed August 21, 2015).

35. U.S. Department of Education, National Center for Education Statistics, "The Condition of Education 2015, Characteristics of Postsecondary Faculty: Fast Facts," 2015, http://nces.ed.gov/fastfacts/display.asp?id=61 (accessed August 21, 2015).

36. "2014 Census," American Society of News Editors, July 29, 2014, http://asne .org/content.asp?pl=121&sl=387&contentid=387 (accessed August 21, 2015).

37. Darnell Hunt, Ana-Christina Ramon, and Zachary Price, "2014 Hollywood Diversity Report: Making Sense of the Disconnect," Ralph J. Bunche Center for African American Studies at UCLA, 2014, www.bunchecenter.ucla.edu/wp-content/uploads /2014/02/2014-Hollywood-Diversity-Report-2-12-14.pdf (accessed August 21, 2015).

38. Who Leads Us?, Reflective Democracy Campaign, http://wholeads.us (accessed August 21, 2015).

39. "National: Few See Improvements in Race Relations Under Obama," Al Jazeera America/Monmouth University Poll, January 19, 2015, www.monmouth.edu/assets /0/32212254770/32212254991/32212254992/32212254994/32212254995/300647710 87/cb87f8b6-582c-4624-8b1c-41916f76bb44.pdf (accessed August 21, 2015).

40. "The Rise of Asian Americans," Pew Research Center: Social & Demographic Trends, www.pewsocialtrends.org/asianamericans-graphics (accessed August 21, 2015).

41. Peter A. Dorsey, *Common Bondage: Slavery as Metaphor in Revolutionary America* (Knoxville: University of Tennessee Press, 2009), 86.

42. See David Armitage, *The Declaration of Independence: A Global History* (Cambridge, MA: Harvard University Press, 2007), 77. Also see Jefferson's "original rough draft" of the Declaration of Independence, Library of Congress, www.loc.gov/exhibits /declara/ruffdrft.html (accessed August 21, 2015).

43. "Fourth Debate: Charleston, Illinois," National Park Service: Lincoln Home, www.nps.gov/liho/learn/historyculture/debate4.htm (accessed August 21, 2015).

44. Eric Foner, "Reconstruction," *Encyclopaedia Britannica*, www.britannica.com/EB checked/topic/493722/Reconstruction/295416/The-end-of-Reconstruction (accessed August 21, 2015).

45. Ira Katznelson, *Fear Itself* (New York: Norton, 2013), 268.

46. Branch, *At Canaan's Edge*, Chapter 6.

47. Peter Applebome, "The 1992 Campaign: Death Penalty; Arkansas Execution Raises Questions on Governor's Politics," *New York Times*, January 25, 1992, www

.nytimes.com/1992/01/25/us/1992-campaign-death-penalty-arkansas-execution-raises
-questions-governor-s.html (accessed August 21, 2015).

48. Paul Rosenberg, "Bill Clinton's Gutsy Apologies: Now He Owes One to Ricky Ray Rector," *Salon*, July 25, 2015, www.salon.com/2015/07/25/bill_clintons_gutsy_apolo gies_now_he_owes_one_to_ricky_ray_rector (accessed August 21, 2015).

49. "Obama Delivers Eulogy in Charleston," *New York Times*, Times Video, June 27, 2015, www.nytimes.com/video/us/100000003767801/obama-delivers-eulogy-in -charleston.html (accessed August 21, 2015).

CHAPTER 4: REQUIEM FOR THE WHITE SWING VOTER

1. Evan McMorris-Santoro and John Stanton, "New Democratic Governors Chair: Party's Priority Shouldn't Be Winning Back White Men," *BuzzFeed News*, March 24, 2015, www.buzzfeed.com/evanmcsan/new-democratic-governors-chair-partys-priority -shoudnt-be-wi#.fjj6r7P57Z (accessed August 21, 2015).

2. Jonathan Martin and Maggie Haberman, "Hillary Clinton Traces Familiar Path, Troubling Party," *New York Times*, June 6, 2015, www.nytimes.com/2015/06/07/us/pol itics/hillary-clinton-traces-friendly-path-troubling-party.html (accessed August 21, 2015).

3. Stanley B. Greenberg, "Goodbye, Reagan Democrats," *New York Times*, November 10, 2008, www.nytimes.com/2008/11/11/opinion/11greenberg.html?_r=2&ref =opinion&oref=slogin (accessed August 21, 2015).

4. Neil MacFarquhar, "What's a Soccer Mom Anyway?," *New York Times*, October 20, 1996, www.nytimes.com/1996/10/20/weekinreview/what-s-a-soccer-mom-anyway.html (accessed August 21, 2015).

5. Peter Wallsten, "Bush Sees Fertile Soil in 'Exurbia,'" *Los Angeles Times*, June 28, 2004, http://articles.latimes.com/2004/jun/28/nation/na-exurban28 (accessed August 21, 2015).

6. Greenberg, "Goodbye Reagan Democrats."

7. Robert Draper, "The Great Democratic Crack Up of 2016," *New York Times Magazine*, May 12, 2015, www.nytimes.com/2015/05/17/magazine/the-great-demo cratic-crack-up-of-2016.html?_r=0 (accessed August 21, 2015).

8. David Brooks, "The Field Is Flat," *New York Times*, March 27, 2015, www.nytimes .com/2015/03/27/opinion/david-brooks-the-field-is-flat.html (accessed August 21, 2015).

9. Alex Roarty, "Can Clinton Win Back the White Working Class?," *National Journal*, November 30, 2014, www.nationaljournal.com/politics/can-clinton-win-back-the -white-working-class-20141130 (accessed August 21, 2015).

10. Stanley Greenberg, "The Average Joe's Proviso," *Washington Monthly*, June/July/August 2015, www.washingtonmonthly.com/magazine/junejulyaugust_2015/features /the_average_joes_proviso055824.php (accessed August 21, 2015).

11. See "Election Polls—Vote by Groups, 1960–1964," Gallup Poll, www.gallup
.com/poll/9454/election-polls-vote-groups-19601964.aspx (accessed July 1, 2015). Also
see "How Groups Voted," Roper Center of the University of Connecticut.

12. In 2012, Obama received 65,915,796 votes to Romney's 60,933,500 votes, winning reelection by a margin of 4,982,296 votes. The Federal Election Commission's
official election results show that 129,085,403 people cast ballots, and according to the
National Exit Poll, Whites comprised 72 percent of all voters. That 72 percent translates
to 92.9 million White voters casting a ballot in 2012. Obama received 39 percent of
those White voters, and 59 percent of them voted for Romney (the other 2 percent voted
for the minor party candidates). What that means is that Obama received 36,247,181
White votes, and Romney received 54,835,479 White votes. The rest of Obama's 66 million votes came from people of color, who cast 29,668,815 ballots to reelect the president. If Obama had received 36.5 percent of the total White votes, his number of White
votes would have fallen from 36,247,181 to 33,923,644, a drop of 2.3 million votes. But
Obama won by a hair shy of 5 million votes, so he could have lost all 2.3 million of those
White voters to Romney and still have had 63,592,259 of all voters, leaving him 335,221
votes ahead of Romney. The bottom line is that with as little as 36.5 percent of the White
vote, Obama would still have won the popular vote in 2012.

13. See Office of the Clerk, U.S. House of Representatives, "Election Statistics,"
http://clerk.house.gov/member_info/electionInfo/ (accessed September 25, 2015).

14. Algernon Austin, *America Is Not Post-racial: Xenophobia, Islamophobia, Racism,
and the 44th President* (Santa Barbara, CA: Praeger, 2015).

15. Lorraine C. Miller, "Statistics of the Presidential and Congressional Election of
November 4, 2008," Office of the Clerk, U.S. House of Representatives, July 10, 2009,
http://history.house.gov/Institution/Election-Statistics/2008election/ (accessed August 21, 2015).

16. Karen L. Hass, "Statistics of the Congressional Election of November 2, 2010,"
Office of the Clerk, U.S. House of Representatives, June 3, 2011, http://history.house
.gov/Institution/Election-Statistics/2010election/ (accessed August 21, 2015).

17. Election 2010 House Map, *New York Times*, http://elections.nytimes.com/2010
/results/house (accessed August 21, 2015).

18. Miller, "Statistics of the Presidential and Congressional Election of November 4,
2008." Also see Karen L. Hass, "Statistics of the Congressional Election of November
4, 2014," Office of the Clerk, U.S. House of Representatives, March 9, 2015, http://
clerk.house.gov/member_info/electionInfo/2014/114-statistics.pdf (accessed August
21, 2015).

19. Hass, "Statistics of the Congressional Election of November 4, 2014."

20. The sources for the raw number of votes for the elections of 2008–2014 can be
found in the immediately preceding footnotes. The exit polls conducted include a national House of Representatives exit poll in midterm elections with a racial breakdown
of the voters, but not a national Senate exit poll. Nonetheless, the Republicans received

6 million fewer votes overall in the 2014 Senate races than in the 2008 Senate races, so their number of Whites would also have obviously gone down, not up.

21. Jonathan Chait, "Dan Pfeiffer's Exit Interview: How the White House Learned to Be Liberal," *New York*, March 8, 2015, http://nymag.com/daily/intelligencer/2015/03 /dan-pfeiffer-exit-interview.html (accessed August 21, 2015).

22. "The Uninsured: A Primer: Key Facts about Americans without Health Insurance," Kaiser Commission on Medicaid and the Uninsured, October 2012, https:// kaiserfamilyfoundation.files.wordpress.com/2013/01/7451-08.pdf (accessed August 21, 2015).

23. "Party Divisions of the House of Representatives," History, Art & Archives, U.S. House of Representatives, http://history.house.gov/Institution/Party-Divisions/74 -Present/ (accessed August 21, 2015).

24. Chris Frates, "CBO: Bend the Cost Curve, What Does That Mean?," *Politico*, October 30, 2009, www.politico.com/livepulse/1009/CBO_Bend_the_cost_curve_what _does_that_even_mean.html (accessed August 21, 2015).

25. "How Will Obamacare Affect Me?," Obamacare Facts, http://obamacarefacts .com/how-will-obamacare-affect-me (accessed August 21, 2015).

26. David Axelrod, *Believer: My Forty Years in Politics* (New York: Penguin Press, 2015), Chapter 25.

27. Rick Cohen, "ACA Implementation and Low Confidence in Government," *Nonprofit Quarterly*, November 25, 2014, https://nonprofitquarterly.org/policysocial -context/25221-aca-implementation-and-low-confidence-in-government.html (accessed August 21, 2015).

28. Barack Obama, "Remarks by the President at the Catholic Health Association Conference," White House, Office of the Press Secretary, June 9, 2015, www.white house.gov/the-press-office/2015/06/09/remarks-president-catholic-health-association -conference (accessed August 21, 2015).

29. Axelrod, *Believer*.

30. *2013 Yearbook of Immigration Statistics*, Department of Homeland Security, Office of Immigration Statistics, August 2014, www.dhs.gov/sites/default/files/publi cations/ois_yb_2013_0.pdf (accessed August 21, 2015).

31. Suzy Khimm, "Obama Is Deporting Immigrants Faster than Bush. Republicans Don't Think That's Enough," *Washington Post*, August 27, 2012, www.washington-post.com/blogs/wonkblog/wp/2012/08/27/obama-is-deporting-more-immigrants-than-bush-republicans-dont-think-thats-enough (accessed August 21, 2015).

32. Seth Freed Wessler, "How Immigration Reform Got Caught in the Deportation Dragnet," *Colorlines*, October 7, 2010, www.colorlines.com/articles/how-immigration -reform-got-caught-deportation-dragnet (accessed August 21, 2015).

33. Mark Hugo Lopez and Paul Taylor, "Latino Voters in the 2012 Election," Pew Research Center, November 7, 2012, www.pewhispanic.org/2012/11/07/latino-voters -in-the-2012-election (accessed August 21, 2015).

34. Jennifer Steinhauer, "Speaker 'Confident' of Deal with White House on Immigration," *New York Times*, November 8, 2012, www.nytimes.com/2012/11/09/us/politics/boehner-confident-of-deal-with-white-house-on-immigration.html (accessed August 21, 2015).

35. Richard Gonzales, "Activists: We Want an Emancipation, not a 'Deporter in Chief,'" NPR, March 29, 2014, www.npr.org/sections/codeswitch/2014/03/29/296290027/activists-we-want-an-emancipator-not-a-deporter-in-chief (accessed August 21, 2015).

36. Benjy Sarlin, "Udall rallies Latinos, but leaders fear it's too little, too late," MSNBC, November 4, 2014, www.msnbccom/msnbc/udall-rallies-latinos-leaders-fear-its-too-little-too-late (accessed August 21, 2015).

37. Hass, "Statistics of the Congressional Election of November 4, 2014," Office of the Clerk, U.S. House of Representatives, March 9, 2015, http://clerk.house.gov/member_info/electionInfo/2014/114-statistics.pdf (accessed August 21, 2015). The 2014 exit poll showed that Latinos comprised 14 percent of the 2,041,058 total votes cast in the Senate race, which would be 285,748 Latino voters. See also "America's Choice 2014: Election Center, Senate," www.cnn.com/election/2014/results/state/CO/senate (accessed August 21, 2015). As of 2013, there were 497,000 Latinos who were eligible to vote. See also U.S. Census Bureau, Current Population Survey, November 2012; Table 4b. Reported Voting and Registration, by Sex, Race and Hispanic Origin, for States: November 2012.

38. Jason Zengerle, "Alison Lundergan Grimes Is Running the Worst Senate Campaign of the Year," *New Republic*, October 12, 2014, www.newrepublic.com/article/119800/alison-lundergan-grimes-2014-senate-campaign-disaster (accessed August 21, 2015).

39. Ruben Navarrette Jr., "Latinos Aren't a Cheap Date for Democrats Anymore," *Daily Beast*, November 11, 2014, www.thedailybeast.com/articles/2014/11/11/latinos-aren-t-a-cheap-date-for-democrats-anymore.html (accessed August 21, 2015).

40. "Lorraine Hansberry—The Black Revolution and the White Backlash: Forum at Town Hall sponsored by The Association of Artists for Freedom," American Radioworks, American Public Media, http://americanradioworks.publicradio.org/features/blackspeech/lhansberry.html (accessed August 21, 2015). Also see James Baldwin's essay "Sweet Lorraine," in *To Be Young, Gifted and Black: Lorraine Hansberry in Her Own Words*, adapted by Robert Nemiroff (New York: Vintage Books, 1995), xviii.

CHAPTER 5: FEWER SMART-ASS WHITE BOYS

1. "Young Regrets His Choice of Words but Not His Message," UPI, August 24, 1984, www.upi.com/Archives/1984/08/24/Young-regrets-his-choice-of-words-but-not-his-message/6604462168000 (accessed August 21, 2015).

2. See Timothy J. Minchin and John A. Salmond, *After the Dream: Black and White Southerners Since 1965* (Lexington: University Press of Kentucky, 2011), 134.

3. Richard Prince's Journal-isms "Right About Smart-Ass White Boys: Andrew Young, at NABJ, Stands by Words of 30 Years Ago," Maynard Institute, August 1, 2014, http://mije.org/richardprince/right-about-smart-ass-white-boys (accessed August 21, 2015).

4. See Who Leads Us?, Reflective Democracy Campaign, http://wholeads.us (accessed August 21, 2015). Also see "Election Results 2008, Exit Polls," *New York Times*, November 5, 2008, http://elections.nytimes.com/2008/results/president/exit-polls (accessed August 21, 2015).

5. And, for the record, some of my best friends are White guys.

6. For purposes of the audit report, "Democratic Party" or "Party" referred, collectively, to all three of the largest Democratic Party committees: the Democratic National Committee (DNC), the Democratic Congressional Campaign Committee (DCCC), and the Democratic Senatorial Campaign Committee (DSCC). The audit looked at money spent on procurement and contracting, defined as outside purchase of goods or services necessary for the electoral program operations of the Party. See Julie Martinez Ortega and Steve Phillips, "2014 Fannie Lou Hamer Report: Analysis and Review of Democratic Spending," PowerPAC+, 2014, http://www.powerpacplus.org/2014_fannie_lou _hamer_report (accessed August 25, 2015).

7. Branch, *Pillar of Fire*, Chapter 34, "A Dog in the Manger—The Atlantic City Compromise."

8. Ortega and Phillips, "2014 Fannie Lou Hamer Report."

9. The party committees spent a total of $476 million in 2014. The party committees spent $193 million in 2014 on consulting firms. The party committee expenditures went to 108 consulting firms, 15 of which were minority-owned/senior leadership is minority. Minority-owned consulting firms earned 2.1 percent of party committees' expenditures to consulting firms and 0.9 percent of total expenditures made. The analysis of 2014 spending was conducted by PowerPAC+, but the results have not been released publicly.

10. Getting an accurate read on election spending requires art, science, and a little bit of magic. The reporting rules are porous and inconsistent, with little prospect of imminent improvement. Nevertheless, the $200 million figure comes from combining the information at opensecrets.org and the FEC's site showing that NextGen Climate action spent $74 million in 2014. For more information, see "2014 Outside Spending, by Group," OpenSecrets.org, www.opensecrets.org/outsidespending/summ.php ?cycle=2014&type=p&disp=O (accessed August 21, 2015). Also see the Federal Election Commission's Candidate and Committee Viewer, www.fec.gov/finance/disclo sure/candcmte_info.shtml (accessed August 21, 2015).

11. See "Partners," in "About Us: Leadership" on GMMB's website, www.gmmb .com/about/leadership (accessed August 21, 2015). The Partners are the top level of leadership at the company.

12. Tom McGinty and Brody Mullins, "Political Spending by Unions Far Exceeds Direct Donations," *Wall Street Journal*, July 10, 2012, www.wsj.com/articles/SB100014 24052702304782404577488584031850026 (accessed August 21, 2015).

13. To determine the number of AFL–CIO unions run by White men, I used pictures and biographies for all fifty-six of the presidents of the unions to determine their race and gender.

14. Paul Frymer, *Black and Blue: African Americans, the Labor Movement, and the Decline of the Democratic Party* (Princeton, NJ: Princeton University Press, 2007), Chapter 6.

15. Sarah Hansen, "Cultivating the Grassroots: A Winning Approach for Environment and Climate Funders," National Committee for Responsive Philanthropy, February 2012, http://ncrp.org/files/publications/Cultivating_the_grassroots_final_lowres.pdf (accessed August 21, 2015).

16. Dorceta E. Taylor, "The State of Diversity in Environmental Organizations," Green 2.0, July 2014, http://diversegreen.org/wp-content/uploads/sites/4/2014/07/FullReport_Green2.0_FINAL.pdf (accessed August 21, 2015).

17. Chris Mooney, "Environmental Groups Are Spending an Unprecedented $85 Million in the 2014 Elections," *Washington Post*, October 27, 2014, www.washingtonpost.com/blogs/wonkblog/wp/2014/10/27/environmental-groups-are-spending-an-unprecedented-85-million-in-the-2014-elections (accessed August 21, 2015).

18. "State of the Work, Executive Summary: Tackling the Tough Challenges to Advancing Diversity, Equity, and Inclusion," D5 Coalition, 2014, p. 4, www.d5coalition.org/wp-content/uploads/2014/07/D5-State-of-the-Work-Executive-Summary-2014.pdf (accessed August 21, 2015).

19. Gwen Ifill, "The Transition; Clinton Chooses 2 and Deplores Idea of Cabinet Quotas," *New York Times*, December 22, 1992, www.nytimes.com/1992/12/22/us/the-transition-clinton-chooses-2-and-deplores-idea-of-cabinet-quotas.html (accessed August 21, 2015).

20. William J. Baumol et al., *Good Capitalism, Bad Capitalism, and the Economics of Growth* (New Haven, CT: Yale University Press, 2007), 228.

21. David Carr, "How Obama Tapped into Social Networks' Power," *New York Times*, November 9, 2008, www.nytimes.com/2008/11/10/business/media/10carr.html (accessed August 21, 2015).

22. Susan Yaochum, "At the Other End of Brown's 800 Line," *San Francisco Chronicle*, April 1, 1992. For an image of the article, see Peter Hartlaub, "Jerry Brown's 1-800 presidential hotline still works!," *SFGate*, October 2, 2013, http://blog.sfgate.com/thebigevent/2013/10/02/breaking-jerry-browns-1-800-presidential-hotline-still-works (accessed August 21, 2015).

23. Hartlaub, "Jerry Brown's 1-800 presidential hotline still works!"

24. Michael Cornfield, "The Internet and Campaign 2004: A Look Back at the Campaigners," Pew Internet Research Center, www.pewinternet.org/files/old-media/Files/Reports/2005/Cornfield_commentary.pdf.pdf (accessed August 21, 2015).

25. Gary Wolf, "How the Internet Invented Howard Dean," *Wired*, January 2004, http://archive.wired.com/wired/archive/12.01/dean.html (accessed August 21, 2015).

26. Katharine Q. Seelye, "How to Sell a Candidate to a Porsche-Driving, Leno-Loving Nascar Fan," *New York Times*, December 6, 2004, www.nytimes.com/2004/12/06 /politics/06strategy.html (accessed August 21, 2015).

27. Branch, *Pillar of Fire*, Chapter 40, "Saigon, Audobon and Selma."

28. See Denis Brennan, *The Making of an Abolitionist: William Lloyd Garrison's Path to Publishing The Liberator* (Jefferson, NC: McFarland, 2014), 148. And see "Pro-Slavery Mob Destroys Abolitionist's Printing Press," National Constitution Center, http://con stitutioncenter.org/timeline/html/cw04_11999.html (accessed August 21, 2015).

29. Jon Meacham, *American Lion: Andrew Jackson in the White House* (New York: Random House, 2008), 305.

30. "Obama's Inner Circle Shares Inside Story," CBS News, November 7, 2008, www.cbsnews.com/news/obamas-inner-circle-shares-inside-story (accessed August 21, 2015).

31. Trey Ellis, "No Matter What We Say Now Every Black Person in America Will Vote for Obama," *Huffington Post*, August 14, 2007, www.huffingtonpost.com/trey-ellis /no-matter-what-we-say-now_b_60369.html (accessed August 22, 2015).

32. Bill Schneider, "Poll: As Thompson's Star Fades, Clinton's on the Rise," CNN, October 16, 2007, www.cnn.com/2007/POLITICS/10/16/schneider.poll/index.html (accessed August 22, 2015).

33. Ellis, "No Matter What We Say."

34. John M. Broder, "Obama and Clinton Settle In for the Long Run," *New York Times*, February 6, 2008, www.nytimes.com/2008/02/06/us/politics/06cnd-campaign .html?_r=0 (accessed August 22, 2015).

35. See Election Guide 2008, "Results: Democratic Delegate Count," 2008, *New York Times*, http://politics.nytimes.com/election-guide/2008/results/delegates/ (accessed August 22, 2015).

36. Ibid. Also see Leonie Huddy and Tony E. Carey Jr., "Group Politics Redux: Race and Gender in the 2008 Democratic Presidential Primaries," *Politics & Gender* 5, no. 1 (2009), https://rooneycenter.nd.edu/assets/16534/huddy_carey2009pol_gender.pdf (accessed August 22, 2015).

37. "2008 Democratic Delegates," Real Clear Politics, www.realclearpolitics.com /epolls/2008/president/democratic_delegate_count.html (accessed August 22, 2015).

38. Mark Hugo Lopez and Paul Taylor, "Dissecting the 2008 Electorate: Most Diverse in History," Pew Research Center, April 30, 2009, www.pewhispanic.org/2009/04/30 /dissecting-the-2008-electorate-most-diverse-in-us-history (accessed August 22, 2015).

39. William H. Frey, "10 Maps That Explain the Next Election," *Politico*, November 18, 2014, www.politico.com/magazine/story/2014/11/10-maps-that-explain-the -next-election-113002.html#.VWgaAmDAzCk (accessed August 22, 2015).

40. Christopher Edley Jr., "Race in America Roundtable Round One: Opening Remarks," *Atlantic*, November 13, 1997, www.theatlantic.com/past/docs/unbound/forum /race/edley1.htm (accessed August 22, 2015).

41. "Financial Release: Starbucks Unveils Accelerated Global Growth Plans," Starbucks Investor Relations, December 5, 2012, http://investor.starbucks.com/phoenix .zhtml?c=99518&p=irol-newsArticle&ID=1764541 (accessed August 22, 2015).

42. Helen H. Wang, "Five Things Starbucks Did to Get China Right," *Forbes*, August 12, 2012, www.forbes.com/sites/helenwang/2012/08/10/five-things-starbucks -did-to-get-china-right (accessed August 22, 2015).

43. "Starbucks' Quest for Healthy Growth: An Interview with Howard Schultz," *McKinsey Quarterly*, March 2011, www.mckinsey.com/insights/growth/starbucks_quest _for_healthy_growth_an_interview_with_howard_schultz (accessed August 23, 2015).

44. Amnon Cavari, Richard J. Powell, and Kenneth R. Mayer, eds., *The 2012 Presidential Election: Forecasts, Outcomes, and Consequences* (Lanham, MD: Rowman & Littlefield, 2014), 26.

45. "Jeremiah Wright," *Bill Moyers Journal*, PBS, April 25, 2008, www.pbs.org/moyers /journal/04252008/profile.html (accessed August 23, 2015).

46. Brian Ross and Rehab El-Buri, "Obama's Pastor: God Damn America, U.S. to Blame for 9/11," ABC News, March 13, 2008, http://abcnews.go.com/Blotter/Democratic Debate/story?id=4443788 (accessed August 23, 2015).

47. "Obama's Brain Trust Speaks," *Huffington Post*, December 11, 2008, www.huff ingtonpost.com/2008/11/10/obamas-brain-trust-speaks_n_142606.html (accessed August 23, 2015).

48. Heather E. Harris, ed., *The Obama Effect: Multidisciplinary Renderings of the 2008 Campaign* (Albany: State University of New York Press, 2010), 32. See also Axelrod, *Believer*, Chapter 18.

49. "Text of Obama's Speech: A More Perfect Union," *Wall Street Journal*, March 18, 2008, http://blogs.wsj.com/washwire/2008/03/18/text-of-obamas-speech-a-more -perfect-union (accessed August 23, 2015).

50. Ibid.

51. "Transcript for March 18, 2008," *Hardball with Chris Matthews*, MSNBC, www .nbcnews.com/id/23707778/ns/msnbc-hardball_with_chris_matthews/t/hardball-chris-matthews-march/#.VWglI2DAzCk (accessed August 23, 2015).

52. "Mr. Obama's Profile in Courage," *New York Times*, March 19, 2008, www.nytimes .com/2008/03/19/opinion/19wed1.html/ (accessed August 23, 2015).

53. Teresa Wiltz, "Obama Has Jay-Z on His iPod and the Moves to Prove It," *Washington Post*, April 19, 2008, www.washingtonpost.com/wp-dyn/content/article /2008/04/18/AR2008041803282.html (accessed August 23, 2015). For the speech itself, see "Barack Obama in Raleigh, NC," YouTube, www.youtube.com/watch ?v=FlR9DNfqGD4 (accessed August 23, 2015).

54. Rida Hamida, personal communication, March 25, 2015.

55. For more on the efforts of many Arab Americans to improve the census forms, see Jens Manuel Krogstad, "Census Bureau Explores New Middle East/North Africa Ethnic Category," Pew Research Center, March 24, 2014, www.pewresearch.org/fact-tank

/2014/03/24/census-bureau-explores-new-middle-eastnorth-africa-ethnic-category/ (accessed August 17, 2015).

CHAPTER 6: INVEST WISELY

1. See "2012 Presidential Race," Center for Responsive Politics, OpenSecrets.org, www.opensecrets.org/pres12/index.php (accessed August 23, 2015).

2. See "Democratic Party: Fundraising Overview 2014," Center for Responsive Politics, OpenSecrets.org, www.opensecrets.org/parties/totals.php?cycle=2014&cmte =DPC (accessed August 23, 2015).

3. Stephen Labaton, "The 1992 Campaign: Campaign Finances; Despite Economy, Clinton Sets Record for Funds," New York Times, October 24, 1992, www.nytimes .com/1992/10/24/us/1992-campaign-campaign-finances-despite-economy-clinton -sets-record-for-funds.html (accessed August 23, 2015).

4. See Philip Elliott, "Barak Obama: First President Who Fails to Raise as Much Money as Opponent?," Christian Science Monitor, July 18, 2012, www.csmonitor.com /USA/Elections/From-the-Wires/2012/0718/Barack-Obama-First-president-who-fails -to-raise-as-much-money-as-opponent (accessed August 23, 2015). Also see Abby Liv-ingston, "President Obama, Democrats Have Best Fundraising Month of Cycle," Roll Call, October 6, 2012, http://atr.rollcall.com/president-obama-democrats-have-best -fundraising-month-of-cycle (accessed August 23, 2015). Also see Byron Tau, "Obama Campaign Final Fundraising Total: $1.1 Billion," Politico, January 19, 2013, www.politico .com/story/2013/01/obama-campaign-final-fundraising-total-1-billion-86445.html (accessed August 23, 2015).

5. Gabriel DeBenedetti, "Hillary Clinton Rakes In $45 Million in Her First Quarter," Politico, July 1, 2015, www.politico.com/story/2015/07/hillary-clinton-campaign-fund raising-first-quarter-119636.html (accessed August 23, 2015).

6. Kenneth P. Vogel, Big Money: 2.5 Billion Dollars, One Suspicious Vehicle, and a Pimp—on the Trail of the Ultra-Rich Hijacking American Politics (New York: Public-Affairs, 2014), Chapter 1.

7. See "2012 Presidential Race," Center for Responsive Politics, OpenSecrets.org, www.opensecrets.org/pres12/index.php (accessed August 23, 2015). Also see Tau, "Obama campaign final fundraising total: $1.1 billion."

8. See "Mobile Technology Fact Sheet," Pew Research Center: Internet Science & Tech, October 2014, www.pewinternet.org/fact-sheets/mobile-technology-fact-sheet (accessed August 23, 2015).

9. Aaron Smith, "Real Time Charitable Giving," Pew Research Center: Internet, Science & Tech, January 12, 2012, www.pewinternet.org/2012/01/12/real-time-chari table-giving (accessed August 23, 2015). And see "Mobile Technology Fact Sheet," Pew Research Center.

10. Mike Roberts and Lauren Barley, "Four VCs on Evaluating Opportunities," Working Knowledge: The Thinking that Leads, Harvard Business School, May 2, 2005, http://hbswk.hbs.edu/item/4780.html (accessed August 23, 2015).

11. Tim Higgins, "Apple iPhones Sales in China Outsell the U.S. for First Time," *Bloomberg Business*, April 27, 2015, www.bloomberg.com/news/articles/2015-04-27 /apple-s-iphones-sales-in-china-outsell-the-u-s-for-first-time (accessed August 23, 2015).

12. See Lindsay Hixon, Bradford B. Hepler, and Myoung Ouk Kim, "The White Population: 2010," U.S. Census Bureau, September 2011, www.census.gov/prod/cen2010 /briefs/c2010br-05.pdf (accessed August 23, 2015). And see Sonya Rastogi, Tallese D. Johnson, Elizabeth M. Hoeffel, and Malcolm P. Drewery Jr., "The Black Population: 2010," U.S. Census Bureau, September 2011, www.census.gov/prod/cen2010/briefs /c2010br-06.pdf (accessed August 23, 2015); Elizabeth M. Hoeffel, Sonya Rastogi, Myoung Ouk Kim, and Hasan Shahid, "The Asian Population: 2010," U.S. Census Bureau, March 2012, www.census.gov/prod/cen2010/briefs/c2010br-11.pdf (accessed August 23, 2015); Jeffrey S. Passel, D'Vera Cohn, and Mark Hugo Lopez, "Hispanics Account for More than Half of Nation's Growth in Past Decade," Pew Research Center: Hispanic Trends, March 24, 2011, www.pewhispanic.org/2011/03/24/hispanics -account-for-more-than-half-of-nations-growth-in-past-decade (accessed August 23, 2015).

13. See Anna Brown and Mark Hugo Lopez, "Mapping the Latino Population, By State, County, and City," Pew Research Center: Hispanic Trends, August 29, 2013, www.pewhispanic.org/2013/08/29/mapping-the-latino-population-by-state-county -and-city (accessed August 23, 2015). And see Aaron M. Renn, "The Shifting Geography of Black America," New Geography, August 5, 2011, www.newgeography.com /content/002371-the-shifting-geography-black-america (accessed August 23, 2015).

14. Matt Bloch, Matthew Ericson, and Kevin Quealy, "Census 2010: Gains and Losses in Congress," *New York Times*, 2010, www.nytimes.com/interactive/2010/12/21/us /census-districts.html?_r=0 (accessed August 23, 2015).

15. Had Kerry won Ohio, he would have won the presidency. He lost Ohio by just 118,000 votes. According to the exit polls, the African American vote total was 10 percent of all 5.6 million votes cast. Had Kerry received 96 percent of those votes instead of the 84 percent he garnered, that would have resulted in a switch of 135,000 votes, tipping the election—and the White House—to Kerry.

16. U.S. Census Bureau, Current Population Survey, November 2012; Table 4b.

17. Michael Lewis, *The Big Short: Inside the Doomsday Machine* (New York: Penguin Books, 2011), 127.

18. A good glossary of many of these and other terms can be found at the Roper Center's Public Opinion Archives site, www.ropercenter.uconn.edu/education/polling _fundamentals_glossary.html (accessed August 23, 2015).

19. Keith Ellison, personal communication, July 22, 2015.

20. According to the exit polls, Whites comprised 75 percent of the 4,136,821 votes cast in the Senate contest, which would mean that 3,102,616 White people voted. Hagan received the support of 39 percent of those White voters—1,210,020 people—and those White voters comprised 54 percent of Hagan's 2,249,311 total voters. The other 46 percent of her votes, then, came from people of color. See National Election Pool, "National Exit Poll," CNN, November 4, 2008, http://www.cnn.com/ELECTION/2008/results/polls/#val=NCS01p1 (accessed August 25, 2015).

21. Kathy Kiely, "Outside Interests Pour $37 Million into N.C. Senate Race," Sunlight Foundation, October 7, 2014, http://sunlightfoundation.com/blog/2014/10/07/outside-interests-pour-37-million-into-n-c-senate-race (accessed August 23, 2015).

22. $18.8 million would pay for 392 staffers at a full-time salary of $40,000/year, with 20 percent added for benefits (coming to a total of $48,000 per staffer). If each of those staffers got 3 additional votes per week, that would add up to 1,176 votes identified per week by all of the staffers. Over 50 weeks, that's 58,800 votes, 13,191 more than the 45,609 she lost by.

23. David Brookman and Joshua Kalla, "Experiments Show This Is the Best Way to Win Campaigns. But Is Anyone Actually Doing It?" *Vox*, November 13, 2014, www.vox.com/2014/11/13/7214339/campaign-ground-game (accessed August 23, 2015).

24. "More Outside Spending in Senate Races Goes to Digital," *New York Times*, October 16, 2014, www.nytimes.com/interactive/2014/10/16/upshot/100000003177162.embedded.html (accessed August 23, 2015).

25. Walter Shapiro, "The Greedy Truth about Media Consultants," *Salon*, March 9, 2006, www.salon.com/2006/05/09/campaign_consultants (accessed August 23, 2015).

26. Zac Moffat, "$80 Million in Broadcast Has Been Delivered to Voters in the Wrong Congressional Districts . . . since Labor Day," Targeted Victory, October 17, 2014, www.targetedvictory.com/2014/10/17/80-million-broadcast-delivered-voters-wrong-congressional-districts-since-labor-day (accessed August 23, 2015).

27. Paul Taylor, Mark Hugo Lopez, Jessica Hamar Martinez, and Gabriel Velasco, "When Labels Don't Fit: Hispanics and Their Views of Identity," Pew Research Center, Pew Hispanic Center, April 4, 2012, www.pewhispanic.org/files/2012/04/PHC-Hispanic-Identity.pdf (accessed August 23, 2015).

28. "Statistical Portrait of Hispanics in the United States, 2012: Population by Race and Ethnicity: 2000 and 2012," Pew Research Center, Pew Hispanic Center, www.pewhispanic.org/files/2014/04/FINAL_Statistical-Portrait-of-Hispanics-in-the-United-States-2012.pdf (accessed August 23, 2015). I say "at least 73 percent" because that number refers to U.S.-born Latinos, and more than 5 million foreign-born Latinos also speak English very well. (There is inadequate data on what percentage of foreign-born Latinos are eligible to vote, so we can't arrive at a more precise figure.)

29. "The Rise of Asian Americans," Pew Research Center, April 4, 2013, www.pewsocialtrends.org/files/2013/04/Asian-Americans-new-full-report-04-2013.pdf (accessed

August 23, 2015). See also "The Asian American Vote: A Report on the Multilingual Exit Poll from the 2012 Presidential Election," Asian American Legal Defense and Education Fund, 2013, http://aaldef.org/AALDEF%202012%20Exit%20Poll%20 Presentation.pdf (accessed August 23, 2015).

30. "The State of the Asian American Consumer: Growing Market, Growing Impact," Nielsen Company, Quarter 3, 2012, www.nielsen.com/content/dam/corporate /us/en/microsites/publicaffairs/StateoftheAsianAmericanConsumerReport.pdf (accessed August 23, 2015).

31. Ken Auletta, *Googled: The End of the World as We Know It* (New York: Penguin Books, 2009), 5.

32. Ginny Goldman, "By the numbers—EARLY VOTE," Texas Organizing Project, October 31, 2014, e-mail.

33. "Democratic Victory Task Force Preliminary Findings," Democratic National Committee, 2015, www.scribd.com/doc/256467123/Democratic-Victory-Task-Force -Preliminary-Findings (accessed August 23, 2015).

34. Inclusv, www.inclusv.com.

35. Dorceta E. Taylor, PhD, "The State of Diversity in Environmental Organizations," Green 2.0, July 2014, 71, http://diversegreen.org/wp-content/uploads/sites/4 /2014/07/FullReport_Green2.0_FINAL.pdf (accessed August 23, 2015).

36. Dominic Pulera, *Sharing the Dream: White Males in Multicultural America* (New York: Continuum International, 2004), 185.

37. John Cook, "This Seattle Angel Investor just Declared that He'll only Back Startups with at Least One Female Founder," *Geek Wire*, May 20, 2015, www.geekwire .com/2015/this-seattle-angel-investor-just-declared-that-hell-only-back-startups-with-at -least -one-female-founder (accessed August 23, 2015).

38. Anthony Thigpenn, personal communication, August 4, 2015.

39. Adam Nagourney, "Obama Camp, Seeing Shift, Bets on Long Shot in Arizona," *New York Times*, April 15, 2012, www.nytimes.com/2012/04/16/us/politics/obama-campaign -turns-attention-on-arizona.html?pagewanted=all&_r=1 (accessed August 23, 2015).

40. See "Georgia Senate Race," Center for Responsive Politics, OpenSecrets.org, www .opensecrets.org/races/summary.php?cycle=2014&id=GAS1 (accessed August 23, 2015).

41. See Darren Sands, "With Eye Toward South In '16, Democrats Launch Training Program For Staffers of Color," Buzzfeed, September 23, 2015, http://www.buzzfeed .com/darrensands/with-eye-toward-southern-states-in-16-democrats-launch-diver (accessed September 23, 2015).

CHAPTER 7: WHAT IS JUSTICE? POLICY PRIORITIES FOR THE NEW AMERICAN MAJORITY

1. "Prepared Remarks of First Lady Michelle Obama for White House Convening on Creating Opportunity for Native Youth," Office of the First Lady, White House, April 8,

2015, www.whitehouse.gov/the-press-office/2015/04/08/prepared-remarks-first-lady
-michelle-obama-white-house-convening-creatin (accessed August 23, 2015).

2. Today's values for both houses based on Zillow. See www.zillow.com/homes/2637
-dartmoor-road-cleveland-heights-ohio_rb (accessed August 25, 2015) and www.zillow
.com/homes/3256-East-128th-Street-Cleveland,-OH_rb (accessed August 25, 2015).

3. See Ray Boshara, William R. Emmons, and Bryan J. Noeth, "The Demographics of Wealth: Essay No. 1: Race, Ethnicity, and Wealth," Federal Reserve Bank of St.
Louis, February 2015, www.stlouisfed.org/household-financial-stability/the-demo
graphics-of-wealth/essay-1-race-ethnicity-and-wealth (accessed August 23, 2015). For
Native American wealth estimates, see Jessica Gordon Nembhard, PhD, "Wealth Inequality and Racial Wealth Accumulation," Insight Center for Community Economic
Development, 2007, http://ww1.insightcced.org/uploads////assets/Gordon_Nemb
hard_Jessica/GordonNembhard%20Wealth%20Accumulation%20Communities
%20of%20Color%20Overview.pdf (accessed September 23, 2015). The Federal Reserve Bank of St. Louis defines wealth as follows: "Wealth is a family's net worth,
consisting of the excess of its assets over its debts at a point in time. Total assets
include both financial assets, such as bank accounts, mutual funds and securities,
as well as tangible assets, including real estate, vehicles and durable goods. Total
debt includes home-secured borrowing (mortgages), other secured borrowing (such
as vehicle loans) and unsecured debts (such as credit cards and student loans). Debt
incurred in association with a privately owned business or to finance investment
real estate is subtracted from the asset's value, rather than being included in the
family's debt."

4. See Boshara, Emmons, and Noeth, "The Demographics of Wealth: Essay No. 1:
Race, Ethnicity, and Wealth." Also see Karthick Ramakrishnan and Farah Z. Ahmad,
"State of Asian Americans and Pacific Islanders Series," Center for American Progress,
April 23, 2014, www.americanprogress.org/issues/race/report/2014/04/23/87520
/state-of-asian-americans-and-pacific-islanders-series (accessed August 23, 2015).

5. "What Is the Average Annual Return for the S&P 500?," Investopedia, www.invest
opedia.com/ask/answers/042415/what-average-annual-return-sp-500.asp (accessed
August 23, 2015). As the article outlines, it is difficult to calculate a precise estimate of
stock market returns, but the S&P average since inception is a reasonable reflection of
the fact that, over time, the stock market has gone up, and 10 percent is as good a ball-
park as there is—based on historical data—of what investments in stocks will yield.

6. According to the Compound Interest Calculator at the U.S. Securities and Exchange's website, $134,000 earning a 10 percent return (with no additional invest-
ments) would grow to $2,125,654.46 in 28 years while $11,000 at 20 percent would
increase to $1,813,291.29. See Compound Interest Calculator, Investor.gov: U.S. Se-
curities and Exchange Commission http://investor.gov/tools/calculators/compound
-interest-calculator (accessed September 2, 2015).

7. George Yancy and Joe Feagin, "American Racism in the 'White Frame,'" *New York Times*, July 27, 2015, http://opinionator.blogs.nytimes.com/2015/07/27/american -racism-in-the-white-frame (accessed August 23, 2015).

8. See Sven Beckert, *Empire of Cotton* (New York: Knopf, 2014). Also see Harold Myerson, "How the American South Drives the Low-Wage Economy," *American Prospect*, Summer 2015, http://prospect.org/article/how-american-south-drives-low-wage -economy (accessed August 23, 2015).

9. Virginia Groark, "Slave Policies," *New York Times*, May 5, 2002, http://www.ny times.com/2002/05/05/nyregion/slave-policies.html (accessed September 2, 2015). See also ABS Staff, "15 Major Corporations You Never Knew Profited from Slavery," *Atlanta BlackStar*, August 26, 2013, http://atlantablackstar.com/2013/08/26/17-major -companies-never-knew-benefited-slavery/ (accessed September 2, 2015).

10. See Ida M. Tarbell, *The History of the Standard Oil Company* (New York: McClure, Phillips, 1904), https://archive.org/details/historyofstandar00tarbuoft (accessed August 25, 2015).

11. Ira Katznelson, *When Affirmative Action Was White* (New York: Norton, 2005), Chapter 5, "White Veterans Only."

12. Glenn C. Altschuler and Stuart M. Blumin, *The GI Bill: A New Deal for Veterans* (New York: Oxford University Press, 2009), Introduction.

13. Michael J. Bennett, *When Dreams Came True: The GI Bill and the Making of Modern America* (Washington, DC: Brassey's, 1996), Preface, Chapter 1, "A New Life."

14. Katznelson, *When Affirmative Action Was White*, Chapter 5.

15. Robert Putnam, *Bowling Alone* (New York: Simon & Schuster, 2000).

16. Katznelson, *When Affirmative Action Was White*, Chapter 5.

17. Charles G. Bolte and Louis Harris, *Our Negro Veterans* (New York: Public Affairs Committee, Pamphlet #128, 1947), 28.

18. Katznelson, *When Affirmative Action Was White*.

19. Thom Massey, "Being Black at Stanford: A Personal Reflection, Part 1," *Stanford Magazine*, Summer 1984, quoted in and viewable at Steve Phillips, *Justice and Hope: Past Reflections and Current Visions of the Stanford Black Student Union* (Stanford, CA: Black Student Union, 1990), https://studentaffairs.stanford.edu/sites/default /files/bcsc/files/Justice%20and%20Hope-%20Scanned.pdf (accessed August 25, 2015).

20. Melissa Murray, "When War Is Work: The G.I. Bill, Citizenship, and the Civic Generation," *California Law Review* 96, no. 4 (August 2008), http://scholarship.law .berkeley.edu/californialawreview/vol96/iss4/3 (accessed August 23, 2015).

21. Melvin Oliver and Thomas Shapiro, *Black Wealth/White Wealth* (New York: Routledge, 1996), Chapter 1, "Race, Wealth, and Equality."

22. Ibid.

23. Ibid.

24. Robert Rosenblatt and James Bates, "High Minority Mortgage Denial Rates Found," *Los Angeles Times*, October 22, 1991, http://articles.latimes.com/1991-10-22 /news/mn-119_1_denial-rate (accessed August 17, 2015).

25. Nikole Hannah-Jones, "Housing Crisis: Widespread Discrimination; Little Taste for Enforcement," ProPublica, June 11, 2013, www.propublica.org/article/housing -crisis-widespread-discrimination-little-taste-for-enforcement (accessed August 23, 2015).

26. The Editorial Board, "How Racism Doomed Baltimore," *New York Times*, May 9, 2015, www.nytimes.com/2015/05/10/opinion/sunday/how-racism-doomed-baltimore .html (accessed August 23, 2015).

27. Claire Zillman, "Microsoft's New CEO: One Minority Exec in a Sea of White," *Fortune*, February 4, 2014, http://fortune.com/2014/02/04/microsofts-new-ceo -one-minority-exec-in-a-sea-of-white/ (accessed September 24, 2015).

28. Crystal Goss, "Pledge of Allegiance in Schools: Not Required in These 5 States," Take Part, August 13, 2012, www.takepart.com/photos/these-five-states-do-not-require -pledge-allegiance-schools/new-pledge-allegiance-requirements-nebraska (accessed August 23, 2015).

29. "2014 Annual Social and Economic Supplement," Current Population Survey, U.S. Census Bureau, www.census.gov/hhes/www/cpstables/032014/hhinc/hinc01_000 .htm (accessed August 23, 2015). The Census Bureau unfortunately does not have household income data for Native Americans.

30. See Karthick Ramakrishnan and Farah Z. Ahmad, "State of Asian Americans and Pacific Islanders Series," Center for American Progress, April 23, 2014, www .americanprogress.org/issues/race/report/2014/04/23/87520/state-of-asian-americans -and-pacific-islanders-series (accessed August 23, 2015).

31. Meizhu Lui, "Laying the Foundation for National Prosperity: The Imperative of Closing the Racial Wealth Gap," Insight Center for Community Economic Development, March 2009, www.insightcced.org/uploads/CRWG/LayingTheFoundation ForNationalProsperity-MeizhuLui0309.pdf (accessed August 23, 2015).

32. Evan J. Mandery, "End College Legacy Preferences," *New York Times*, April 24, 2014, www.nytimes.com/2014/04/25/opinion/end-college-legacy-preferences.html (accessed August 23, 2015).

33. Scott Jaschik, "Legacy of Bias," *Inside Higher Ed*, September 22, 2010, www .insidehighered.com/news/2010/09/22/legacy (accessed August 23, 2015).

34. Tracy Loeffelholz Dunn and Jeff Neumann, "40 Acres and a Mule Would be at Least $6.4 Trillion Today—What the U.S. Really Owes Black America," *Yes! Magazine*, May 14, 2015, www.yesmagazine.org/issues/make-it-right/infographic-40-acres-and-a -mule-would-be-at-least-64-trillion-today (accessed August 23, 2015).

35. See Bilal Qureshi, "From Wrong to Right: A U.S. Apology for Japanese Internment," *Code Switch*, NPR, August 9, 2013, www.npr.org/sections/codeswitch/2013/08 /09/210138278/japanese-internment-redress (accessed August 23, 2015). Also see

Leslie T. Hatamiya, *Righting a Wrong: Japanese Americans and the Passage of the Civil Liberties Act of 1988* (Stanford, CA: Stanford University Press, 1993), 108–9.

36. Ta-Nehisi Coates, "The Case for Reparations," *Atlantic*, June 2014, www.theatlantic.com/features/archive/2014/05/the-case-for-reparations/361631 (accessed August 23, 2015).

37. Linda Darling-Hammond, *The Flat World and Education: How America's Commitment to Equity Will Determine Our Future* (New York: Teachers College Press, 2010), 38.

38. Ibid., 7.

39. Ibid., 43.

40. See Diane Ravitch, *Reign of Error: The Hoax of the Privatization Movement and the Danger to America's Public Schools* (New York: Vintage Books, 2013).

41. Mae Ngai, "Reforming Immigration for Good," *New York Times*, January 29, 2013, www.nytimes.com/2013/01/30/opinion/reforming-immigration-for-good.html (accessed August 23, 2015).

42. David Bacon, "What Real Immigration Reform Would Look Like," *The Progressive*, July 2013, http://www.progressive.org/news/2013/07/183149/what-real-immigration-reform-would-look (accessed September 2, 2015).

43. Bill Ong Hing, *Ethical Borders: NAFTA, Globalization and Mexican Migration* (Philadelphia: Temple University Press, 2010).

44. Janet Murguia, "A Commonsense Solution for Immigration Reform Must Be Enacted This Year," National Council of La Raza, April 22, 2013, www.nclr.org/images/uploads/publications/nclrtestimony_sjc_42213_1.pdf (accessed August 23, 2015).

45. Lisa García Bedolla, "California Online Voter Registration for the November 2012 Election," PowerPAC.org, June 2013.

46. "Online Voter Registration: Trends in Development and Implementation," Pew Charitable Trusts, May 13, 2015, www.pewtrusts.org/en/research-and-analysis/issue-briefs/2015/05/online-voter-registration (accessed August 23, 2015).

47. "Brennan Center Highlights New Proposal to Modernize Voting System, Bill Introduced Today," Brennan Center for Justice, January 23, 2013, www.brennancenter.org/press-release/brennan-center-highlights-new-proposal-modernize-voting-system-bill-introduced-today (accessed August 23, 2015).

48. Maria L. La Ganga, "Under New Oregon Law, All Eligible Voters Are Registered unless They Opt Out," *Los Angeles Times*, March 17, 2015, www.latimes.com/nation/la-na-oregon-automatic-voter-registration-20150317-story.html (accessed August 23, 2015).

49. Sandhya Somashekhar, Wesley Lowery, and Keith L. Alexander, "Black and Unarmed," *Washington Post*, August 8, 2015, www.washingtonpost.com/sf/national/2015/08/08/black-and-unarmed (accessed August 16, 2015).

50. Rich Juzwiak and Aleksander Chan, "Unarmed People of Color Killed by Police, 1999–2014," *Gawker*, December 8, 2014, http://gawker.com/unarmed-people-of-color-killed-by-police-1999-2014-1666672349 (accessed August 23, 2015).

51. Peter Wagner, Leah Sakala, and Josh Begley, "States of Incarceration: The Global Context," Prison Policy Initiative, June 2014, http://www.prisonpolicy.org/global/ (accessed August 25, 2015).

52. See Molly Weasley, "Black Lives Matter Offers 10-Point Plan to Curb Police Killing," *DailyKos*, August 21, 2015, http://www.dailykos.com/story/2015/08/21/1414302/-Black -Lives-Matter-offers-10-point-plan-to-curb-police-killing# (accessed September 2, 2015).

53. David Siders, "Jerry Brown Signs Bill Banning Grand Juries in Police Use-of-Force Cases," *Sacramento Bee*, August 11, 2015, www.sacbee.com/news/politics-government /capitol-alert/article30736917.html (accessed August 15, 2015).

54. See Erika Harrell, "Black Victims of Violent Crime," U.S. Department of Justice, August 2007, www.bjs.gov/content/pub/pdf/bvvc.pdf (accessed August 23, 2015). Also see Callie Marie Rennison, "Hispanic Victims of Violent Crime, 1993–2000," U.S. Department of Justice, April 2002, http://bjs.gov/content/pub/pdf/hvvc00.pdf (accessed August 23, 2015). Also see Jennifer L. Truman, "Criminal Victimization, 2010," U.S. Department of Justice, September 2011, www.bjs.gov/content/pub/pdf/cv10.pdf (accessed August 23, 2015).

55. Denise McKeon, "Research Talking Points on Dropout Statistics," National Education Association, February 2006, www.nea.org/home/13579.htm (accessed August 23, 2015).

56. J. B. Wogan, "But What Did Cory Booker Actually Accomplish in Newark?," *Governing*, December 2013, www.governing.com/topics/politics/gov-what-cory-booker -accomplished.html (accessed August 23, 2015).

57. See "United States of America," World Prison Brief, International Centre for Prison Studies, www.prisonstudies.org/country/united-states-america (accessed August 23, 2015).

58. See "Top PACs," Center for Responsive Politics, OpenSecrets.org, www.open secrets.org/pacs/toppacs.php?cycle=2014&Type=E&filter=P (accessed August 23, 2015).

59. See Michelle Alexander, *The New Jim Crow* (New York: The New Press, 2010).

60. For more information, see the Cooper Drum Company page on the U.S. Environmental Protection Agency site, http://yosemite.epa.gov/r9/sfund/r9sfdocw.nsf /ViewByEPAID/CAD055753370 (accessed August 23, 2015).

61. "State and County QuickFacts: South Gate (city), California," U.S. Census Bureau, http://quickfacts.census.gov/qfd/states/06/0673080.html (accessed August 23, 2015).

62. M. Linda Jaramillo and Carlos J. Correa Bernier, "Toxic Wastes and Race at Twenty, 1987–2007," United Church of Christ, March 2007, http://d3n8a8pro7vhmx .cloudfront.net/unitedchurchofchrist/legacy_url/491/toxic-wastes-and-race-at-twenty -1987-2007.pdf (accessed August 23, 2015).

63. J. Stephen Powell, "Political Difficulties Facing Waste-to-Energy Conversion Plant Siting," prepared by Cerrell Associates, 1984, www.ejnet.org/ej/cerrell.pdf (accessed August 23, 2015).

64. Wendy Culverwell, "Derek Smith Stepping Down as CEO of Clean Energy Works," *Portland Business Journal*, March 31, 2015, www.bizjournals.com/portland/blog /sbo/2015/03/derek-smith-stepping-down-as-ceo-of-clean-energy.html (accessed August 23, 2015).

65. "Green Infrastructure for Climate Resiliency," Office of Water, U.S. Environmental Protection Agency, July 2014, http://water.epa.gov/infrastructure/greeninfra structure/upload/climate_res_fs.pdf (accessed August 23, 2015).

66. "Greenhouse Gas-Reduction Investments to Benefit Disadvantaged Communities," California Environmental Protection Agency, February 9, 2015, www.calepa .ca.gov/EnvJustice/GHGInvest (accessed August 23, 2015).

67. See Martin Luther King Jr., *Where Do We Go From Here?* (Boston: Beacon Press, 2010), Chapter 5.

68. Valerie Jarrett and Broderick Johnson, "My Brother's Keeper: A New White House Initiative to Empower Boys and Young Men of Color," White House Blog, February 27, 2014, www.whitehouse.gov/blog/2014/02/27/my-brother-s-keeper-new-white -house-initiative-empower-boys-and-young-men-color (accessed August 23, 2015).

69. Emanuel Saez and Gabriel Zucman, "Wealth Inequality in the United States since 1913: Evidence from Capitalized Income Tax Data," National Bureau of Economic Research, October 2014, http://gabriel-zucman.eu/uswealth (accessed August 23, 2015) and http://gabriel-zucman.eu/files/SaezZucman2014.pdf (accessed August 23, 2015).

70. Bryce Covert, "It Would Actually Be Very Simple to End Homelessness Forever," Think Progress, October 9, 2014, http://thinkprogress.org/economy/2014/10 /09/3577980/end-homelessness/ (accessed September 1, 2015).

71. Julie Hirshfeld Davis and Tamar Lewin, "Obama Plan Would Help Many Go to Community College Free," *New York Times*, January 8, 2015, www.nytimes.com /2015/01/09/us/politics/obama-proposes-free-community-college-education-for-some -students.html (accessed August 23, 2015).

72. Alan S. Blinder and Mark Zandi, "How the Great Recession Was Brought to an End," Economic & Consumer Credit Analytics, Moody's Analytics, July 27, 2010, www .economy.com/mark-zandi/documents/End-of-Great-Recession.pdf (accessed August 23, 2015).

73. "Health Insurance Coverage and the Affordable Care Act," Office of the Assistant Secretary for Planning and Evaluation, U.S. Department of Health and Human Services, May 5, 2015, http://aspe.hhs.gov/health/reports/2015/uninsured_change /ib_uninsured_change.pdf (accessed August 23, 2015).

74. "Health Coverage by Race and Ethnicity: The Potential Impact of the Affordable Care Act," Kaiser Family Foundation, March 13, 2011, http://kff.org/disparities-policy /issue-brief/health-coverage-by-race-and-ethnicity-the-potential-impact-of-the-afford able-care-act (accessed August 23, 2015).

75. "Poverty in the United States: A Snapshot," National Center for Law and Economic Justice, www.nclej.org/poverty-in-the-us.php (accessed August 23, 2015).

76. Barack Obama, "A More Perfect Union," Speech at Philadelphia Constitution Center, March 18, 2008, http://constitutioncenter.org/amoreperfectunion/ (accessed August 25, 2015).

77. Sean Sullivan, "The Fix's Best Fundraiser of 2012," *Washington Post*, December 13, 2012, http://www.washingtonpost.com/news/the-fix/wp/2012/12/13/the-fixs-best-fundraiser-of-2012/ (accessed August 25, 2015).

78. Editorial, "Elizabeth Warren's Appeal," *New York Times*, October 16, 2011 (accessed August 23, 2015).

CHAPTER 8: CONSERVATIVES CAN COUNT

1. Henry Barbour, Sally Bradshaw, Ari Fleischer, Zori Fonalledas, and Glenn McCall, "Growth and Opportunity Project," GOP, 2013, 4, http://goproject.gop.com/RNC_Growth_Opportunity_Book_2013.pdf (accessed August 23, 2015).

2. Jim Rutenberg, "A Dream Undone," *New York Times*, July 29, 2015, www.nytimes.com/2015/07/29/magazine/voting-rights-act-dream-undone.html (accessed August 23, 2015).

3. Wendy R. Weiser and Lawrence Norden, "Voting Law Changes in 2012," Brennan Center for Justice, 2011, www.brennancenter.org/sites/default/files/legacy/Democracy/VRE/Brennan_Voting_Law_V10.pdf (accessed August 23, 2015).

4. Justin Levitt, "A Comprehensive Investigation of Voter Impersonation Finds 31 Credible Incidents out of One Billion Ballots Cast," *Washington Post*, August 6, 2014, www.washingtonpost.com/blogs/wonkblog/wp/2014/08/06/a-comprehensive-investigation-of-voter-impersonation-finds-31-credible-incidents-out-of-one-billion-ballots-cast (accessed August 23, 2015).

5. Aaron Blake, "Everything You Need to Know about the Pennsylvania Voter ID Fight," *Washington Post*, October 2, 2012, www.washingtonpost.com/blogs/the-fix/wp/2012/10/02/the-pennsylvania-voter-id-fight-explained (accessed August 23, 2015).

6. Author's calculations based on Pennsylvania 2012 exit polls. See "President Exit Polls," *New York Times*, 2012, http://elections.nytimes.com/2012/results/president/exit-polls?state=pa (accessed August 23, 2015).

7. "Take Your Souls to the Polls: Voting Early in Ohio," ACLU, www.aclu.org/podcast/take-your-souls-polls-voting-early-ohio (accessed August 23, 2015).

8. Weiser and Norden, "Voting Law Changes in 2012."

9. See "Section 4 of the Voting Rights Act," U.S. Department of Justice, www.justice.gov/crt/about/vot/misc/sec_4.php (accessed August 23, 2015).

10. Tomas Lopez, " 'Shelby County': One Year Later," Brennan Center for Justice, June 24, 2014, www.brennancenter.org/analysis/shelby-county-one-year-later (accessed August 23, 2015).

11. Ethan Magoc, "Flurry of Photo ID Laws Tied to Conservative Washington Group," News 21, August 12, 2012, http://votingrights.news21.com/article/movement/ (accessed August 23, 2015).

12. "Voting Newsletter: How Voting Restrictions Impacted the 2014 Election, Federal Ruling on Registration Law," Brennan Center for Justice, November 14, 2014, www.brennancenter.org/newsletter/voting-newsletter-how-voting-restrictions-impacted-2014-election-federal-ruling (accessed August 23, 2015). And see Greg Palast, "Jim Crow Returns: Millions of minority voters threatened by electoral purge," Al Jazeera America, October 29, 2014, http://projects.aljazeera.com/2014/double-voters/index.html (accessed August 23, 2015).

13. See "Elections: Issues Related to State Voter Identification Laws," U.S. Government Accountability Office, September 2014, www.gao.gov/assets/670/665966.pdf (accessed August 23, 2015).

14. In that same time period, Hawaii elected Governor David Ige and Senator Mazie Hirono, while California, in a bit of a rainbow bonanza, elected Attorney General Kamala Harris, Secretary of State Alex Padilla, Controller Betty Yee, and Treasurer John Chiang.

15. See "United States—Black Population Percentage by State," Index Mundi, 2010, www.indexmundi.com/facts/united-states/quick-facts/all-states/black-population-percentage#chart (accessed August 23, 2015). Also see "Election Guide 2008: Maryland Primary Results," New York Times, http://politics.nytimes.com/election-guide/2008/results/states/MD.html (accessed August 23, 2015).

16. Kevin Robillard, "Harry Reid Backs Chris Van Hollen in Maryland Senate Race," Politico, March 6, 2015, www.politico.com/story/2015/03/harry-reid-backs-chris-van-hollen-senate-bid-115836.html (accessed August 23, 2015).

17. See "Presidente Bush: Nos Concemos," YouTube, April 16, 2012, www.youtube.com/watch?v=xHghAjADiXc (accessed August 23, 2015).

18. Kerry was the first Democrat to opt out of the public financing system set up after Watergate in 1974. That system limited the amount that a candidate could spend if they accepted public financing, which is why Kerry could spend so much more. George Bush also opted out, and he bested Kerry by spending $270 million. See Federico Subervi-Velez, The Mass Media and Latino Politics: Studies of U.S. Media Content, Campaign Strategies, and Survey Research: 1984–2004 (New York: Routledge, 2008), 303. See also Ed Hornick, "Why do U.S. elections cost so much?," October 13, 2011, CNN, www.cnn.com/2011/10/13/politics/us-election-costs (accessed August 23, 2015).

19. See Hector Amaya, Citizenship Excess: Latinos/as, Media, and the Nation (New York: New York University Press, 2013), 71.

20. Voter News Service, "Florida Election Day Exit Poll," CNN, November 3, 1998, http://www.cnn.com/ELECTION/1998/states/FL/G/exit.poll.html (accessed August 23, 2015).

21. Boer Deng, "Can Texas Republicans Make a Red State Redder?" *Slate*, September 26, 2014, www.slate.com/articles/news_and_politics/politics/2014/09/greg_abbott_is_campaigning_for_texas_hispanics_can_the_state_s_republicans.html (accessed August 23, 2015).

22. See National Election Pool exit poll conducted by Edison Research, November 5, 2014, accessed via 2014 Election Center, CNN, www.cnn.com/election/2014/results/state/TX/governor#exit-polls (accessed August 23, 2015).

23. Josh Dawsey and Heather Haddon, "Black, Latino Leaders Cool on Christie," *Wall Street Journal*, April 27, 2015, www.wsj.com/articles/some-groups-cool-on-christie-1430097711 (accessed August 23, 2015).

24. David Freelander, "How Chris Christie Is Winning Over Hispanics," *Daily Beast*, November 3, 2013, www.thedailybeast.com/articles/2013/11/03/can-christie-win-latinos.html (accessed August 23, 2015).

25. "Election 2013: Exit Polls, N.J. Governor," *New York Times*, November 5, 2013, www.nytimes.com/projects/elections/2013/general/new-jersey/exit-polls.html (accessed August 23, 2015).

26. Rand Paul, "Rand Paul: We Must Demilitarize the Police," *Time*, August 14, 2014, http://time.com/3111474/rand-paul-ferguson-police (accessed August 23, 2015).

27. Mike Allen, "Paul: African American Leaders May Not Yet Embrace GOP," *Politico*, October 17, 2014, www.politico.com/story/2014/10/rand-paul-african-americans-111975.html (accessed August 23, 2015).

28. Alice Ollstein, "Inside the Koch Brothers' Multi-Million Dollar Campaign to Win Over Latinos," Think Progress, September 30, 2014, http://thinkprogress.org/election/2014/09/30/3573291/koch-libre-latinos (accessed August 23, 2015).

29. See Ibid.

30. See "The Libre Initiative: The Koch Brothers' Focus on Latino Voters," People for the American Way, www.pfaw.org/rww-in-focus/libre-initiative-koch-brothers-new-focus-winning-latino-voters (accessed August 23, 2015).

31. Mara Liasson, "GOP Tries New Effort to Bring in Hispanic Voters," NPR, January 13, 2011, www.npr.org/2011/01/13/132873320/gop-tries-new-effort-to-bring-in-hispanic-voters (accessed August 23, 2015).

32. See "American Action Network/American Action Forum," FactCheck.org, February 26, 2014, www.factcheck.org/2014/02/american-action-networkamerican-action-forum (accessed August 23, 2015). Also see Hispanic Leadership Network, http://hispanicleadershipnetwork.org (accessed August 23, 2015).

33. Kenneth P. Vogel, "Karl Rove vs. the Koch Brothers," *Politico*, October 10, 2011, www.politico.com/news/stories/1011/65504_Page4.html (accessed August 23, 2015).

34. See Future Majority Project, http://futuremajorityproject.gop (accessed August 23, 2015).

35. "GOP Minority Outreach: 'Future Majority Caucus,' " NPR, February 11, 2013, www.npr.org/2013/02/11/171704904/gop-minority-outreach-future-majority-caucus (accessed August 23, 2015).

36. Adrian Carrasquillo, "This Group Helped Get Dozens of Diverse Republican Candidates Elected and They're Back for 2016," *BuzzFeed News*, June 17, 2015, www.buzzfeed.com/adriancarrasquillo/this-group-helped-get-dozens-of-diverse-republican-candidate#.kjmzlo270B (accessed August 23, 2015).

37. Henry Barbour, Sally Bradshaw, Ari Fleischer, Zori Fonalledas, and Glenn McCall, "Growth and Opportunity Project," GOP, 2013, 4, http://goproject.gop.com/RNC_Growth_Opportunity_Book_2013.pdf (accessed August 23, 2015).

38. Jonathan Capehart, "Rep. Mo Brooks Talks 'War on Whites' as the GOP Loses the Battle for Votes," *Washington Post*, August 4, 2014, www.washingtonpost.com/blogs/post-partisan/wp/2014/08/04/rep-mo-brooks-talks-war-on-whites-as-the-gop-loses-the-battle-for-votes/ (accessed August 23, 2015).

39. Chris Cillizza, "The Democratic Party's Autopsy Is Largely Useless. Except for This One Point," *Washington Post*, February 23, 2015, www.washingtonpost.com/blogs/the-fix/wp/2015/02/23/the-democratic-partys-autopsy-is-largely-useless-except-for-this-one-point/ (accessed August 23, 2015). The Democrats' final report was originally to be released in May 2015 and then late July 2015, but as of the end of September 2015, there was no sign of the final report.

40. ORC International, "CNN/ORC International Poll," CNN.com, August 18, 2015, http://i2.cdn.turner.com/cnn/2015/images/08/17/rel8a.-.gop.2016.pdf (accessed August 24, 2015).

41. Ian Haney-Lopez, *Dog Whistle Politics: How Coded Racial Appeals Have Reinvented Racism and Wrecked the Middle Class* (New York: Oxford University Press, 2014), Preface.

42. Ibid.

43. Ann Coulter, *Adios America: The Left's Plan to Turn Our Country into a Third World Hellhole* (Washington, DC: Regnery, 2015), Chapter 2.

44. Ronald Brownstein and Janie Boschma, "The GOP's Control of Congress Is Only Getting Stronger," *National Journal*, January 8, 2015, www.nationaljournal.com/next-america/newsdesk/the-gop-s-control-of-congress-is-only-getting-stronger-20150108 (accessed August 23, 2015).

CONCLUSION: FROM FEAR TO HOPE

1. Jewelle Taylor Gibbs and Teiahsha Bankhead, *Preserving Privilege: California Politics, Propositions, and People of Color* (Westport, CT: Praeger, 2001).

2. "Two Students Arrested at Cannery Protest," *Stanford Daily*, February 24, 1986, http://stanforddailyarchive.com/cgi-bin/stanford?a=d&d=stanford19860224-01.2.12 (accessed August 23, 2015).

3. Miles Corwin, "Canning Workers' Bitter Strike Devastates Lives, Economy of Watsonville," *Los Angeles Times*, September 14, 1986, http://articles.latimes.com/1986 -09-14/news/mn-12455_1_production-workers (accessed August 17, 2015).

4. Gibbs and Bankhead, *Preserving Privilege*.

5. Jonathan Martin and Maggie Haberman, "Hillary Clinton Traces Friendly Path, Troubling Party," *New York Times*, June 6, 2015, www.nytimes.com/2015/06/07/us /politics/hillary-clinton-traces-friendly-path-troubling-party.html (accessed August 17, 2015).

6. Axelrod, *Believer*, Chapter 25.

7. Sean Sullivan, "Schumer: Democrats 'Blew' Opportunity by Focusing on 'Wrong Problem'—Health Care," *Washington Post*, November 25, 2014, www.washingtonpost .com/news/post-politics/wp/2014/11/25/schumer-democrats-blew-opportunity-by -focusing-on-wrong-problem-of-health-care (accessed August 19, 2015).

8. Lerone Bennett Jr., "Of Time, Space, and Revolution," *Ebony*, August 1969, https://books.google.com/books/about/Ebony.html?id=AtsDAAAAMBAJ (accessed September 22, 2015).

9. WGBH Interactive, "Africans in America," PBS, 1998, http://www.pbs.org/wgbh /aia/part4/4p1561.html (accessed August 24, 2015).

10. Martin Luther King Jr., "1964 Nobel Peace Prize Acceptance Speech," December 10, 1964, www.nobelprize.org/nobel_prizes/peace/laureates/1964/king-accep tance_en.html (accessed August 19, 2015).

11. Martin Luther King Jr., "I've Been to the Mountaintop," April 3, 1968, http:// www.americanrhetoric.com/speeches/mlkivebeentothemountaintop.htm (accessed August 25, 2015).

APPENDIX A: MATH AND METHODOLOGY

1. "How Groups Voted in 2012," Roper Center of the University of Connecticut, www .ropercenter.uconn.edu/polls/us-elections/how-groups-voted/how-groups-voted-2012 (accessed August 21, 2015).

2. Samuel Best and Brian Krueger, "Gallup(ing) Away from the Herd," Monkey Cage, November 7, 2012, http://themonkeycage.org/2012/11/galluping-away-from-the -herd (accessed August 23, 2015); Samuel J. Best and Brian S. Krueger, *Exit Polls: Surveying the American Electorate, 1972–2010* (Washington, DC: CQ Press, 2012), 18.

3. Best and Krueger, *Exit Polls*, 19.

4. William H. Frey, "Minority Turnout Determined the 2012 Election," Brookings Institution, May 10, 2013, www.brookings.edu/research/papers/2013/05/10-election -2012-minority-voter-turnout-frey (accessed August 23, 2015).

APPENDIX B: WHAT'S IN A NAME?

1. Lori L. Tharps, "The Case for Black with a Capital B," *New York Times*, November 18, 2014, www.nytimes.com/2014/11/19/opinion/the-case-for-black-with-a-capital -b.html (accessed August 23, 2015).

2. Currently, the Census Bureau equates the terms "Hispanic" and "Latino," defining both as "a person of Cuban, Mexican, Puerto Rican, South or Central American, or other Spanish culture or origin, regardless of race."

3. Dunbar-Ortiz, *An Indigenous Peoples' History of the United States*.

INDEX

North Carolina, 113
  2008 election, 10
  2014 election, 19, 75–76, 103–4, 218n20
  Native Americans in, 32
  progressive Whites in, 41
North Dakota, 34
Nunn, Michelle, 100, 113

Obama, Barack, xiv–xv, xvii–xviii
  Charleston shooting, 59
  Cuba reset, 22
  health care reform, 69–72
  immigration reform, 58, 72–75, 134–35
  My Brother's Keeper initiative, 143
  presidential election of 2008
    (see election of 2008)
  presidential election of 2012
    (see election of 2012)
  White swing voters and, 62–63, 65–75, 69
Obama, Michelle, 116, 119
Occupy Wall Street, 118–19, 146, 147
Ohio
  2004 election, 100, 217n15
  2008 election, 152
  2010 election, 152
  2012 election, 153
Oklahoma, 32
Oliver, Melvin, 123
1–800 numbers, use in 1992 election, 84
Only the Paranoid Survive (Grove), 83
Open Society Foundation, 133
Oregon, 12, 137, 142
Ortega, Julie Martinez, 16, 20–21, 177
Ozawa v. United States, 51

Pacific Islander Americans, 28–29, 188–89
Palestinian Americans, 36
Paul, Rand, 157–58
Pennsylvania
  Puerto Ricans in, 22
  voter ID laws, 136
Perception Institute, 53
Perot, Ross, 24, 168

persuasion, 102–4, 105
Peters, Scott, 112
Pew Research Center, 43, 106
Pfeiffer, Dan, 69
Phillips, Doris C., 16–17, 116–17, 122
Phillips, James L., Sr., 16–17, 116–17, 122
Pinckney, Clementa, 59
Pittsburgh Steelers, 111
Plessy v. Ferguson, 50–51
Podesta, John, 110, 175
police murders, 53, 124, 137–38, 139
police officer body cameras, 138
policy priorities, 116–48
  comprehensive immigration reform, 132–35
  criminal justice reform, 137–40
  democracy reforms, 135–37
  education, 130–32
  environmental equity, 140–43
  Justice and Equality Fund, 143–45
  racial wealth gap, 117–20
  See also economic justice
Political campaigns, 101–7, 114–15
  gearing toward White swing voters, 74–77
  See also political investing
political consultants. *See* White consultants
political investing, 96–115
  asking tough questions, 101–9
  budget matching plan, 104–7
  tracking progress, 107–9
  "What is our plan?," 101–4
  in growing markets, 98–100
  for the long term, 109–14
politics
  of African Americans, 18–20
  of Arab Americans, 38
  of Asian Americans, 28–29
  of Latinos, 22–25
  of Native Americans, 33–34
  of progressive Whites, 41–43
Polk, James, 21
Polluter Pays, 130, 142, 166

ABOUT THE AUTHOR

Steve Phillips is a national political leader, civil rights lawyer, and senior fellow at the Center for American Progress. Active in political and social change for thirty years, in 1992 he became the youngest person ever elected to public office in San Francisco and went on to serve as president of the Board of Education, where he authored pathbreaking legislation making San Francisco the first school district in the country to incorporate books by writers of color into the required reading in the literature curriculum. He is the co-founder of PowerPAC.org, a social justice and advocacy organization that conducted the largest independent voter mobilization efforts backing Barack Obama, Cory Booker, and Kamala Harris. In 2014, he co-authored the first-ever audit of Democratic Party spending and was named one of "America's Top 50 Influencers" by *Campaigns and Elections* magazine.

Phillips has appeared on multiple national radio and television networks, including NBC, CNN, Fox News, and TV One. He was a featured speaker at the City Club of Cleveland in 2014, and his address on race and politics was nationally broadcast on C-SPAN. Phillips has written extensively, with his work appearing in *Campaigns & Elections,* the *Huffington Post, San Jose Mercury News,* the *San Francisco Chronicle,* the *San Francisco Examiner,* and the *Cleveland Plain Dealer,* among other national and state publications.

Phillips holds a JD from Hastings College of the Law and a BA from Stanford University. He lives in San Francisco with his wife and two cats.

Publishing in the Public Interest

Thank you for reading this book published by The New Press. The New Press is a nonprofit, public interest publisher. New Press books and authors play a crucial role in sparking conversations about the key political and social issues of our day.

We hope you enjoyed this book and that you will stay in touch with The New Press. Here are a few ways to stay up to date with our books, events, and the issues we cover:

- Sign up at www.thenewpress.com/subscribe to receive updates on New Press authors and issues and to be notified about local events
- Like us on Facebook: www.facebook.com/newpressbooks
- Follow us on Twitter: www.twitter.com/thenewpress

Please consider buying New Press books for yourself; for friends and family; or to donate to schools, libraries, community centers, prison libraries, and other organizations involved with the issues our authors write about.

The New Press is a 501(c)(3) nonprofit organization. You can also support our work with a tax-deductible gift by visiting www.thenewpress.com/donate.